NONGRADEDNESS

Robert H. Anderson
Barbara Nelson Pavan

NONGRADEDNESS
HELPING
IT TO
HAPPEN

TECHNOMIC
PUBLISHING CO., INC.
LANCASTER · BASEL

Nongradedness
a **TECHNOMIC**®publication

Published in the Western Hemisphere by
Technomic Publishing Company, Inc.
851 New Holland Avenue
Box 3535
Lancaster, Pennsylvania 17604 U.S.A.

Distributed in the Rest of the World by
Technomic Publishing AG

Printed in the United States of America
10 9 8 7 6 5 4 3 2 1

Main entry under title:
  Nongradedness: Helping It to Happen

A Technomic Publishing Company book
Bibliography: p.
Includes index p. 235

Library of Congress Card No. 92-62813
ISBN No. 0-87762-980-3

Contents

Preface

IN the 1990s, the prospects for widespread acceptance and implementation of nongradedness seem to be greater than they have been in this century, although this is not to say that there is already a strong movement in that direction. In perhaps 5 to 10 percent of elementary schools, including nearly all of those in Kentucky and Oregon, there seem to be significant efforts in motion under the force of legislative mandates or, preferably, awareness that gradedness is a dead cause. In a sense these efforts represent a "revival" of programs that were launched between roughly 1955 and 1975, although in actuality the numbers of such programs probably never exceeded 1,500 to 2,000 and it cannot be said that in those days nongradedness became a major movement. However, significant literature did surface and attract national attention, and through such excellent efforts as Individually Guided Education (both the Wisconsin and the Kettering-/I/D/E/A/ versions) there came to be a small number of well-designed and well-managed nongraded programs. Most of the best examples also involved team teaching and multi-aged grouping, for reasons that this present volume hopes amply to explain.

By 1975 or 1980, it seemed that many of the nongraded programs had lost their momentum and had become less visible. Had the idea lost its saliency? Did the programs fail to produce better results? Was nongradedness just a bandwagon that lost its wheels? Did parents cause nongradedness to falter? Is gradedness, after all, a better arrangement? These and other questions surfaced, and for a while it was not easy to deal with them. As the 1980s wrapped up, however, interest in nongradedness picked up dramatically, and the once-puzzling questions seemed easier to answer.

It needs to be remembered that American schools have gone through a very, very difficult quarter century. For a decade or so bandwagons were indeed rumbling all over the place, and many of them fell apart.

Teachers were scarce for a while, and upgrading teacher education was not on the national agenda. Teacher inservice programs were almost totally inadequate, both in substance and in funding. Federal and foundation dollars began to dry up or to be diverted away from structural changes. Severe budget cuts led to reductions in force and to staff reassignments. Pressure groups became more and more assertive with respect to school programs and practices, and calls for "back to basics" seemed much louder than calls for qualitative improvements in services to children. The general increase in societal pathologies had a depressing effect on school staffs. The political atmosphere was generally non-supportive of schools and geared to accountability crudely defined. The numbers of children considered to be "at-risk" reached astronomical proportions. The entertainment industry, and even the sports world, became a largely corrupting influence on young people, and a decline in ethical standards in government offices and corporate headquarters left its mark on public morale. It was, in short, a time when the energy required for transforming schools into nurturant environments was in short supply.

With specific reference to nongradedness, it seems that the historic mobility of the school workforce played a major role in the evaporation of pilot efforts. Most of these efforts unfortunately had been launched top-down by enthusiastic administrators who did not provide their staffs with sufficient orientation, training, and ongoing supervisory assistance. As these career-oriented leaders left for other jobs, commitment diminished; and as some of the "original" pilot-program staff members also moved on or retired, their replacements were less able, or willing, to carry on. That most teachers continued to work in self-contained classrooms was probably the single strongest impediment to successful implementation of nongradedness. Next strongest was continuing teacher reliance on conventional graded textbooks and materials. The fade-away of nongradedness therefore is not too difficult to explain. Conditions for its full development over a sufficient period of time simply did not exist.

It should be noted that except in perhaps a half-dozen isolated situations—these usually involving suspicious right-wing critics—parental reactions to nongradedness programs were generally positive. Furthermore, we are unaware of any instances where pupil test results or other conventional indicators clearly indicated that the pilot programs had failed. Even when imperfectly implemented, nongraded programs have at least held their own against graded classes. And as far as the general literature was concerned, there never surfaced any argument against the concept of nongradedness. To our knowledge there is not, and there has not been, any philosophical or research-based support for continuation of graded structure. That gradedness persists is certainly not due to the advice of scholars/researchers/experts in the educational community. Its advocates are primarily the textbook publishers, the testing industry, and various bureaucrats who feed on the statistics that graded schools generate. Perhaps its advocates also include some thousands of teachers whose grade-related habits are, alas, very firmly entrenched.

Although the parallel may seem harsh, staying with gradedness in the 1990s is somewhat similar to what smoking tobacco was about a decade ago: a self-destructive habit, distressingly hard to abandon, and encountering insufficient national outrage to generate policies against it. National awareness about the dangers of smoking *did* emerge, however, and tobacco smoke is disappearing from buses, planes, trains, public buildings, and most workplaces. In the 1990s the eventual demise of the tobacco industry seems anything but far-fetched. This volume seeks to accelerate the demise of yet another self-destructive habit—the graded school. We want to help that to happen.

CHAPTER 1
The Time Is Now

ONE of the problems with *today* is that soon it will be *yesterday*. This happens to *this year* also: soon it will be *last year*. Similarly, decades and then centuries fade away. And so, at least as often as not, do movements and ideas that may once have had their *heyda* (a Middle English term) or heyday.

This book derives from, and supports, the hope that graded schools, as American children have known them for much more than one hundred years, have had their heyday. Put another way, gradedness has done sufficient mischief in the twentieth century so that its imminent demise will be cause for celebration. Also to be celebrated at still uncertain future moments will be (among other things) the decline and fall of age stratification in schooling, of the literal self-contained classroom, of the rigid lock-step curriculum that accompanies gradedness, and of the foolish notion that children in school should compete rather than cooperate with each other. Whether it is true that new heydays will be dawning for alternatives to such concepts, of course, remains to be discovered. It will be exciting to see what schooling arrangements will be in place by the time Century XXI rolls around.

When Century XIX rolled around, there wasn't anything even closely resembling an American public school system. Such schools as there were served only a small fraction of children, usually males headed for religious careers, and literacy was mostly a family responsibility. By mid-century, however, urbanization and industrialization had created a dramatic need for expansion of schools at a cost shared among taxpayers. The earliest of these schools accepted children of all ages, and (faithful to classic descriptions of the Little Red Schoolhouse) it was not unusual to see three- and four-year-olds in the same classroom as teenagers (Angus, Mirel, and Vinouskis, 1988). However, as Goodlad and Anderson (1987) have pointed out, there were a number of efforts to establish a more orderly and regimented structure, of which new textbooks including The *McGuffey Eclectic Readers* (after 1836) and the English monitorial system were prime examples. There was a rather steady progression toward classifying young people and providing them with progressively-more-difficult materials of instruction. By mid-century, therefore, the stage had already been set for the formal adoption of full-fledged graded schools.

The person usually associated with such schools is Horace Mann of Massachusetts, whose advocacy of graded structure was fueled by its apparent success in Germany. The famous Quincy Grammar School in Boston, founded in 1848, became not the first but by far the most remarkable example, after which thousands of elementary schools were patterned. The building, unusual for its day, was four stories high (and by the way, it was so solid that it remained in use in Boston for more than 120 years). Each teacher had a separate room. There was a large assembly hall, and the school was unified as well as graded. Pupils were sorted in "grades" of like achievement and they either "passed" or "failed" at the end of the year. A full-time principal, John T. Philbrick, administered the school.

Within the next fifteen to twenty years, especially in the cities, the graded pattern crystallized into a structure that almost every adult in America, even today, would recognize from his/her own youthful experience. By approximately 1870, however, the concept of graded schools was being questioned, even attacked, by various prominent educators. Sad to say, gradedness stubbornly survived these attacks and remained solidly in place for much longer than a century. In the 1990s, in fact, it remains a formidable challenge to reformers.

In retrospect, it must be admitted that for a time gradedness served a somewhat useful purpose. Out of what must have been chaos it created order, at least in the form of sequences that had some plausible relationship to the successive maturational levels of students. Since teachers were invariably ill-trained (if at all), grade levels made it possible for each teacher to "specialize" by learning the material of a single grade instead of the entire curriculum. Parenthetically on this point, it is probable that some teachers who managed to hold their own in, say, fourth grade, might have been lost in one of the lower grades. Aggregating children in each class of the same age, and following the (false) assumption that everyone in each class could profit from the same instruction, gradedness permitted teachers to work with larger groups instead of with just a few at a time, and this had economic if not educational advantages. A system of teacher-up-front, didactic instruction developed, and having children seated at fixed desks in straight rows combined with the threat of poor marks and non-promotion tended to be seen as supportive of discipline.

Of interest on this point is that society in general, and school people and clerics in particular, tended in those days to view children as especially vulnerable to the many temptations that could spell their downfall. Such views persist in the late twentieth century as well; but only among religious extremists is there now such a negative perception of morality and motivation in children as prevailed at that time. *The McGuffey Readers* were full of reminders that sin must be avoided, diligence and resistance to bad thoughts and behaviors must prevail, and reward belongs to the virtuous. Less subtle were descriptions in some textbooks on graded schools, of "dullards" and "laggards" on the one hand and mischievous and precocious children on the other, both perceived as being in the clutches of the Devil ("The Olde Deluder Satan") and therefore unable or unwilling to function as dutiful students.

Many educators and philosophers of that period would have been astonished to read late twentieth century accounts of human variability, psychosocial characteristics of children and youth, motivation for learning, "effective schools," and child growth and development. They would have been equally amazed to hear modern educators describing the ideal school as a "happy place" for children, and "success for every child K–12" as an attainable goal.

Another factor in the graded school movement, elementary level, was that the routinized and systematic approach made it easier to supervise teachers, most of whom were females who in those days had much less choice of careers than their male counterparts and who were, and long remained, available for low salaries. As the only so-called profession, outside of the military and other governmental employees, subject to taxpayer-enforceable wage controls, teachers found themselves at great disadvantage in seeking better working conditions or improvements in the learning atmosphere for their pupils. Teacher preparation institutions such as the Normal Schools had low status, and over a century or so as teacher education was gradually absorbed into the university system it almost never achieved status equal to other "professional" preparation units. Furthermore, in harmony with taxpayer resistance to adequate funding of public schools, controlling forces such as state legislatures and the university power structure prevented teacher education from keeping pace with the increasing complexity of fully educating America's children.

EDUCATION FOR . . . ALL?

This brings us to the question, not much debated prior to mid-twentieth century, of "Who shall be educated?"

In a sense, the argument that *all* American children are entitled to a sufficient tax-supported education was not much in dispute during the latter half of the nineteenth century, but it should be realized that "sufficient" had a very narrow definition. Secondary schools were not everywhere in place until the end of the century, and even then they served only a small fraction of the population. It took a long time before compulsory attendance laws, child labor laws, and societal recognition of several terrible inequities led to new ways of thinking about universal public education.

To jump a step ahead of our story, it has also taken a very long time for the American employment market to change from one requiring only a small fraction of well-educated and technically proficient workers to one which, rather suddenly so it seems, has an almost insatiable demand for such graduates. The same employers and politicians who, only a generation ago, saw no need to upgrade school services are now complaining about the "shameful failure" of the school system to provide enough good employees.

Well, some of the "failure" may indeed be blamed on the school people; and this book seeks to illuminate some of the problems that educators have brought upon themselves and that they can, and must, fix. But let us return to the question of who should be educated. We will do this by suggesting that some good things have recently been happening and that our ability to comprehend and deal with our educational responsibilities has recently been strengthened.

CAUSES FOR CELEBRATION

For a long time, American society has been struggling with three basic education-related questions: (1) Which American children are entitled to full educational services? (2) How should the fact of individual differences (of many sorts) be taken into account in schooling practices? and (3) How far should the notion of a truly educated citizenry be taken?

As we read educational history, we see that it was not until after World War I that the concept of universal, tax-supported, quality education became part of serious public discourse. Furthermore, it was only after World War II that public education began to be identified directly with the nation's economic, political, and social well-being.

Not incidentally, it was also after World War II that American society began to deal in earnest with the educational (and other) needs of large segments of its population: minority children, handicapped/disadvantaged/deprived ("at risk") children, children whose family situation and/or environment is stressful, children oppressed by physical or chemical abuse, children whose talents and propensities do not fit the usual schooling practices, children of migrant workers, and various others who in past decades were either ignored by the school system or provided with an early exit.

Although in some ways the children from such situations remain at risk and even in peril (as forcefully documented by Jonathan Kozol in *Savage Inequities*, 1991), educators have reason to give thanks for some major events that were intended to be helpful and that have in fact made a positive difference. These include the Civil Rights Act of 1964, withholding federal dollars from segregated schools; the Chapter I program; Head Start; the *Brown vs. Topeka* decision; Public Law 94-142; and various related state actions/decisions that have supported the national effort to provide better opportunities to children previously denied them.

There is also reason for educators to celebrate the additional knowledge that is available to them in the 1990s. Although no one would claim that it is now adequate (the more you know, the more you know that you don't know!), there is a rich literature now available in the areas of human development, human learning, instructional methodology, school and classroom management, organizational dynamics, and also in the disciplines that support the educational endeavor. It would be impossible to quantify, much less appraise, but the sheer amount of educational research that is being done each year would have been unimaginable twenty or twenty-five years ago. Furthermore, educators know perhaps ten times more now than they did even ten years ago about what works, what doesn't work, what may be worth piloting, and what further questions need to be asked.

We hope that readers of this book will conclude, at the end, that what we have just said about R&D in general is very true about nongradedness versus gradedness.

There are still other things that teachers might well celebrate. We are pleased that the term "restructuring" has become a familiar, albeit multidimensional, topic not only within education but also in public discussion. We are equally pleased that the concept of site-based decision making is gaining ground, and that the top-down, "quick fix" solutions of only a few years ago are giving way to long-term, fundamental changes. Except in the funding area, state legislatures are behaving more responsibly, in recognition of these factors, and more and more states are making it possible for schools to function as decision-making units and for teachers, at last, to have a stronger role in deciding what should be taught, and in what ways. This is a good trend worth celebrating.

Also worth celebrating is the progress being made toward recognizing and acting upon the need for continuous, intensive, and meaningful inservice education. An intra-professional–growth focus is replacing the old top-down, scattershot inservice that so many teachers hated; and a broad-gauged, coordinated approach to human resource development is firmly in place in many districts.

Perhaps even more welcome is that, as indicated above, prevailing views of human potential and human motivation are much more enlightened in the 1990s. The old moralistic, good-vs.-evil thinking on which many school practices were based is giving way to a more optimistic view of children as essentially moral, essentially eager to learn and to fulfill their potential, and essentially teachable. Benjamin Bloom's (1976) conclusion that 95 percent of children are capable of significant success in our schools is gaining in acceptance among teachers, and mechanisms that prevent children from succeeding are gradually being abandoned. These include literal gradedness, practices of tracking children, practices of retaining children, use of competitive ABCDF marking systems, and other arrangements that cause children to be frustrated, to learn less, and eventually to drop out. These are forces that our book seeks to destroy.

Perhaps American educators should be especially grateful to the Japanese and the Germans because they helped the American taxpayer to realize that unless American schools do a better job of fully educating *all* children, our workforce will not be strong enough to compete in the international marketplace. We are, slowly but surely, moving from minimalism (the "basics" at the lowest level) to the view that each child is an essential human resource for the nation's well-being, and even survival. There has been less movement, so far, toward realizing that a truly enlightened citizenry is even more important to the good life than a skillful workforce—but at least we seem to be making some progress.

We should celebrate also that society is beginning to view teaching as a more significant and dignified profession. Whereas once we were satisfied if teachers were good disciplinarians and able deliverers of a curriculum that came top-down, we now are coming to see teachers as responsible, creative, skillful professionals who coordinate, manage, and inspire a very dynamic process.

Principals and supervisors, too, enjoy higher status these days. As the coordinators and managers of the dynamic programs that are emerging, they are more and more appreciated for the leadership roles they play.

Worth celebrating are some of the trends in the ways schools are being organized. Once again, and perhaps this time with far more intensity, American schools are questioning the graded structure and seeking to make "continuous progress" a reality in the lives of children. Once again, there is a strong trend toward bringing teachers out of their isolated self-contained classrooms and into teams of various kinds. Even more exciting is that pupils are being organized much more frequently into teams, as the advantages of cooperative learning become more evident. Educators are beginning to accept the idea that children are best served in a group that is basically heterogeneous (both age-wise and in terms of sociocultural makeup), and therefore multi-age grouping is increasingly apparent. At the same time, the old notion that children should sit still and not talk to each other is going out the window, and today's best classrooms are regular beehives of activity and conversation. These developments are surely worth celebrating!

In many ways, we hope that this book helps the reader to appreciate the significance of the celebration, while recognizing what remains to be done before the *ultimate* celebration (of *every* child succeeding in school) is warranted.

THE TIME FACTOR IN EDUCATIONAL CHANGE

One of the most common remarks, especially by naysayers, about efforts to promote or develop a structural or other change is, "We've already tried it, and it didn't work." A similar, related question often is

"Why change what is working well enough?" (variant: If it ain't broke, don't fix it). A more dangerous sort of comment would be "That (arrangement) won't be good for kids," and of course there sometimes are remarks such as "I'm already working too hard as it is, and this is just one more bandwagon to live through."

These and similar reactions to proposed changes usually have some validity, at least within the context of a school district's long-term history. Often enough, ideas have indeed been tested and found wanting. Sometimes programs in place seem to be working well. Some suggested practices may actually be hurtful, or at least nonbeneficial, for children. And, perhaps especially, most teachers *do* work very hard and they know that many flimsy "bandwagons" have rumbled down the educational corridors over the years. Skepticism and resistance, when yet another rumble is heard, is therefore not altogether surprising.

We have already noted that, unlike most other so-called professionals, educators receive insufficient preservice preparation for the extremely complex and challenging work they must carry out. Most of what teachers eventually incorporate in their operational repertoires is learned on the job. Compounding the problem is what virtually every researcher or observer of life in schools comments on, namely the disappointingly low level of professional interaction in schools and the pervading use of obsolete instructional behavior and practices. Many of these habits have been carried forward from previous centuries, when very little was known about how human beings really learn. Most observers also are struck by the deliberate isolation of teachers from each other and the absence of what, in 1990s terms, would be called a healthy work culture.

That great numbers of children and youth are unenthusiastic about their school experiences and, worse, are not well served by those experiences, is widespread public knowledge. Unfortunately, there is also a widespread public assumption, reflected in legislative mandates and school board policies, that the conventional/traditional system of schooling remains appropriate and that any decline in educational productivity is due mainly to the lack of effort (variant: self-discipline) among students and even teachers.

Unfortunately teachers, most of whom were attracted into teaching because they valued the conventional definitions of schooling and teaching, tend to remain loyal to those definitions. Therefore they are uncomfortable with efforts to redefine their roles or their pedagogy.

Since such efforts only rarely are accompanied by intensive training to insure understanding and success, each new idea or arrangement tends to be pursued with neither skill nor enthusiasm, and soon enough it falters or breaks down. In other words, the bandwagon winds up in the junkyard.

There are, however, moments in history when "new" ideas or arrangements are met with favor, even enthusiasm, and changes are made that were once unthinkable. In many such instances, perhaps most, the "new" thought or practice has a prior history of rejection or failure— but the difference is that this time around, the legitimacy and/or usefulness of the idea is better understood and the context is more favorable. Nongradedness may well be one such idea: it has a long in-and-out history, but it is at last enjoying clearer definition, and it is returning to the scene at a time when many forces, including the national press for restructuring, are providing a strong support base.

The brilliant American anthropologist Loren Eiseley more than three decades ago wrote about the difficult progress of ideas in science. Students of scientific history, he noted, learn that "a given way of looking at things, a kind of unconscious conformity which exists even in a free society, may prevent a new contribution from being followed up, or its implications from being fully grasped" (Eiseley, 1960, p. 6). He cited as examples Mendel (genetics), Darwin (evolution), and Semmelweis (childbed fever), all creative thinkers whose discoveries were ridiculed, or worse, by intolerant and prejudiced colleagues. Scientists, he noted, "have occasionally persecuted other scientists, and they have not always been able to see that an old theory, given a hairsbreadth twist, might open an entirely new vista to the human reason." Eiseley observed that to see things differently from other persons, to step outside the intellectual climate of one's age or time, is therefore difficult and even dangerous; but eventually that climate may evolve in such a way that previously rejected theories and ideas will prevail.

In the same way, educational reformers will encounter diehard loyalty to graded structure, to competitive marking practices, to age-graded groupings, to promotion-and-retention policies, and to the self-contained classroom. All of these obsolescent arrangements have long been deeply entrenched and earnestly endorsed. They have staunchly resisted numerous reform efforts, whose heroes have included John Dewey, Helen Parkhust, Francis W. Parker, and Carleton Washburne, over most of this century. All of these reformers, in their time, were apparently seen as incompatible with the prevailing intellectual, social, and political climates.

Now those climates have shifted. The entire nation is caught up in intensive reexamination of schooling practices, with the term "restructuring" as a label under which various reforms, including nongradedness, are being pursued.

The motivation behind many of these current reforms is largely economic and political, as America's competitive standing in the world market has declined and as the schools have borne much of the blame for the shortage of skilled and industrious workers. However, there has also been a big and welcome change in the nation's awareness of the unmet educational (and other) needs of large segments of the population, as noted previously.

Also claimed previously was that educational research and development has been increasing in quality and quantity. Not so very long ago, research in our field was ignored, even scorned, in ways such as Eiseley has documented. By 1992, however, the national climate has changed and some of the "old theories" such as those disputing gradedness in its many dimensions have, let us hope, been given the "hairsbreadth twist" that "might open an entirely new vista to the human reason."

We therefore perceive that the time is at last ripe for a serious onslaught on literally graded practice. In subsequent chapters we will share what the continuing flow of research has to say about the rigid lockstep, about promotion and retention, about the typical competitive atmosphere and the ABCDF marking system that symbolizes it, about unit-age classroom groupings, about cooperative learning, and about the usefulness of team arrangements for teachers and children. We will offer practical suggestions for setting outmoded systems and practices aside. We hope that what we have to say will be sufficiently persuasive, and will seem sufficiently plausible, so that many of our readers will find themselves embracing nongradedness. In this closing phase of the twentieth century, let the graded school structure as we have known it, especially in its extreme dimensions, be laid to rest.

REFERENCES

Angus, David L., Jeffrey E. Mirel and Maris A. Vinouskis. 1988. "Historical Development of Age Stratification in Schooling," *Teachers College Record*, 90:211–233.

Bloom, Benjamin. 1976. *Human Characteristics and School Learning*. New York, NY: McGraw-Hill.

Eiseley, Loren. 1960. *The Firmament of Time*. New York, NY: Atheneum Publishers.

Goodlad, John I. and Robert H. Anderson. 1987. *The Nongraded Elementary School*. New York, NY: Teachers College Press; Harcourt Brace and World, 1959 and 1963.

Kozol, Jonathan. 1991. *Savage Inequities*. New York, NY: Crown.

CHAPTER 2

Considering Our Preparedness for Major Change

WHEN approaching the prospect of a major change in one's professional life, there is inevitably a mixture of doubt, enthusiasm, apprehension, confidence, curiosity, uncertainty, and other emotions swirling together in one's head. If the change involves adjusting to new relationships with peers and new or different ways of dealing with clients (in our case, pupils and their parents), it is all the more likely that the emotions will be intense.

There are also important intellectual questions that accompany change, and to the extent that one is either unable to identify those questions or unable to answer them with confidence, one will be less than eager to proceed.

Already suggested in Chapter 1 is that previous efforts to break away from the graded structure did not make sufficient headway because surrounding conditions were not favorable. Prevailing outdated views of what schools should do and be, of how children's school progress is best stimulated, of how the work of teachers can best be organized, and of the human interactions that ought to occur in a well-managed school environment, tended to contradict or diminish the arguments for adopting different approaches. This book contends that views now in ascendance are far more compatible with nongradedness, and the prospects for its implementation are therefore much better.

Such a conclusion, however, requires verification in each specific school and/or school district situation, and one of the first steps any staff should take before venturing into a nongraded program is to check out the mindsets of its members. In this chapter, we present suggestions for managing that process.

INVENTORY OF EDUCATIONAL BELIEFS AND IDEAS

In order to facilitate photocopying, we are providing in Supplement One (which appears at the back of the book, with perforated edges for

easy removal), an inventory that contains seventy-five statements designed to provoke the reader into agreeing with, disagreeing with, or
acknowledging uncertainty about the beliefs and ideas represented.

The statements have been written in language that sometimes states
the opposite of what we (the authors) believe to be true. Therefore any
reader whose views coincide exactly with ours will agree with many of
the statements, will disagree with many others, and in some cases will
find it difficult or impossible (as we do) to agree or disagree with some
of the statements. A list of the authors' own responses is given in Appendix A (p. 217).

Our suggestion is that individual readers should respond to the instrument privately, subsequently taking note of the extent to which they
and the authors are in agreement. In order to understand how the
authors themselves have responded to each statement, there is provided
(on pp. 15–27) a discussion that shows either Disagree, Agree, or Uncertain as the "preferred response" in each case and then provides an
explanation for the preference. In order to make the explanations more
readable, only a few of them make reference to research or researchers;
but it should be noted that for (almost) every preferred response there
is in fact a body of supporting research evidence. At the end of this
chapter are cited some of the references that were used in putting the
questions together.

In a few cases, the response admittedly is geared to a strongly held
opinion rather than to empirical research data. The reader should be
aware that there remains room for uncertainty about some of the statements. Overall, however, it seems reasonable to proclaim that school
personnel who are comfortable with all or most of the authors'
preferred responses will find it much easier, as well as more tempt-
ing, to move forward with nongradedness than will those who have
doubts or reservations. The inventory, then, is a helpful device for
measuring the collective readiness of a school or a school district for
making changes.

GET READY, GET SET, GET ON YOUR MARKS . . .

Step One

Turn now to Supplement One (the inventory) in the back of the book.
Carefully remove the inventory and the response sheet. Make as many
photocopies as will be needed, if you plan to invite colleagues to partic-

ipate in the inventorying process. Then, with appropriate explanation, have each person respond to the instrument privately.

Step Two

Either as a total staff or in smaller groups, sit together and compare/tabulate the responses. This might begin with questions such as:

(1) Which of these statements were the most difficult to "assess?"
(2) Which statements deal with policies/practices that are nearest and dearest to our professional hearts?
(3) Which statements appear to be the most controversial among educators?

Such discussion might help group members to discover topics on which there is reasonable consensus, items on which viewpoints differ rather markedly, and also items where mystery or uncertainty may prevail.

Step Three

Now that you and your colleagues have made a statement to each other about the ideas and beliefs identified in the inventory, it may be interesting to see how your views do or do not coincide with the views of those who put the inventory together. Turn, therefore, to the material that follows. It might be helpful for someone to first read off the seventy-five code responses (1 = D; 2 = A; 3 = A; 4 = A; 5 = D; etc.) so that everyone could circle the numbers of the ones they got "right" and mark the ones they got "wrong," as a quick check. Then, as time and interest permit, the "official" explanations as provided below could be debated.

INVENTORY OF EDUCATIONAL BELIEFS AND IDEAS

Code A = Agree; D = Disagree; ? = Uncertain

1. Students who move in and out of nongraded programs may be placed at a disadvantage when they move to a middle or junior high school.

DISAGREE: *Not if they have learned how to learn, and to believe in themselves, both of which are likely.*

2. A school in which grade labels and related organizational practices are used, can in fact be superior to a school that has officially abandoned the grade structure.

   AGREE: *Officially abandoning grade labels is a good first step, but it takes skill and effort to make nongradedness a reality.*

3. A nongraded program is essential for students even beyond the primary level.

   AGREE: *The benefits of nongradedness, in the form of a good and appropriate education, should not be denied to students at the intermediate and middle school levels.*

4. Student evaluation records that consist of frequent anecdotal notations and dated samples of a child's work may be a more effective "reporting system" than the traditional letter grades.

   AGREE: *Standardized tests and formal check lists evaluate children on conformity rather than diversity. A "portfolio" evaluation program provides the teacher and parent with more insight into the child's progress.*

5. A nongraded or continuous progress program can be built on a system of "defined levels."

   DISAGREE: *"Defined levels" are a little different in concept from "grade levels."*

6. It could be harmful to children if their school work during the first three or four years is nearly always successful.

   DISAGREE: *Most researchers claim that continuing success is beneficial. Keep in mind, however, that real learning results from making lots of errors and mistakes along the way.*

7. Discipline problems tend to increase when teachers assume most of the responsibility for directing the learning process.

   AGREE: *Teacher-directed learning and external rules do not increase self control.*

8. Children can learn without liking their teachers.

   UNCERTAIN: *On this point it's hard to be entirely sure. What we know is that the teacher must believe and communicate to all children that they can achieve and accomplish great things.*

9. A competitive learning environment increases motivation, achievement, and self-improvement.

DISAGREE: *Often just the opposite. When the goal is simply to avoid failure in a competitive situation, learning and achievement suffer. Recent evidence points to significant advantages for students when they experience a mostly collaborative school involvement.*

10. Understanding the culture and ethnicity of students matters little in creating instructional strategies.

    DISAGREE: *Teachers need to become more aware of the intrinsic and distinct "character" of different cultures.*

11. Strong research evidence supports the recommendation that elementary school classes should not exceed (approximately) twenty-five pupils.

    DISAGREE: *A 25–1* ratio *seems desirable, but not the* class size *of twenty-five. Many different group sizes are needed. Twenty-five to thirty is a poor group size for almost any instructional purpose. The specific task, materials required, and student needs determine the number of students that may be profitably engaged in any given educational experience.*

12. Multi-age classes allow students to develop both leadership and followership skills.

    AGREE: *A younger student has less understanding of expectations and procedures and so starts as a follower. Over time, the student matures and becomes more comfortable in assuming a leadership role in the classroom.*

13. Studies have provided evidence that "age segregation" in classrooms increases competition and aggression of students.

    AGREE: *Many schools cling tenaciously to "age segregation" even though studies reveal that multi-age grouping promotes a more natural, harmonious, and nurturing environment.*

14. The use of computer-assisted instruction may increase the isolation and alienation of students, even in the nongraded school.

    UNCERTAIN: *We don't know enough yet to answer this question definitively, but some research shows that students learn more when they use the computer together rather than individually.*

15. In an open classroom, the materials provided have a prescribed usage determined by the curriculum.

    DISAGREE: *This is true only to a small extent—the teacher may have a purpose for providing certain materials, but should be flexi-*

ble enough to adapt instruction according to the children's own responses to the materials.

16. While the student takes an active part in an activity-centered or open classroom, the teacher is equally active in stimulating children's interest.

AGREE: *The teacher is responsible for providing a broad range of materials that will help stimulate the many interests of the child. Unless children have been exposed to an educational activity, they do not have the opportunity to learn.*

17. Sequenced curriculum materials are very helpful and should be followed by all students, especially in the skill areas of mathematics and reading.

DISAGREE: *Sequence of learning must be determined by the teacher and each individual student as there is little logical or inherent sequence in the various curriculum areas; no predetermined sequence is appropriate to all learners; and individual differences in level of competence and interest are constantly in flux.*

18. A visit to an "open space" school building will show evidence of nongrading, team teaching, and flexibility in action.

DISAGREE: *Unfortunately, even though the open space building facilitates a flexible, nongraded team teaching approach, it does not guarantee that the staff will develop this type of program.*

19. Typically, teachers are trained and prepared to make the most effective use of non-professional assistants in the schools.

DISAGREE: *New roles for paraprofessionals and teacher-aides are emerging. Many of these adults live in the neighborhood of the school and "know" the students well. Teachers should be encouraged to utilize the skills, experience, and even colleagueship of paraprofessionals.*

20. One of the purposes of team teaching is to make possible the easy scheduling of a greater number of "homogeneous" groups of children than is possible in self-contained class programs.

DISAGREE: *This is a trick question, because it's partly true. Teaming allows both teachers and children to experience many types of groups and to have contact with a great variety of people each day.*

21. Team teaching is difficult when the team members have a variety of opinions and ideas to contribute to lesson planning.

DISAGREE: *Variety is the spice of life. Differing opinions and ideas are in fact necessary if good programs are to emerge.*

22. Teachers often feel lonely and unappreciated.

    AGREE: *All too many teachers work in self-contained isolation, closed off from adult contact for the greater part of the day. Even if the teacher does a good job, no one else really knows.*

23. The recent wave of site-based management schools will have little effect on incorporating new and innovative instructional strategies.

    UNCERTAIN: *It is too early to tell. In some cases radical and exciting changes have been made in school policy, including adopting a nongraded philosophy, while in other cases only cosmetic and superficial changes have resulted, maintaining the status quo.*

24. When innovations are being considered, classroom teachers should be involved in preliminary planning and in all phases of implementation.

    AGREE: *Yes! Teachers must clearly understand the* rationale *behind any innovation, and must have sufficient time, support, and resources to successfully implement the new strategy.*

25. Most parents tend to understand the philosophy and goals behind a nongraded or team-teaching school.

    DISAGREE: *No. Unfortunately, most parents do not have adequate or sufficiently recent information on the goals and strategies of nongraded schools, and the schools they attended were graded with self-contained classrooms.*

26. A "nongraded first grade" and "nongraded reading" are acceptable forms of nongradedness.

    DISAGREE: *Can a "grade" be made nongraded? If nongrading is good for one subject, why not all subjects? In other words, this is a case where* all *of the loaf—not just a part—is important.*

27. Research studies in nongradedness have increased steadily from the early 1960s right up to the present.

    DISAGREE: *Literature searches reveal only a relatively small number of recent studies in nongradedness. The majority of studies were published between 1968 and 1976. Unfortunately, there was a definite return to "traditional" ways of thinking during the late 1970s and the 1980s.*

28. There are concepts and skills that must be mastered at each grade level if the pupil is to progress in school.

DISAGREE: *Eventually, all the concepts and skills must be mastered; but children learn at different rates and in different sequences. Progress should be noted on a continuum, not in segments.*

29. Used with care and discretion, ABCDF report cards can be a useful mechanism in the school's educational and public relations program.

DISAGREE: *Never, never, never! Kids learn less from competition with each other than from cooperation with each other. ABCDF perpetuates an unhealthy and unproductive way of viewing and describing pupil growth and progress.*

30. The main reason to have a strong evaluation and assessment program is so that the school can fully inform the parents of the child's progress and status.

DISAGREE: *No, it is even more important to evaluate for programmatic and child-oriented purposes. Evaluation by the teacher and/or the child is done for diagnostic purposes and results in the formulation of new educational objectives.*

31. Elementary-aged students should not be involved in making up rules of behavior and discipline under which they will operate— this process should occur mainly at the high school level.

DISAGREE: *Children at any age do not respond or take kindly to rules that are simply laid down by teachers or adults. The involvement of students in developing the rules that will "govern" their class or school pays dividends in many ways.*

32. Children in the primary unit (formerly grades 1-2-3) rarely need to have continued exposure to kindergarten type experiences.

DISAGREE: *Since children develop at individual rates and sequences, how can a sharp division be made between kindergarten and primary activities?*

33. Learning goals are obscured when a variety of activities are being carried on simultaneously during a given class period.

DISAGREE: *Different children learn in different ways. Therefore, a variety of activities is* necessary *for maximum learning.*

34. Usually, children are not given sufficient responsibility for establishing and pursuing their learning goals.

AGREE: *Unfortunately this is true. Commitment to learning depends, in part, on self selection of goals. Let's place more trust in the kids!*

35. The teacher-student relationship, more than any other single factor, determines how much learning will actually take place.

UNCERTAIN: *It is important, but we cannot be sure it is* the *most important factor, especially if instructional strategies might include cooperative learning, computer-assisted learning, or continuous progress learning.*

36. Group cohesiveness is lost when children in a classroom are not of approximately the same age.

DISAGREE: *On the contrary, age variance can be a real advantage. Children's natural play groups are composed of children spanning several age years.*

37. In the typical school, setting up classroom groups by ability is necessary and desirable.

DISAGREE: *Studies reveal that positive interactions and beneficial peer modeling between high ability and low ability students* can *increase the achievement of lower ability students. However, the usage of homogeneous skills groups is useful as long as these are* temporary *and* flexible. *The unit or class with which the student has permanent identification must be heterogeneous.*

38. There is a direct relation between promotion/retention practices and student performance.

DISAGREE: *Just the opposite. There is no valid evidence that demonstrates retention has beneficial impact on low achieving students. Research shows that non-promoted children learn less than those who were promoted.*

39. Textbooks are used the same way in nongraded and graded schools.

DISAGREE: *Not only do textbooks nurture conformity, but the fortunes of the textbook industry are tied to selling complete sets of textbooks for* each *grade level. Research has shown that graded textbooks are stumbling blocks to individual progress, and therefore would be less important in a nongraded school.*

40. A "cooperative learning" environment will increase the academic achievement of every student in the classroom.

UNCERTAIN: *Cooperative learning will increase the academic achievement for all students, including the gifted. Further, cooperative learning teaches students how to work together.*

41. The availability of materials for students is crucial to the success of individualized programs.

AGREE: *Not only must materials be available, but there must be a wide variety to accommodate different learning needs and styles.*

42. It is highly desirable for all children to formulate their own individual learning goals with guidance from their teachers.

AGREE: *Even young children can make good decisions about what to learn. The unique needs, interests, and abilities, as well as the rates, styles, and patterns of learning for each child will determine his/her individual curriculum.*

43. Some teachers keep their classroom doors tightly shut to avoid criticism and evaluation of their teaching.

AGREE: *Yes, but this is a self-defeating behavior. Interaction and interchange are necessary for growth. Working on a team helps teachers receive constructive suggestions, see other teachers' ways of teaching, and become a more confident teacher.*

44. School buildings with self-contained classrooms cannot house team teaching and nongradedness.

DISAGREE: *It is a little harder to team when space is inflexible, but teachers and administrators can be very creative when confronted with old-fashioned schools built to house old-fashioned ideas.*

45. Team teaching programs cannot function effectively unless the role of the principal changes to that of group facilitator.

AGREE: *Well-informed, supportive, skillful leadership enables teachers to more successfully adopt new teaching procedures.*

46. About 90 percent of the professional knowledge a career teacher can possess will have to be acquired after entering the profession as a newly certified teacher.

AGREE: *This points up the need for team teaching, which permits a continuing on-the-job seminar, and a good staff development program.*

47. Flexible scheduling means having periodic changes in a "set" schedule.

DISAGREE: *No, it means much more than that. Besides, a "set" schedule is probably a bad thing. Keep things as "open" and "loose" as you can!*

48. In moving into a nongraded structure, it is best to nongrade the primary division first.

UNCERTAIN: *This is usually true, since primary teachers do seem to be the ones most amenable to change. However, the whole school staff has to be involved eventually, and sometimes it is upper-grade teachers who are most ready for the change.*

49. The majority of elementary school buildings are either obsolete or greatly inhibit team teaching concepts, collaborative learning, and other new instructional strategies.

AGREE: *Sad, isn't it? Better leadership is needed in planning for flexible school buildings in the twenty-first century. Meanwhile, renovations are possible in most situations.*

50. Staff development, training, and coaching are crucial if a nongraded, team-taught program is to succeed.

AGREE: *To change habitual patterns, new skills and techniques are required. Time, resources, and support must be provided, on an ongoing basis, as teachers develop, practice, and assess new skills and strategies.*

51. A portfolio of a student's work can be an effective assessment tool.

AGREE: *What could be more informative than examining the student's actual work? Original essays, science projects, and other evidence of mastery provide insight—something that no "ABCDF" type of mark could ever do.*

52. A student evaluation should concentrate on the weaknesses of the student—and offer strategies to improve the problem areas.

DISAGREE: *There is good reason to believe that concentrating on strengths is good, and focusing on weaknesses can be harmful. A good assessment program must, however, take constructive note of weaknesses.*

53. Uniform achievement standards must be maintained if a school is to be considered a good school.

DISAGREE: *Uniform achievement standards too often become maximum limits. The important idea is to help each child attain optimum performance.*

54. The greatest single difficulty in accomplishing the goals of the "nongraded school" involves solving the curriculum problems that this organizational scheme raises.

AGREE: *This is true. That is why interdisciplinary strategies such as "writing-across-the-curriculum" are so valuable.*

55. A nongraded program enables a school to "cover" the standardized curriculum faster and better.

DISAGREE: *A nongraded program is* not *based on speed but on the needs and interests of each student. Committed teachers work hard to avoid "covering" the curriculum superficially.*

56. The most appropriate type of competition in the school is where children compete with themselves.

AGREE: *There are many children who prefer either doing their own work in their own way, or working in collaborative groups with other children. Competition can often be harmful—especially in competing with other children for high grades.*

57. The teacher should try to keep a close watch over all children to make sure they are doing what they are supposed to do.

DISAGREE: *In this way teachers dominate children, refuse to allow them opportunities to develop responsibility for their own learning, and discourage initiative. Yet most teachers indicate these goals are important.*

58. Teachers should never say to a student, "I don't know."

DISAGREE: *Those involved in the school enterprise are co-learners, especially teachers and students. No one knows everything, but one can ask other students or teachers and use resource material to help the questioner and oneself find the answer.*

59. Modern concepts of curriculum and instruction see teachers as resource persons rather than transmitters of knowledge.

AGREE: *The teacher is a facilitator of learning. This means that the teacher* supports *a child's development by helping each child formulate goals, diagnose problem areas, suggest alternative plans of action, provide resource materials, and give encouragement or support or prodding as needed.*

60. Student failure is often due to teacher attitude and low expectations.

AGREE: *High teacher expectations reflect respect for the child's potential, and do seem to be connected to student achievement and improvement. If teachers expect poor performance, they'll usually get it—the "Pygmalion effect."*

61. Research studies have shown a positive causal relationship between the self-contained classroom and the personal-social-emotional well-being of younger children.

    DISAGREE: *The research shows just the opposite. It's not organization that influences well-being, but the way children are treated. The opportunity to associate with more teachers and more kids apparently has a positive relationship to individual well-being.*

62. In general, gifted children or slow-learning children are best served in special, separate classes.

    DISAGREE: *No, not on a permanent basis. It is best when they can sometimes be together, and at other times mix with children of other abilities.*

63. Academic achievement should be the chief criterion for pupil placement in a nongraded program.

    DISAGREE: *No, it is only one of many. Learning style, interest, speed of learning, ability, motivation, friendships, and probably other factors are criteria also to be considered.*

64. The curriculum should be organized to develop the understanding of concepts and methods of inquiry rather than to emphasize specific content learning.

    AGREE: *Detailed subject matter learning may be soon forgotten, but the understanding of concepts and methods of inquiry can be applied in new situations.*

65. As a general rule, a "messy" classroom reinforces children's bad habits.

    DISAGREE: *Learning is the result of childrens' interactions with the world they inhabit. An individual learns by direct experience and with manipulation of the learning environment. Therefore the child must be allowed to explore, to experiment, to mess around, to play, and to have the freedom to err.*

66. A cooperative learning procedure promotes more positive cross-sex and cross-ethnic relationships than does individualistic or competitive learning.

    AGREE: *Competition, including intergroup competition, promotes less positive cross-sex and cross-ethnic relationships than does a cooperative environment. When cooperation dominates an instructional situation, positive relationships among heterogeneous students result.*

67. Since manipulative materials are so important in open and non-graded classrooms, there must be enough of each item for each child.

DISAGREE: *No, this could be wasteful. Diversity in usage and types of material is encouraged to meet different interests and learning styles.*

68. Having more than one teacher will probably confuse a good many children.

DISAGREE: *Having only one teacher may also confuse or frustrate a child, especially a child who finds it easier to learn from a "teaching style" different from the one used by the classroom teacher. The "one teacher best for the child" concept is a myth and a fallacy. Most children are easily able to adjust to working with several teachers.*

69. Teacher empowerment has more to do with issues of money and recognition than with curriculum or instruction.

DISAGREE: *Many teachers have been recently fighting for the right to implement curriculum and teaching techniques that are more student-centered than those currently in place at their schools.*

70. Fear of failure is a greater "motivator" than "guaranteed success."

DISAGREE: *No, not for most people. Students are less likely to perform well when the "stakes" are too high. A cooperative teaching team will help its members plan successful lessons by working together. Team members will analyze "failures" in a supportive manner and use coaching techniques to improve the instructional practices of each team member.*

71. Hierarchical structure is a necessary ingredient of full-fledged team teaching.

UNCERTAIN: *It depends on the team teaching model. In some cases there is never a teacher leader, while in others, there is a rotating system. In reality there does need to be someone in charge. Usually the teacher with the best organizational skills becomes the team leader, regardless of the official designation.*

72. Team teaching is a form of departmentalization.

DISAGREE: *This is a frequent misconception. A team of teachers is responsible for the entire instructional program of all students on their team. Teachers plan, teach, and evaluate together. Individual team members, however, should each play an "expert" or specialist role within the program.*

73. Strategically, before officially launching a nongraded program in a school, it is very helpful to first implement a cooperative, team teaching model.

AGREE: *Yes. Teachers often need to informally experiment with developing methods of cooperation, team teaching, and materials sharing before being asked to implement a full-fledged nongraded program.*

74. Parents are usually reluctant to accept children's greater freedom of choice and movement in a school that adopts the "open classroom" or nongraded approach.

DISAGREE: *Some may object at first, but parents are happy when their children are happy, confident, and achieving. Parents will give more support to the idea of flexibility and student choice than teachers might expect. In fact, research reveals that* involved *and* informed *parents can be a crucial component in developing a successful educational strategy.*

75. Unless one is nearly certain of the results, a new school program should not be tried out.

DISAGREE: *If that was accepted as true, no one would have walked on the moon, or even on shoes. What we should guard against are new programs that have a poor research or support base, or a poor chance of succeeding. Nongradedness and team teaching have a very strong research/support base.*

A FINAL STEP IN USING INVENTORY INFORMATION

These seventy-five statements cover a variety of topics that fall roughly into six categories: (1) continuous progress; nongradedness; (2) individual differences; (3) pupil grouping; (4) curriculum, methods, and materials; (5) team teaching; and (6) site-based management.

After you and your colleagues have identified levels of agreement with the authors' preferred responses, look again at the response sheet (Appendix A, page 217), and draw five parallel lines (from left to right) as follows:

(1) Under items 5, 30, and 55. The fifteen numbers above the line (1–5, 26–30, and 51–55) represent statements having to do with *nongradedness and continuous progress.*

(2) Under items 10, 35 and 60. The fifteen numbers (6–10, 31–35, and 56–60) belong to *individual differences.*

(3) Under items 13, 38, and 63. Nine items (11–13, 36–38, 61–63) deal with *pupil grouping.*

(4) Under items 17, 42 and 67. Twelve items: *curriculum, methods, and materials.*

(5) Under items 22, 47 and 72. Fifteen items: *team teaching.*

The remaining nine items (23–25, 48–50, 73–75) relate to school-based management.

You and your colleagues can now make some estimates of the *categories* of questions with which you were most "comfortable," as compared with those that proved to be problematic. If, for example, there was a higher proportion of statements in the *pupil grouping* category on which you and your colleagues tripped up, that information could be helpful as you seek to learn more about current research trends. If the fifteen "team teaching" items made good sense to most of you, this could reinforce all of you in taking steps away from your self-contained classrooms.

The inventory, it should be remembered, is intended mostly as a stimulant to your thinking. By the time you and your colleagues have wrestled with it for a while, you should all have a clearer view of which areas and practices bind you together, and which will require a certain amount of further study and negotiation.

SOME WORDS OF REASSURANCE

By the time a staff has considered all of the ramifications that could be involved in making as major a change as the move to nongradedness, it may feel somewhat overwhelmed. Using the inventory and/or other instruments to discover where there are shared convictions and/or perceptions, and where there may be need for gathering more information or dealing with potentially sensitive concerns, can be an important first step toward a proactive, confident stance.

We (the authors) perceive that teachers will disagree with each other less often on fundamental values—for example the "right" of each precious child to develop his/her full potential within a nurturing educational environment—than they will on procedural/operational matters where entrenched habits (not beliefs) are challenged in some way. For example, having worked in isolation for so many years, the prospect of more active adult colleagueship may at first seem to some teachers as less than wonderful. Having long used conventional report cards and promotion-retention mechanisms as presumably useful motivating devices, changing to a more personalized and less competitive strategy may seem like a dubious move. Having discouraged pupils from moving around too much and chatting with each other, a livelier and noisier classroom may seem like an invitation to discipline problems. Having faithfully followed the rigid curriculum sequences of a graded program, a more flexible and integrated curriculum may seem to offer less substance. Perhaps most important of all, having already learned that a conscientious teacher's work is never done, the unpredictable time demands of the proposed new program may seem unbearable.

Happily, we can offer some reassurances on most of these points, and also identify some real advantages that are built into the restructured setting.

First of all, when you have been giving your best to the teaching role for a long time, your energy meter has already gone up as high as it can go. Of course, there have always been some teachers who do not work as hard or as earnestly as they should, and for whom cutting corners and making only a marginal contribution to the school's success is more or less habitual. In a restructured school, such teachers tend to become uncomfortable, and their foot-dragging could become a burden to their high-minded colleagues. Their griping about "so much extra work" might even come to be seen as legitimate, especially since it is probably true for them.

But teachers long accustomed to a heavy workload should not be misled by the protestations of marginal people. It is true that the workload will become different in several ways, and perhaps during the first few months the emotional load will seem heavier than usual; but once some operational decisions have been worked out and some routines are established, life in the school should if anything become more tolerable. Under the old graded paradigm, there are/were some built-in frustrations for children and for teachers that in the new nongraded paradigm have been cleansed away. Within the nongraded environment there should be a happier, success-oriented, productive atmosphere that makes classroom management less stressful and teachers' sense of accomplishment stronger.

One possible danger, which we will discuss again later in the book, is that teachers—once involved in the excitement of a new program—might voluntarily bite off more "extra" work than they can really chew, for example in curriculum revision or in developing new teaching strategies. They may need to be reminded periodically that, as the saying goes, "Rome wasn't built in a day!" Creating a new and better world for children is a long, painstaking, trial-and-error process, and every day/week/month/year decisions have to be made about what needs doing *now*, what needs doing *within the month* (or so), and what can be *postponed* until higher-priority work has been accomplished.

Despite the national and state politicians who are constantly calling for a quick fix, repair and renewal of the American school system needs to be recognized as a long-term project. Getting a good, authentic nongraded program started and running is at least a two- or three-year project, and completing the fine tuning will require a number of years after that. Understanding and accepting that a manageable pace is both honorable and practical can be a great relief to everyone.

Site-based decision making, which is a major national trend, happens to be uniquely compatible with the trend toward nongradedness. Inherent in transferring more responsibility for operational decisions to front-line workers is a belief that better decisions can and will be made by those "closest to the action." It therefore represents, literally, a vote of confidence in the motivation and in the skills of such persons. Historically, teachers have been uncommonly vulnerable to top-down management, and all too often the administrators have enforced uniformity of instruction even to the point where, say, a fourth grade teacher whose class is not up to Chapter 5 in the mathematics textbook by Thanksgiving is considered to be delinquent.

Freed of such unintelligent supervisory expectations, teachers can address the learning needs of their pupils in a greater variety of ways. Freed of the tyranny of a timetable geared to gradedness, teachers can be much more responsible to pupil learning rates and styles. All in all, endowing teachers with the authority to pursue defined goals according to their own best judgment may seem revolutionary, but it is in fact a belated acknowledgement that intelligence and wisdom resides in the teaching force to a remarkable degree.

One of the strongest messages in this book is that teachers as well as children are more productive within a cooperative framework than within a framework of isolation. Teachers who have already had some experience with teaming probably need little or no reassurance on this point. Those with only self-contained experience, however, may need some initial bolstering. Perhaps they do not yet realize how much easier it is to tackle a challenging task when one has colleagues to share the burden. Perhaps the concept of synergy (loosely defined as a situation where the energy of one person plus the energy of another person plus the energy of yet another person can add up to the energy of five persons!) has not yet caught their imagination. In fact, perhaps they have not tried to calculate how much easier their recent professional experiences could have been if they had had more chances just to talk problems over, and exchange big or little success stories, with colleagues. We almost envy these persons for the pleasant surprises and the great new ideas that lie in store for them.

Finally, we hope it is reassuring to teachers to discover how thoroughly consistent the concept/practice of nongradedness is with their most deeply held convictions about children. In the past, these convictions have often been at odds with prevailing societal views and expectations. However, in the 1990s the need for abandoning bad schooling practices such as gradedness and top-down policy making is widely recognized. Probably there has not been a better time in this century for teachers to announce proudly that they are ready and willing to rescue the schools from these destructive habits.

The following books, articles, and authors were among those used as references in putting together the survey questions (see also references attached to Chapters 3 and 4).

REFERENCES

Bloom, Benjamin. 1981. *All Our Children Learning: A Primer for Parents, Teachers, and Other Educators*. New York, NY: McGraw-Hill.

Clinchy, Evans. 1987. *A Consumer's Guide to Schools of Choice: For Parents and Other Educators*. Boston, MA: Institute for Responsive Education.

Dar, Yetiezkel and N. Nurg Resh. 1986. "Classroom Intellectual Composition and Academic Achievement," *American Educational Research Journal*, 23(3):357–374.

Freeman, Jayne. 1984. "How I Learned to Stop Worrying and Love My Combination Class," *Instructor*, 93(7):48, 54.

Goodlad, John and Robert H. Anderson. 1987. *The Nongraded Elementary School*. New York, NY: Teachers College Press.

Labaree, David. 1983. *Setting the Standard: The Characteristics and Consequences of Alternative Student Promotional Policies*. Citizens Committee on Public Education in Philadelphia.

Ornstein, Allan C. 1989. "The Nature of Grading," *The Clearinghouse*, 62(April): 365–369.

Pratt, David. 1983. *Age Segregation in Schools*, paper presented at *The Annual Meeting of the American Educational Research Association*.

Veldman, Donald J. and Julie P. Sanford. 1984. "The Influence of Class Ability on Student Achievement and Classroom Behavior," *American Educational Research Journal*, 21(3):629–644.

Warring, Douglas, David Johnson, Geoffrey Maruyama and Roger Johnson. 1985. "Impact of Different Type of Cooperative Learning on Cross-Ethnic and Cross-Sex Relationships," *Journal of Educational Psychology*, 77(1):53–59.

CHAPTER 3

What Does the Research Say about Nongradedness?

MUCH is known about how children learn and what schooling practices foster child growth and learning. This chapter provides a background of evidence to show that nongraded schools are most likely to benefit children from all circumstances and in all ability ranges. First presented is a brief piece on learning theory and development, followed by the issue of success as more motivating than failure. Research on promotion, ability grouping, and tracking is then followed by an extensive meta-analysis of the studies that compare nongraded and graded schools on academic achievement and mental health standardized tests.

LEARNING THEORY AND DEVELOPMENT

No two students arrive at school with identical dispositions to learn. They differ in physical development (for example, eye-hand coordination) and in life experiences both as to content and as to level of their success in negotiating their environment. As children commence the essential task of learning to read, it is clear that some have already acquired many critical prerequisites, but others have not. Differences in levels of attention and motivation are readily apparent. Some make rapid gains while others need more time before progress is noted (see Figure 3.1).

The "school ready" child begins already having mastered much of the standard kindergarten curriculum and probably gains little during this first school year. She (the "ready" child is most likely to be a girl from a home where the parents have provided many of the usual beginning school activities) then progresses year by year through the expected school curriculum and completes her fourth year as expected. On the other hand, the "late bloomer" has not been socialized to the expected

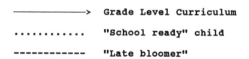

Grade 3				
Grade 2				
Grade 1				
Kindergarten				
Chronological Age	5	6	7	8
School Year	1	2	3	4

———————→   **Grade Level Curriculum**

· · · · · · · · · · ·   **"School ready" child**

— — — — — — — —   **"Late bloomer"**

FIGURE 3.1 Grade level curriculum and student learning rates.

school rules such as waiting for a turn and raising his hand before speaking. He (as unready students are most likely to be boys and/or from homes that are unable to assist their children in school readiness activities) is unlikely to be willing to focus on teacher-directed tasks, but strives to move toward other more active activities. Quite frequently, this child suddenly (or so it appears) "catches on" and advances through several years of the standard curriculum if he has been placed in a continuous progress situation that allows this type of advancement.

Less rapid gains (even a loss) or a plateau in achievement may occur as the skills are being refined or if a shift to a new more efficient technique is being mastered. Fatigue, illness or absence will also negatively impact on performance. Repetition of errors or focus on the wrong part of the task may also impede learning rates.

In *Toward a Theory of Instruction*, Bruner (1966) wrote, "There is no unique sequence for all learners, and the optimum in any particular case will depend upon a variety of factors, including past learning, stage of development, nature of the material, and individual differences." Because there is "no single ideal sequence," effective curriculum "must contain different ways of activating children, different ways of presenting sequences, different opportunities for some children to 'skip' parts while others work their way through, different ways of putting things." Bruner suggests that teachers need to observe children in order to see "what they are making of the material and how they are organizing it" as knowledge of their achievements is insufficient.

For example, two very young children when faced with a plate of five chocolate chip cookies will very quickly divide the cookies between themselves, and after viewing the remaining cookie will carefully divide it into two equal halves. These children understand the concepts of division and fractions long before they are able to give the correct answers to a sheet of addition problems from a workbook.

In addition, the particular activities that the teacher has designated for a specific child and the environment (ethos, climate) of the school are factors affecting learning. Learning curves for individuals are sawtoothed with up and down progress rather than smooth like those typically given in educational psychology textbooks. The better the match between an individual's learning dispositions and the learning experiences, the more likely the student will progress. Gordon (1988) states that educational programming based on characteristics such as social/economic status, sex and gender, ethnicity, culture, and language have been unsuccessful due to the variation within each designated group. Instead, more emphasis on individual differences in functioning such as interests, cognitive styles and rates, motivation, work habits, previously developed skills, and temperament all need to be considered within the environmental context.

Time is one element that may be varied. Not all students in grade one will master the first grade curriculum. However, if students are allowed three years to demonstrate the achievement expected at the end of third grade, many more students will be able to do so than if evaluated at the end of each grade (McLoughlin, 1969).

Recently intelligence has been defined by Gardner (1983) to include not only the verbal (linguistic) and mathematical constructs, but also musical, spacial, bodily-kinesthetic, interpersonal, and intrapersonal intelligences. These intelligences (which may be modified through experience) require more active performance than paper and pencil exercises for both learning and assessment. Student projects (Blythe and Gardner, 1990) are suggested as a major vehicle for learning. Caine and Caine's (1991) synthesis of research on the human brain led them to the same instructional recommendation (themes and projects) based on the need for meaning and patterns, parts and whole processed simultaneously, and the uniqueness of each brain. (See Chapter 7 for more discussion.)

SUCCESS OR FAILURE

Most children come to school eager to learn and believing that they are capable of learning. Their positive self-concepts and high levels of self-esteem are based on their past experiences, in which their efforts and interactions with the environment were successful. While it has not been documented that tactics for raising self-esteem will result in increased academic achievement (Scheirer and Kraut, 1979), the two factors are positively correlated (Holly, 1987). Especially for the early years, Bloom (1981) recommends that learning tasks be planned so that children will succeed and so that failure is the result of insufficient di-
᠁᠁sis or inappropriate instructional strategies. He indicates that the continuous progress concept of the ungraded school as described by Goodlad and Anderson (1963), which also eliminates the failure of retention, would foster that success.

McClellan (1985), noted for his life-long work on achievement and motivation, says that in schools where children are effectively motivated, the teachers' and children's own expectations for themselves are high enough to demand the child's best efforts, but not so high that excessive frustration and discouragement result (p. 663). Hope of success translates into a productive tension, which leads to sustained efforts on the task. Fear of failure leads to avoidance of the task, especially when a public failure may lead to rejection by others.

Success raises self-esteem, thereby increasing the willingness to work, which then raises the level of achievement. The tasks accomplished, however, must be challenging and perceived as valuable and not trivial to gain this sense of personal efficacy. In addition, Beane (1991) notes that personal efficacy is connected to collective efficacy so that students need to know they (as individuals and as a group) are important and have power. He suggests that a school that enhances self-esteem would have a problem-centered curriculum collaboratively developed and not have tracking, competition, or autocratic procedures.

Some of the conventional wisdom on motivating students is questioned in a 1991 *ASCD Update*. Brophy says that extrinsic rewards convey the idea that learning is unpleasant. Instead teachers should be conveying the attitude that learning after a challenge is a reward. Too much sympathy over failure, praise for trivial tasks, and unsolicited help from the teacher may send the message that the teacher believes the student has low ability, suggests Graham.

PROMOTION AND NONPROMOTION

After reviewing research on promotion and nonpromotion published between 1909 and 1962, Goodlad and Anderson (1963:41) summed up as follows:

> The arguments favoring promotion or nonpromotion fit into four major categories: pupil achievement, pupil attitudes toward school and schooling, pupil social-personal adjustment, and the teacher's view of the school's function. The evidence from research comparing nonpromoted pupils with promoted pupils in these first three areas is overwhelming. Promoted slow-learning children achieve at higher levels, are involved less often in aggressive acts toward school and schooling, get along better with their peers, and appear to have more wholesome feelings of personal worth. Upper grade achievement levels are higher in schools that have low nonpromotion rates. A major area of tension among promoted slow-learners appears to be associated with fear of failure. They express worry over their school progress, believe their parents to be similarly concerned, and frequently resort to cheating as a way of assuring higher achievement.

The introduction to the 1987 edition of Goodlad and Anderson (p. xxii) cites additional recent research that once again affirms the negative effects of retention. Because we feel that the elimination of retention and promotion policies is crucial for the implementation of nongradedness, a number of the major research studies are reviewed here.

Jackson (1975) made a systematic review of the research literature on retention published between 1929 and June 1973. He located thirty original research studies that compared promoted and nonpromoted students quantitatively on achievement or adjustment and concluded: "There is no reliable body of evidence to indicate that grade retention is more beneficial than grade promotion for students with serious academic or adjustment difficulties" (p. 627).

The meta-analysis by Holmes and Matthews (1984) was based on forty-four studies comparing promoted and retained students with sufficient data to compute an effect size. They found that the promoted groups outperformed the retained groups by the following effect sizes or standard deviation units.

Academic achievement	+ .44
Personal adjustment	+ .27
Self-concept	+ .19
Attitude toward school	+ .16

Their powerful conclusions seem to have been ignored:

Those who continue to retain pupils at grade level do so despite cumulative research evidence showing that the potential for negative effects consistently outweighs positive outcomes. Because this cumulative research evidence consistently points to negative effects of nonpromotion, the burden of proof legitimately falls on proponents of retention plans to show there is compelling logic indicating success of their plans when so many other plans have failed. (Holmes and Matthews, 1984: 232)

Holmes' follow-up study published in 1989 (Shepard and Smith) yielded nineteen additional studies, but reached the same conclusion as noted above. Only nine of the sixty-four studies had positive results for retention, but these studies were based on more able populations who received intensive remediation after retention, which resulted in higher achievement only the year after retention. In a few years all benefits for retention disappeared as the older retained child then performed on the same level as the younger promoted student.

Peterson, DeGracie, and Ayabe (1987) found that retained students who received remedial help made better scores on first grade achievement tests taken in their second year of first grade than similar low achievers did in their first year of first grade. These differences disappear by grade three. However, the retained students have now spent an extra year in school and achieve no better than the promoted students.

There has been a widely held belief that kindergarten might be the best time to retain a child, or even that a younger child might be better not to start kindergarten with his/her age mates. Possibly these "red-shirted" students, if boys, will even have a better chance for the football team! Educators who make such recommendations generally believe that children become physiologically "ready for school" and that this cannot be altered by experiences. Other teachers accept children into their classrooms and fit the instruction to the child's needs. Smith and Shepard (1987) have found that whether a child is retained is more likely to be based on the teacher's belief system than on the charac-teristics of the child. They also caution (1986) that the two most popular readiness tests (Gesell School and Metropolitan) were not designed for screening or retaining children and have a 50 percent error rate (p. 80). Children who are retained in kindergarten or first grade perform less well than comparable promoted children and have more negative attitudes toward school and self.

Drawing on their book, *Flunking Grades: Research and Policies on Retention*, Shepard and Smith (1990) detail some highlights:

(1) Retained children actually perform more poorly on average when they go on to the next grade than if they had been promoted without repeating a grade.

(2) Dropouts are five times more likely to have repeated a grade than are high school graduates. Students who repeat two grades have a probability of dropping out of nearly 100 percent.

(3) Children in Yamamoto's (1980) study of childhood stressors rated the prospect of repeating a grade as more stressful than "wetting in class" or being caught stealing. The only two life events they felt would be more stressful than being retained were going blind or losing a parent. Both high-achieving and retained students in-terviewed by Byrnes (1989) viewed retention as a necessary pun-ishment for being bad in class or failing to learn.

(4) There are many alternatives to retention that are more effective in helping low achievers. These include remedial help, before- and after-school programs, summer school, instructional aides to work with target children in the regular classroom, and no-cost peer tutoring. Groups of teachers in some schools have developed staffing teams to work out plans with the next-grade receiving teachers about how to address the learning difficulties for students

who otherwise would have been retention candidates. Some schools "place" poor performing students in the next grade with a formally agreed upon Individualized Educational Plan (IEP), akin to the special education model of intervention.

(5) The annual cost to school districts of retaining 2.4 million students per year is nearly $10 billion. Summer school costs only approximately $1,300 per student, compared to $4,051 for a repeated grade. At a wage of $6 an hour for an aide, it would take the savings from only 1.6 retained students to have an extra adult in every classroom full time to give extra attention to low-achieving students.

While Shepard and Smith (1990) declare that approximately half of all ninth grade students have left school or flunked at least one grade, the Office of Educational Research and Improvement (1990) estimates that only 18 percent of the children have repeated at least one grade by the eighth grade. Even this lower figure indicates that too many children suffer the consequences of retention.

Given the overwhelmingly negative effects of retention on academic achievement and attitudes, plus the added cost to school districts, it seems puzzling that retention as a practice has persisted for so many years. Doyle (1989) notes that community leaders' beliefs that elementary school graduation should indicate attainment of a minimum level of achievement and that promotion is a reward to be earned contribute to the persistence of retention policies.

ABILITY GROUPING AND TRACKING

A best-evidence synthesis of the research studies on ability grouping and elementary school academic achievement was compiled by Slavin (1987). In order to look only at the effects of ability grouping compared to heterogeneous grouping using standard instructional practices, he excluded studies that included gifted or special education classes, nongraded or multi-age programs, open classrooms, team teaching, and instructional practices such as cooperative learning, continuous progress-instruction, individualized instruction, and mastery learning. A median effect size of .00 was found when students were assigned to self-contained classes on the basis of ability. Cross-grade ability grouping for reading (Joplin Plan) provided a median effect of + .45, and within-class ability grouping in mathematics yielded an effect size of + .34 (Slavin, 1987). Based on this study and including the research on nongrading reviewed in 1986, he made the following general suggestions:

(1) Students are assigned to heterogeneous classrooms for all subjects except some reading and mathematics lessons, where similar performance levels are required.

(2) Regrouping for homogeneity is for teaching specific skills only.

(3) These small groups will be assessed frequently so that students no longer needing such instruction will be assigned to different groups.

(4) Teachers need to use different instructional techniques based on the specific skill and group taught (Slavin, 1988:71).

Kulick and Kulick in 1984 had indicated that ability-grouped students gained somewhat more than ungrouped ones and that gifted students in special classes with enriched instruction benefited the most. The difference between these two studies is the Kulicks' inclusion of gifted students, which accounted for the positive effect of ability grouping.

Parents of the gifted and educators who specialize in programs for the gifted speak out against untracking, nongradedness, and cooperative learning instructional strategies, as they believe that the gifted students will benefit by segregation from other students. Kulick and Kulick (1987) obtained a + .10 median for high-ability students in separate groups while Slavin (1987) found a median effect size of + .04. Researchers consider an effect size of less than + .20 to be educationally insignificant. High achievers would be the top 33 percent, while the gifted are in the top 5 percent. Slavin (1991) notes that research comparing gifted students in enrichment programs to those who are not, commonly uses as a control group students rejected from gifted placement but with similar IQ or prior achievement. The only study found with randomly assigned students was conducted by Mikkelson in 1962 and found small differences favoring heterogeneous placement.

Comparisons of gifted students in two control schools and two cooperative-learning elementary schools reported by Slavin (1991) found higher test scores for the gifted students in the cooperative learning situation for all reading and math subtests except language mechanics. Process writing was the instructional strategy in the cooperative learning school, which doesn't stress mechanics out of context. Slavin concludes that skills grouping within heterogeneous classes may be used to differentiate instruction and that enrichment benefits all students. The research does not support ability grouping or non-usage of cooperative learning as beneficial to higher achievers or the gifted.

Special education parents and teachers also display concerns about mainstreaming and other forms of nongrading. They fought hard for the passage of Public Law 94-142, which required school districts to provide the instruction needed by handicapped students, and they are rightly concerned that small class sizes and individual tutoring will no longer be available as needed. However, most are aware of both the social and academic stigma that result from the special education label and the segregation of special education students. Far too many mildly handicapped students have not been returned to regular education placements. Research (Madden and Slavin, 1983) on the mildly academic handicapped (IQ above 70) suggests that placement in regular education classes utilizing individualized instruction or cooperative learning techniques along with resource teachers in the classroom is more beneficial than full- or part-time special education placement in terms of academic achievement, self-esteem, social behavior, and emotional adjustment.

Beckerman and Good (1981) noted that both low- and high-aptitude students had higher achievement if at least one-third of the students were high aptitude and no more than one-third were low aptitude in the classroom. In Cincinnati (Lewis and Moore, 1990), where the classrooms of sixty elementary schools were grouped as to number of low-, average-, and high-achieving students, all three groups had highest gains on the California Achievement Test when in rooms with a majority of high achievers.

It is quite possible that the higher achievement gains made in high-aptitude classrooms or groups are due to the instructional treatment that they receive. Grant and Rothenberg (1986) observed that higher groups are given more complex materials at a faster pace, are interrupted less often, are given more opportunities to speak, and are allowed more self-direction. Instruction in special education classes or low-ability groups most frequently is restricted to the basic skills, presented in small increments and reviewed until mastered. On the other hand, gifted classes and high achievers are more likely to work on self-directed projects conceived as part of a thematic unit that requires problem-solving skills. Maybe all students would learn more if afforded the same rich curriculum and opportunities to learn that are generally allowed only to gifted students.

COMPARISONS OF GRADED AND NONGRADED SCHOOLS

The research studies on nongraded, multigraded, and ungraded grouping support the viability of this organizational concept. In most cases, students in schools organized in one of the above styles do as well as or better than students in traditional self-contained classes in terms of both academic achievement and mental health measures. This is in spite of the fact that the instruments used to measure achievement and mental health often are standardized on students in traditionally structured schools.

The true philosophy of nongradedness is the belief that individuals are unique and need different treatments to reach their maximum growth potential. Some nongraded programs reflect this belief, whereas others have demonstrated a limited acceptance of this belief by allowing students to set only their own pace with materials, methods, and goals predetermined.

Degree of implementation of nongradedness is believed to be an important factor influencing student performance. Very few studies make any attempt to evaluate or assess the degree to which the stated procedure was actually operative. Further research should include this dimension as an integral part of the study.

Multi-age or multigrade groups may be formed as an administrative device to solve negotiated-contract problems of equal class size or as a result of a commitment to having students of varying ages working together. Team Teaching (TT) may be a cooperative teaching arrangement with two or more teachers participating, or it may be part of a hierarchical organization, such as in differentiated staffing. Departmental arrangements are generally not considered to be the same as team teaching, but rather involve subject-matter division of the teaching load.

Individually Guided Education (IGE) consists of two major elements: (1) the instructional program component based on the diagnosis of students and placement on the appropriate level regardless of age, and (2) the multiunit organizational component, in which a group of teachers with a designated leader works with a multi-aged group of students (TT). In some IGE schools only the instructional levels component seemed operational. Open Space (OS) refers only to the building facility in which the education takes place, and not necessarily to a program of open education. As with nongradedness, the strength of teachers' commitment and the degree of implementation all too frequently are not stated in research reports. This complicates analysis. Length of time the program has been in operation and length of time a given student has been in the program also may be significant factors.

GENERAL CONCLUSIONS

Research reports continue to be favorable to nongraded schools. Analysis of the research leads to five conclusions:

(1) Comparisons of graded and nongraded schools using standardized achievement tests continue to favor nongradedness.

(2) Attendance in a nongraded school may improve the students' chances for good mental health and positive attitudes toward school.

(3) Longitudinal studies indicate that the longer students are in a nongraded program, the more likely it is that they will have positive school attitudes and better academic achievement.

(4) A nongraded environment is particularly beneficial for blacks, boys, underachievers, and students of lower socioeconomic status in terms of academic achievement and mental health.

(5) Further research is needed that includes an assessment of the actual practices in the allegedly graded or nongraded schools in order to determine if the labels as described are accurate.

Data Gathering Procedures

A survey of all research studies comparing nongraded and graded elementary schools published between 1968 and 1971 was compiled (Pavan, 1973) and published in the *Elementary School Journal*. That article reported the generally very positive effects on academic achievement and mental health for the students in nongraded schools. Sixteen studies were presented in that original article.

To gather documents to update that review, *Research in Education, Current Indexes to Journals in Education, Dissertation Abstracts*, and *Educational Index to Periodicals* catalogs were searched from January 1968 through the summer of 1976 using as research terms these descriptors: nongraded, multigraded, and ungraded. Only studies that compared nongraded and graded students and that used some form of standardized objective measures were then reported. The *Texas Tech Journal of Education* published that review, which consisted of thirty-seven studies (Pavan, 1977). Once again, the positive effects on students in nongraded schools were noted.

As all the indexes mentioned previously except the *Educational Index to Periodicals* are now accessible through computers, this latest update has been much less tedious. In order to uncover more studies, nine descriptors have been used: nongraded, nongrading, ungraded, nongradedness, continuous progress, multiunit, individually guided education, multi-age, and mixed age. ERIC has been searched from 1976 when the service began, and *Dissertation Abstracts* has been searched back to 1968. Due to this expanded list of descriptors and searching years previously manually reviewed by computer, research has been uncovered that might have been published in the earlier articles. In addition, the bibliographies of obtained studies were reviewed for other sources.

The criteria used to determine inclusion in this review of research studies on nongradedness are as follows:

(1) Students in nongraded schools must be compared to those in graded schools or a pre-/post-test of the same students, with the pre-testing conducted before entering a nongraded program.

(2) Students must have been in a nongraded program for at least one academic year.

(3) The nongraded label is assumed to be accurate unless either the researcher or a reading of the study very clearly indicates that the structure was not actually in operation.

(4) There must be more than one nongraded classroom in operation. In cases where the sample size appears small, the study is reviewed to ascertain if matched pairs or a random sample had been obtained from a larger population.

(5) The entire school program must be nongraded, not just one subject area. Data are acceptable from only one subject area, however, and multiple subject data are preferable.

(6) Standard measures of academic achievement, mental health, and attitude are required.

(7) Only studies conducted in the United States and Canada are included.

(8) Students were in nongraded programs in their elementary school years, commonly called grades one to six.

(9) Some evidence was needed as to initial comparability of nongraded and graded schools in the study.

(10) Studies should have been published since 1968.

By following the above criteria, sixty-four research studies published between January 1968 and December 1990, comparing nongraded and graded students, were obtained and are summarized in Appendix B. In addition to nongradedness, thirteen studies were individually guided education (IGE) programs, eleven include open space (OS) components meaning that some of the experimental students are housed in open space buildings or open classroom pods, and eleven studies refer to teacher teaming (TT).

Academic Achievement

Of the sixty-four studies reviewed herein, fifty-seven used standardized achievement tests to compare graded and nongraded schools. Only nine of the ninety-four comparisons favored the graded school. All others either favored the nongraded school or indicated no statistically significant differences between groups. Because many studies used more than one achievement test, because differing age groups were included in the study, or because testing was carried out over a long time span, comparisons of experimental groups (nongraded) and control groups (graded) were made. Sixty comparisons (64 percent) favored nongradedness, twenty-five (27 percent) indicated that both experimental and control groups performed in a similar manner, and nine (9 percent) found that the nongraded pupils did not perform as well. Of the fifty-seven research studies, fifty-two (91 percent) indicated that for all comparisons, the nongraded groups performed better (58 percent) or

Table 3.1. Percentage of studies favoring nongraded programs over graded programs.

	Better	Same	Worse
Academic Achievement	58%	33%	9%
Mental Health	52%	43%	5%
IGE—Achievement	46%	38%	16%
IGE—Mental Health	67%	22%	11%

as well as (33 percent) the graded groups on measures of academic achievement.

The nongraded concept was developed to deal with the fact that individuals are different and different treatments are needed to maximize each individual's potential. Schools that operate under this tenet probably would not be concentrating on high student performance on standardized tests. By contrast, the graded school usually requires each child in a given grade to be exposed to the same materials and to test items of the type that will be found on standardized achievement tests. The finding that pupils in nongraded schools did as well as, or better than, pupils in graded schools is therefore rather remarkable. Standardized tests tend to emphasize mastery of content and attitudes such as social and psychological adjustment to the present standards of traditional education. There should no longer be concern that placing children in nongraded programs might be detrimental to their academic achievement. Overwhelmingly, nongraded groups perform as well as and possibly better than graded groups on achievement tests designed for the graded schools!

Mental Health and School Attitudes

Of the sixty-four reports using standard measures being reviewed herein, forty-two contained a mental health component. All these studies except two either favored (in whole or in part) the nongraded groups or reported no significant differences between the groups. Because many studies used more than one instrument, eighty-one comparisons of experimental (nongraded) and control groups (graded) were reported. Forty comparisons favored nongradedness, thirty-one indicated that both groups performed in a similar manner, and only ten found that nongraded pupils were not as adequate.

The ten negative comparisons were found in eight studies of which six also reported positive or no significant differences on other mental health measures. Three of the negatives involved school anxiety. Otto's works (1969, 1971) and Chandler's dissertation (1969) found that anxiety seemed to increase over the school year for older pupils in the nongraded program. However, the differences were so small as to be easily attributable to chance. Ward (1970), measuring school anxiety by Draw-a-Man analysis, found younger nongraded children less anxious than those in graded schools. Gumpper (1971) found that nongraded students had higher anxiety than graded students on the Piers-Harris

Anxiety Scale, while Guarino (1982) found the opposite result. Using the anxiety scale of the Children's Personality Questionnaire, Patterson (1975) found nongraded students to have more anxiety while Bell (1976) found lower anxiety than in the graded schools. Therefore it seems that there is no clear-cut correlation between anxiety levels and nongradedness.

All but one of the other negatives involve school attitude. Vogel and Bowers (1972) had some negative results on two of the three measures used: Describe Your School, and the Operations section of the Russell Sage Social Relations Test. These negative results were produced because the nongraded pupils did not comply with typical traditional school routines (raising hand, obeying teacher, or not laughing) and attitudes (describing school in glowing terms). Because pupils in nongraded schools showed more skill in cooperative planning as measured by the Russell Sage Social Relations Test, results from these measures can be interpreted in a favorable light when the objectives of nongradedness are considered. Wisecaver (1975) found that nongraded students had a less positive attitude toward school than graded students in a middle socioeconomic status school population, yet Case (1971) found no significant differences in school attitude among all socioeconomic status levels of students on Gordon's "How I See Myself" test. Case also reported positive scores for black students on this test.

Remacle (1971) had negative results for grade six and positive results for grade five nongraded students, while Herrington (1973) and Walker (1973) had totally positive results on the School Morale Scale. The boys in nongraded schools ranked My Classroom Inventory lower than those in graded schools in Ramayya's (1972) Canadian study. Students in an IGE, open space school had a lower School Sentiment Index than those in graded schools (Flowers, 1977).

Several of the positive mental health test results will be examined also. Purkey (1970) made a careful study of two groups of pupils with similar socioeconomic backgrounds. One group attended a traditional school and the other an innovative school. Purkey reported that the pupils had very different self-perceptions as measured by the Coopersmith Self-Esteem Inventory. Pupils in the nongraded school showed more favorable self-esteem. The difference between schools was significant at the .02 level, with the differences between the nongraded and graded students most evident in the older group. Carter (1974) and Walker (1973) used the same instrument with the same positive results, while Anderson (1981) found no differences.

Gumpper (1971), Bradford (1973), Milburn (1981), and Guarino (1982) reported that nongraded groups scored higher than graded groups on the Piers-Harris Children's Self-Concept Scale, while Bowman (1971) found no differences. At least nine other studies used a variety of self-concept or self-esteem instruments and every study except Flowers (1977) found that nongraded students felt better about themselves or not significantly different from students in graded schools. In summary, students in nongraded schools are more likely to have positive self-concepts, high self-esteem, and good attitudes toward school than students in graded schools.

Longitudinal Studies

Seventeen studies presented longitudinal results with most reporting positive results. Of the fifty-eight comparisons made, only two (3 percent) favored the graded schools, while sixteen (28 percent) were similar, and forty (69 percent) comparisons favored the nongraded schools. Apparently, the longer a student is in a nongraded school, the more likely it is that good things will happen: more favorable school attitude, less chance of retention, and better academic achievement.

Five studies followed students who had spent three or four years in nongraded primary units compared to the traditional single grade classes from kindergarten to third. Computations using the data for percentage of yearly deceleration from McLoughlin's study (1970) showed that 5 to 10 percent more children enter fourth grade after three years of schooling (not including kindergarten) in nongraded schools than in graded schools. More pupils attending schools with nongraded primary units entered fourth grade with their entering class than did children attending schools with traditional grade-designated classrooms. In other words, with fewer retentions, fewer students failed. Walker (1973) followed student records over a twelve-year period and estimated that slower students from a nongraded primary would be within one year of grade placement of their normal classmates upon graduation. The achievement gap begins to decrease at about the fifth-grade level.

Eells (1970) reported that the longer students remained in a nongraded primary program, the higher their achievement scores were in relation to ability. Perrin (1969) reported increased academic upward mobility after three years in a nongraded primary program. Morris, Proger, and Morrell (1971) found that nongraded primary students exceeded graded students academically at the end of the three years and also two years after the program ended.

Students at the intermediate level (the traditional grades from four to six) were the focus of three studies. Nongraded students in IGE intermediate classes had higher student achievement and more positive attitudes toward school, even the low-aptitude students (Price, 1977). Another IGE study (Klaus, 1981) noted higher achievement for nongraded students in grades four and five, but no differences in grade six or five years later when students reached the eleventh grade. With only two years in a nongraded program, Anderson (1981) found both groups had similar academic achievement and self-esteem in junior high school.

The remaining nine longitudinal studies were conducted in elementary schools with nongraded programs beginning at age five or six until ages ten to twelve with graded schools from grades one to five or six. Killough (1971) reported higher academic achievement for nongraded students after three years in a nongraded program while Szymczuk (1977) found no differences after two years in a nongraded IGE program (except higher achievement for boys) compared to traditional schools.

Seven studies compared students who had spent their entire elementary school years in the same nongraded or traditional school. The five longitudinal reports that looked at academic achievement (Ramayya, 1972; Yarborough, 1976; Riciotti, 1982; Milburn, 1981; and Schmitt, 1983) found superior performance by nongraded students. On mental health and school attitudinal measures, students from nongraded settings felt more positive or the same as graded school students (Carter, 1973; Ramayya, 1972; Junell, 1971; Yarborough, 1976; and Milburn, 1981) after five or six years in these placements. While Anderson (1981) reported no difference in discipline referrals in junior high after two years in nongraded classes, Schmitt (1983) found significantly fewer for students who had spent five years in a nongraded, open space program.

Disadvantaged Students

Only eighteen research studies on nongradedness have attempted analysis to see if nongradedness is beneficial to the disadvantaged: boys, blacks, underachievers, and students of low socioeconomic status. Data suggest that boys in nongraded schools, compared with boys in graded schools, make better scores on achievement tests (Morris, 1971; Szymczuk, 1977; and Ramayya, 1972) while Wilt (1971) found negative results. Junell (1971) noted that nongraded boys have better attitudes toward self and school, yet boys scored lower on My Classroom Inventory (Ramayya, 1972).

Case (1971) found that it is an advantage for blacks to be in a non-graded team-taught school rather than in a school with self-contained classrooms. The advantages lay in higher achievement scores, better self-concepts, and more positive attitudes toward school. Burtley (1974) compared inner city schools with predominantly black populations with nongraded blacks having higher academic achievement, yet Givens (1972) found no significant differences between the academic achievement of blacks in the experimental and control groups of his study. He indicated that the multigraded students were instructed in a form of individualized instruction for the duration of his study. It appears unlikely that this constitutes an effective nongraded program even though the study did show some positive attitudes toward school, teachers, and learning.

Underachievers with six years of multigraded elementary school education had better self-concepts and attitudes toward school than underachievers with a graded elementary school education (Junell, 1971 and Yarborough, 1976). These same positive attitudes by below-average-ability nongraded students were also reported by Walker (1973), Price (1977), and Milburn (1981). Higher academic achievement by nongraded below-average students was noted by Price (1977), Higgins (1980), and Milburn (1981).

Students of lower socioeconomic status showed greater academic growth, according to the four studies that included this variable for analysis (Perrin, 1969; Herrington, 1973; Marcus, 1971; and Soumokil, 1977).

From the research reported herein, it would appear to be most beneficial for boys, blacks, underachievers, and students of lower socioeconomic status to be placed in nongraded schools.

Assessment of Nongraded Implementation

Very few of the sixty-four studies used some type of instrument to determine if the schools calling themselves nongraded actually were. Five of these studies were conducted in IGE schools and used instruments available as part of the IGE program assessment. Henn (1975) used teacher responses to determine degree of IGE implementation for thirty-two schools and found no relationship between academic achievement and any of the seven IGE outcome clusters. When Patterson (1975), using the same method, compared four high-implementation with three low-implementation schools, students in high-implementation schools had higher self-concepts and higher levels of anxiety than those in low-implementation schools.

Three IGE studies used a Survey of Effective School Practices (SESP), which requires the use of interviews, school observations, and a team of raters. All nine schools were described by Szymczuk (1977) as having amounts of IGEness of 28 percent or less as determined by the SESP with academic achievement more closely linked to socioeconomic status than either years of implementation or degree of IGEness. Using the SESP to designate schools as high, medium, or low implementers of IGE, Price (1977) found students in high-implementation schools had higher academic achievement and more positive attitudes toward school. The most clearly explained IGE study was by Soumokil (1977) whose two schools were statistically significantly different on all measures of IGEness. He found that disadvantaged students in the IGE school had higher academic achievement and a more positive attitude toward school, but a similar locus of control as compared with a standard school. Differences in favor of IGE schools are evident when there is high implementation of the IGE program.

Engel and Cooper (1971) had teachers respond to a nongraded questionnaire developed by Carbone to determine an index of nongradedness. They then compared the most nongraded school with the least and found the academic achievement on vocabulary, comprehension, reading, mechanics of English, and language subtests of California to be significantly higher, with spelling scores the same.

Walker (1973) developed a nongraded assessment scale, wrote program descriptions of six different schools based on interviews, and had independent raters place the schools on a scale from most to least nongraded. Students in the most nongraded program had more positive attitudes toward school, higher self-concepts, and better academic achievement for both normal and slow-progress students.

Using a modified version of an observational instrument developed by Pavan (1972) to document actual nongraded practices, Guarino (1983) located two schools, one clearly nongraded and one clearly graded. Using students matched for age, sex, and IQ, he found that students in the nongraded school had higher academic achievement, lower anxiety, and higher self-concepts than those in the graded school. Of all the studies attempting to ascertain degree of implementation or non-gradedness, this one, which documented observed teaching practices, provides the best evidence.

It is understandable that school observation has played such a small role in these comparative studies, since observation involves a considerable expenditure of time. In fact, the majority of the studies do not even describe the practices of the schools from which their data have been obtained. Although the positive results from nongraded schools over all these research studies provide much evidence, a few in-depth, well-designed studies would be welcomed.

SUMMARY

There is now definitive research evidence to confirm the theories underlying nongradedness. Prior to 1968, research was limited and had conflicting and confusing results. In the period since that time, however, sixty-four research studies have been published. We are now able to bring together for analysis the substantial and generally favorable body of research on nongradedness.

Research studies published between 1968 and 1990 most frequently favored nongradedness on standardized measures of academic achievement and mental health. The results on academic achievement demonstrate that 58 percent of the studies have nongraded students performing better; 33 percent, the same; and only 9 percent worse than graded students. As to the mental health and school attitudes, 52 percent of the studies indicate nongraded schools as better, 43 percent similar, and only 5 percent worse than graded schools. Table 3.1 shows these results and the same pattern for IGE schools.

Boys, blacks, underachievers, and students of lower socioeconomic status were more likely to perform better and to feel more positive toward themselves and their schools in a nongraded environment. The longer pupils were in nongraded programs, the greater the improvement in their achievement scores in relation to ability. More pupils attending schools with nongraded primary units entered the fourth grade with their entering class. Thus research findings on nongraded, multigraded, and ungraded grouping of pupils generally support the use of these organizational arrangements in schools.

REFERENCES

Anderson, Margaret J. 1981. "A Study of the Relationship among Reading Achieve-
    ment, Self-Concept, and Behavior Problems of Junior High School Students
    Instructed in a Continuous Progress Elementary Program and Those Instructed
    in a Traditional Elementary Program," *Dissertation Abstracts*, 41(May):
    4589A.

Beanne, James A. 1991. "Sorting Out the Self-Esteem Controversy," *Educational Lead-
    ership*, 49(1):25–30.

Beckerman, T. and Thomas T. Good. 1981. "The Classroom Ratio of High-and-Low-
    Aptitude Students and Its Effect on Achievement," *American Education Research
    Journal*, 18(Fall):317–327.

Bell, Anne E., Myrna A. Zipursky and F. Switzer. 1976. "Informal or Open-Area
    Education in Relation to Achievement and Personality," *British Journal of Educa-
    tional Psychology*, 46:235–243.

Bloom, Benjamin S. 1981. *All Our Children Learning: A Primer for Parents, Teachers,
    and Other Educators*. New York, NY: McGraw Hill.

Blythe, Tina and Howard Gardner. 1990. "A School for All Intelligences," *Educational
    Leadership*, 47(7):33–37.

Bowman, Betty. 1971. "A Comparison of Pupil Achievement and Attitude in a Graded
    School with Pupil Achievement and Attitude in a Nongraded School 1968–1969,
    1969–1970 School Years," *Dissertation Abstracts*, 32(August):660A.

Bradford, Equilla F. 1972. "A Comparison of Two Methods of Teaching in the Elemen-
    tary School as Related to Achievement in Reading, Mathematics, and Self-
    Concept," doctoral dissertation, Michigan State University.

Brody, Ernest Bright. 1970. "Achievement of First-and-Second-Year Pupils in Graded
    and Nongraded Classrooms," *Elementary School Journal*, 70(April):391–394.

Brooks, Marshall and Paul B. Hounshell. 1975. "A Study of the Locus of Control and
    Science Achievement," *Journal of Research on Science Teaching*, 12(2):175–181.

Brown, Edward K. 1970. *The Nongraded Program at the Powell Elementary School*.
    Philadelphia, PA: Philadelphia School District, ERIC ED 049 298.

Brown, Edward K. and William C. Thelmer, Jr. 1968. *An Evaluation of the Ungraded
    Program at the Powell Elementary School*. Philadelphia, PA: Philadelphia School
    District, ERIC ED 029 368.

Brown, K. G. and A. Martin. 1989. "Student Achievement in Multi-Grade and Single-
    Grade Classes," *Education Canada* (Summer):10–13, 47.

Bruner, Jerome. 1966. *Toward a Theory of Instruction*. New York, NY: W. W. Norton.

Burchyett, James A. 1973. "A Comparison of the Effects of Nongraded, Multi-Age,
    Team Teaching vs. the Modified Self-Contained Classroom at the Elementary
    School Level," *Dissertation Abstracts*, 33(May):5998A.

Burtley, Nathel. 1974. "A Comparison of Teacher Characteristics and Student Achieve-
    ment in Individually Guided Education (IGE) and Traditional Inner City Elemen-
    tary Schools," doctoral dissertation, Michigan State University.

Caine, Renate N. and Geoffrey Caine. 1991. *Making Connections: Teaching and the
    Human Brain*. Alexandria, VA: Association for Curriculum and Supervision De-
    velopment.

Carter, Joy B. 1974. "A Study of the Effects of Multi-Grade Grouping on the Attitudes
    toward Self, Others and School of Selected Third and Fifth Grade Students," *Dis-
    sertation Abstracts*, 34(March):5469A.

Case, David Aree. 1971. "A Comparative Study of Fifth Graders in Elementary Self-Contained Classrooms," *Dissertation Abstracts*, 32(July):86A.

Chandler, Gail E. 1969. "An Investigation of School Anxiety and Nongraded Classroom Organization," *Dissertation Abstracts*, 30(December):2371A.

Chanick, Marion A. 1979. "The Effects of Individually Guided Education on Elementary Students," *Dissertation Abstracts*, 40:2465A.

Dalton, Jerome L. 1974. "A Study of the Development of Creativity and Self-Concept in Graded and Nongraded Elementary Schools," *Dissertation Abstracts*, 35(September):1494A.

Deeb, Jacqueline A. 1971. "A Study of the Academic Self-Concept of Pupils in Selected Graded Schools and Selected Nongraded Schools," *Dissertation Abstracts*, 31(June):6467A.

Doyle, Roy P. 1989. "The Resistance of Conventional Wisdom to Research Evidence: The Case of Retention in Grade," *Phi Delta Kappan*, 71(November), 215–220.

Eells, Calvin E. 1970. "A Study of Academic Ability of Immigrant Pupils over Five Years in a Suburban Nongraded School System," *Dissertation Abstracts*, 31(August):579A.

Engel, Barney M. and Martin Cooper. 1971. "Academic Achievement and Non-gradedness," *Journal of Experimental Education*, 40(Winter):24–26.

Flowers, James R. 1977. "A Comparative Study of Students in Open Space Individually Guided Education (IGE) and Traditional Schools," *Dissertation Abstracts*, 38:4679A.

Gajadharsingh, Joel L. and C. Melvin. 1987. "The Multi-Grade Classroom and Student Achievement," *School Trustee*, 40:4.

Gardner, Howard. 1983. *Frames of Mind*. New York: Basic Books.

Givens, Harry, Jr. 1972. "A Comparative Study of Achievement and Attitudinal Characteristics of Black and White Intermediate Pupils in Individualized, Multigrade and Self-Contained Instructional Programs," *Dissertation Abstracts*, 33(September–October):893A.

Goodlad, John I. and Robert H. Anderson. 1963, 1987. *The Nongraded Elementary School*. New York, NY: Harcourt Brace Jovanovich, 1963, and Teachers College Press, 1987.

Gordon, Edmund W. and Associates. 1988. *Human Diversity and Pedagogy*. New Haven, CT: Center in Research on Education, Culture and Ethnicity Institution for Social and Policy Studies, Yale University.

Grant, Linda and James Rothenberg. 1986. "The Social Enhancement of Ability Differences: Teacher-Student Interactions in First and Second Grade Reading Groups," *Elementary School Journal*, 87(September):29–49.

Guarino, Anthony R. 1982. "An Investigation of Achievement, Self-Concept, and School Related Anxiety in Graded and Nongraded Elementary Schools," doctoral dissertation, Rutgers University.

Gumpper, David C., Joan H. Meyer and Jacob J. Kaufman. 1971. *Nongraded Elementary Education: Individualized Learning-Teacher Leadership-Student Responsibility*. University Park, PA: The Pennsylvania State University Institute for Research on Human Resources, ERIC ED 057 440.

Henn, Dwight C. 1974. "A Comparative Analysis of Language Arts and Mathematics Achievement in Selected IGE/MUS-E and Non-IGE/MUS-E Programs in Ohio," doctoral dissertation, University of Cincinnati.

Herrington, Allen F. 1973. "Perceived Attitudes and Academic Achievement of Reported Graded and Nongraded Sixth-Year Students," doctoral dissertation, University of Miami.

Higgins, Judith J. 1981. "A Comparative Study between the Reading Achievement Levels of Students in a Combination/Ungraded Class and Students in a Graded Class," *Dissertation Abstracts*, 41(9):3806A.

Holly, William J. 1987. *Self-Esteem: Does It Contribute to Students' Academic Success?* Eugene, OR: Oregon School Study Council, University of Oregon.

Holmes, C. T. and K. M. Matthews. 1984. "The Effects of Nonpromotion on Elementary and Junior High Pupils: A Meta-Analysis," *Review of Educational Research*, 54(Summer):225–236.

Jackson, Gregg B. 1975. "The Research Evidence on the Effects of Grade Retention," *Review of Educational Research*, 45(Fall):613–635.

Jeffreys, John Sheppard. 1970. "An Investigation of the Effects of Innovative Educational Practices on Pupil-Centeredness of Observed Behaviors and on Learner Outcome Variables," doctoral dissertation, University of Maryland.

Junell, Joseph Stanley. 1971. "An Analysis of the Effects of Multigrading on a Number of Noncognitive Variables," *Dissertation Abstracts*, 32(July):94A.

Killough, Charles K. 1971. "An Analysis of the Longitudinal Effects That a Nongraded Elementary Program, Conducted in an Open-Space School, Had on the Cognitive Achievement of Pupils," doctoral dissertation, University of Houston.

Klaus, William D. 1981. "A Comparison of Student Achievement in Individually Guided Education Programs and Non-Individually Guided Education Elementary School Programs," doctoral dissertation, University of Missouri-Columbia.

Kuhlman, Carol L. 1985. "A Study of the Relationships between Organizational Characteristics of Elementary Schools, Student Characteristics, and Elementary Competency Test Results," doctoral dissertation, University of Kansas.

Kulik, Chen-Lin and James A. Kulik. 1984. "Effects of Ability Grouping on Elementary School Pupils: A Meta-Analysis," American Psychological Association, Toronto.

Kulik, Chen-Lin and James A. Kulik. 1987. "Effects of Ability Grouping on Student Achievement," *Equity and Excellence*, 23(Spring):22–30.

Lair, Daniel P. 1975. "The Effects of Graded and Nongraded Schools on Student Growth," *Dissertation Abstracts*, 36(December):3358A.

Lawson, Robert E. 1974. "A Comparison of the Development of Self-Concept and Achievement in Reading of Students in the First, Third, and Fifth Year of Attendance in Graded and Nongraded Elementary Schools," *Dissertation Abstracts*, 34(February):4702A.

Lewis, Jack L. and Jerry W. Moore. 1990. "The Impact on Student Achievement Gains of Classroom Compositions Ranging from Heterogeneous to Homogeneous Groupings in the Elementary School," American Educational Research Association, Boston, MA.

Lorton, Larry. 1973. *Reorganizing for Learning at McKinley School—An Experiment in Multi-Unit Instruction*. Paper presented at *The Annual Meeting of The American Educational Research Association*, ERIC ED 075 911.

Madden, Nancy A. and Robert E. Slavin. 1983. "Mainstreaming Students with Mild Handicaps: Academic and Social Overtones," *Review of Educational Research*, 53(Winter):519–569.

Marcus, Marie. 1971. *The Effects of Nongrading, Team Teaching and Individualized Instruction on the Achievement Scores of Disadvantaged Children*. New Orleans, LA: Louisiana State University, ERIC ED 064 234.

McClellan, David C. 1985. *Human Motivation*. Palo Alto, CA: Scott Foresman.

McCoy, Edwardine C. 1972. "A Field Study of a Rural Ungraded Primary School with a Statistical Analysis of Reading Achievement and Personality Adjustment," *Dissertation Abstracts*, 33(September–October):902A.

McLoughlin, William P. 1969. *Evaluation of the Nongraded Primary*. Jamaica, NY: St. Johns University, (April), ED 031 426.

McLoughlin, William P. 1970. "Continuous Pupil Progress in the Nongraded School: Hope or Hoax?" *Elementary School Journal*, 71(November):90–96.

Mikkelson, John E. 1962. "An Experimental Study of Selective Grouping and Acceleration in Junior High School Mathematics," doctoral dissertation, University of Minnesota.

Milburn, Dennis. 1981. "A Study of Multi-Age or Family-Grouped Classrooms," *Phi Delta Kappan*, 62(March):513–514.

Mobley, Charles F. 1976. *A Comparison of the Effects of Multiage Grouping versus Homogeneous Age Grouping in Primary School Classes of Reading and Mathematics Achievement*. Nova University, ED 128 102.

Morris, Vernon R., Barton P. Proger and James E. Morrell. 1971. "Pupil Achievement in a Nongraded Primary Plan after Three and Five Years of Instruction," *Educational Leadership*, 29(March):621–625.

Office of Educational Research and Improvement. 1990. *National Education Longitudinal Study of 1988: A Profile of the American Eighth Grader*. Washington, DC: U.S. Government Printing Office.

Otto, Henry J. 1971. "Research Has a Word: Some Generalizations," in *Curriculum Development in Nongraded Schools*, Edward G. Buffie and John M. Jenkins, eds., Bloomington, IN: University Press, pp. 171–187.

Otto, Henry J., Beeman Phillips, Benjamin Fruchter, Donald H. Williams and Gail E. Chandler. 1969. *Nongradedness: An Elementary School Evaluation*. Austin, TX: Texas University Bureau of Laboratory Schools Monograph No. 21, University of Texas Press, ERIC ED 036 889.

Patterson, John D. 1975. "The Relationships between the Degree of Individually Guided Education Implementation and Student Self Concept and Anxiety," doctoral dissertation, University of Missouri-Columbia.

Pavan, Barbara N. 1972. "Moving Elementary Schools toward Nongradedness: Commitment, Assessment, and Tactics," doctoral dissertation, Harvard University.

Pavan, Barbara N. 1973. "Good News: Research on the Nongraded Elementary School," *Elementary School Journal*, 73(March):233–242.

Pavan, Barbara N. 1977. "The Nongraded School: Research on Academic Achievement and Mental Health," *Texas Tech. Journal of Education*, 4(2):91–107.

Perrin, Jerry D. 1969. "A Statistical and Time Change Analysis of Achievement Differences of Children in a Nongraded and a Graded Program in Selected Schools in the Little Rock Public Schools," *Dissertation Abstracts*, 30(August):530A.

Peterson, Sarah E., James S. DeGracie and Carol R. Ayabe. 1987. "A Longitudinal Study of the Effects of Retention/Promotion on Academic Achievement," *American Educational Research Journal*, 14(Spring):107–118.

Price, David A. 1977. "The Effects of Individually Guided Education (IGE) Processes on Achievement and Attitudes of Elementary School Students," doctoral dissertation, University of Missouri-Columbia.

Purkey, William W., William Graves and Mary Zellner. 1970. "Self-Perceptions of Pupils in an Experimental Elementary School," *Elementary School Journal*, 71(December):166–171.

Ramayya, D. P. 1972. "Achievement Skills, Personality Variables and Classroom Climate in Graded and Nongraded Elementary Schools," *Psychology in the Schools*, 9(January):88–92.

Reid, Ben C. 1973. "A Comparative Analysis of a Nongraded and Graded Primary Program," *Dissertation Abstracts*, 34:(September):1066A.

Remacle, Leo Felix. 1971. "A Comparative Study of the Differences in Attitudes, Self-Concept, and Achievement of Children in Graded and Nongraded Elementary Schools," *Dissertation Abstracts*, 31(May):5984A.

Ricciotti, Joseph A. 1982. "School Organizational Patterns and Reading Achievement," doctoral dissertation, Columbia University Teachers College.

Saunders, Bruce Thomas. 1970. "Emotional Disturbance and Social Position within the Nongraded Classroom," *Psychology in the Schools*, 7(July):269–271.

Schmitt, Rita T. 1983. "The Achievement and Adjustment of Children from Open and Traditional Elementary Schools in Grade Six of Traditional Middle Schools," doctoral dissertation, Temple University.

Schnee, Ronald G. and Joe Park. 1975. "The Open School Improves Elementary Reading Scores in Oklahoma City," *Phi Delta Kappan*, 56(January):366–367.

Schneiderhan, Rosemary M. 1973. "A Comparison of an Individually Guided Education (IGE) Program, and Individually Guided Instruction (IGI) Program, and a Traditional Elementary Educational Program at the Intermediate Level," doctoral dissertation, University of Minnesota.

Sheirer, Mary Ann and Robert E. Kraut. 1979. "Increasing Educational Achievement via Self Concept Change," *Review of Educational Research*, 49(1):131–150.

Shepard, Lorrie A. and Mary Lee Smith. 1986. "Synthesis of Research on School Readiness and Kindergarten Retention," *Educational Leadership*, 44(November):78–86.

Shepard, Lorrie A. and Mary Lee Smith, eds. 1989. *Flunking Grades: Research and Policies on Retention*. London: Falmer Press.

Shepard, Lorrie A. and Mary Lee Smith. 1990. "Synthesis of Research on Grade Retention," *Educational Leadership*, 47(May):84–88.

Sie, Maureen S. 1969. "Pupil Achievement in an Experimental Nongraded Elementary School," doctoral dissertation, Iowa State University.

Slavin, Robert E. 1986. "Ability Grouping and Student Achievement in Elementary Schools: A Best-Evidence Synthesis," American Educational Research Association, San Francisco, CA.

Slavin, Robert E. 1987. "Ability Grouping and Student Achievement in Elementary Schools: A Best-Evidence Synthesis," *Review of Educational Research*, 57(Summer):293–336.

Slavin, Robert E. 1988. "Synthesis of Research on Grouping in Elementary and Secondary Schools," *Educational Leadership*, 46(1):67–77.

Slavin, Robert E. 1991. "Are Cooperative Learning and 'Untracking' Harmful to the Gifted?" *Educational Leadership*, 48(March):68–71.

Smith, Mary Lee and Lorrie A. Shepard. 1987. "What Doesn't Work: Explaining Policies of Retention in the Early Grades," *Phi Delta Kappan*, 69(October):129–134.

Snake River School District. 1972. *Curriculum Change through Nongraded Individualization*. Blackfoot, ID: School District 52, ERIC ED 079 962.

Soumokil, Paul O. 1977. "Comparison of Cognitive and Affective Dimensions of Individually Guided Education (IGE) and Standard Elementary School Programs," doctoral dissertation, University of Missouri-Columbia.

Szymczuk, Michael. 1977. "A Cohort Analysis of Elementary Reading Achievement Scores in Two School Districts Which Implemented the Individually Guided Education Program," doctoral dissertation, Iowa State University.

Turman, Lynette and Bobby Blatt. 1974. *Individualized Instruction through Open Structure: A Child Centered School*. Los Angeles School District, ERIC ED 103 425.

Vogel, Francis W. and Norman D. Bowers. 1972. "Pupil Behaviors in a Multi-Age Nongraded School," *Journal of Experimental Education*, 41(Winter):78–86.

Walker, William E. 1973. "Long Term Effects of Graded and Nongraded Primary Programs," doctoral dissertation, George Peabody College for Teachers.

Ward, Dayton Nissler. 1970. "An Evaluation of a Nongraded School Program in Grades One and Two," *Dissertation Abstracts*, 30(January):2686A.

Wilt, Hiram Jack. 1971. "A Comparison of Student Attitudes toward School, Academic Achievement, Internal Structures and Procedures: The Nongraded School versus the Graded School," *Dissertation Abstracts*, 31(April):5105A.

Wisecaver, Karen L. 1975. "The Effects of School Structure on Student Self-Concept," *Elementary School Guidance and Counseling*, 10(December):132–137.

Yarborough, Betty H. and Roger A. Johnson. 1978. "The Relationship between Intelligence Levels and Benefits from Innovative, Nongraded Elementary Schooling and Traditional, Graded Schooling," *Educational Research Quarterly*, 3(2):28–38.

Yarborough, Betty H. et al. 1976. *A Study of the Relative Effectiveness of Non-Graded and Graded Instruction in the First Six Years of Elementary Schooling*. Norfolk, VA: Old Dominion University, ED 143 669.

CHAPTER 4

Defining Nongradedness

WHAT exactly will and will not change in the transformation to non-gradedness? Certainly, many characteristics of current schools do work, and will be preserved. It is primarily *three* characteristics of graded schools that irritate our professional senses. One is the use of *grade labels* (e.g., *first grade, fourth grade*) to identify boundaries within which it is presumed that typical children of a given age group can and should function academically. The second is the use of a *promotion-retention* system, which requires that a child be demonstrably qualified at the end of each year to cross the boundary between one grade level and the next, or else be retained ("failed") within the lower boundary for yet another academic year. The third is the use of *competitive/comparative evaluation systems*, through which the products of each child's academic efforts are marked or rated with symbols or words that represent points along a scale of acceptability. It is these three features or practices that spawn or support a number of other rigidities, the softening or the abandonment of which must be on the agenda of any enlightened educator.

Below are eleven statements that may serve as a preliminary definition of the nongraded, continuous-progress approach to schooling that this volume seeks to champion. The underlying ideas will reappear in various forms in the remainder of this chapter, as well as in future chapters. Most of them surfaced in the inventory that appeared in Chapter 2. Some describe a philosophical point of view, while others have a practical or procedural dimension. All relate to each other, and to the idealized conception of schooling as a means of helping each child to reach adulthood thoroughly equipped to succeed, in every conceivable role (e.g., worker, family member, citizen, creative contributor), at a high level.

In fairness, it can be conceded that educators in graded schools probably perceive, and have perceived, that their objectives have also been to fulfill human potential. It should not be assumed that advocates of gradedness have less virtue, or less noble aspirations for their students, than advocates of nongradedness. What may well be assumed, however, is that the grade-oriented people have been diminishing, if not destroying, their chances for success by clinging to some dangerously wrong ways of responding to pupil needs and efforts.

A BRIEF OPERATIONAL DEFINITION

In an authentically nongraded school program:

(1) Individual differences in the pupil population are accepted and respected, and there is ample variability in instructional approaches to respond to varying needs.

(2) Learning, which is the "work" of the child, is intended to be not only challenging but also pleasurable and rewarding.

(3) Students are viewed as a whole; development in cognitive, physical, aesthetic, social, and emotional spheres is nurtured.

(4) The administrative and organizational framework, for example with respect to pupil grouping practices, is flexible and provides opportunities for each child to interact with children, and adults, of varying personalities, backgrounds, abilities, interests, and ages.

(5) Students are enabled through flexible arrangements to progress at their own best pace and in appropriately varied ways. Instruction, learning opportunities, and movement within the curriculum are individualized to correspond with individual needs, interests, and abilities.

(6) Curricular areas are both integrated and separate. Instruction, programmatic, and organizational patterns are flexible, with outcomes rather than mere coverage of content as the primary focus.

(7) The expected standards of performance (in terms of outcomes) in the core areas of the curriculum are clearly defined, so that the points to be reached by the end of a designated (e.g., a three- or four-year) period are well known. However, the time taken to reach that end, and the path followed to that end, is allowed to vary for students with different histories and potentialities.

(8) Within the curriculum and related assessment practices, specific

content learning is generally subordinate to the understanding of major concepts and methods of inquiry, and the development of the skills of learning: inquiry, evaluation, interpretation, and application.

(9) Student assessment is holistic, to correspond with the holistic view of learning.

(10) Evaluation of the learner is continuous, comprehensive, and diagnostic. Except for reference purposes as necessary to parental and staff understanding, chronological age and grade norms play a much smaller role in evaluation and reporting activities than does the child's own growth history and potential.

(11) While there are some core components of the curriculum that are especially valued (as reflected in performance standards in the major content areas), the system is largely teacher-managed and controlled. Thus, it empowers teachers to create learning opportunities and to use instructional strategies at their own discretion, based on the perceived needs of the students they are serving. Assessment procedures are similarly flexible, individualized, and teacher-managed.

SOME PARADIGMATIC CONTRASTS

In Table 4.1, we seek to show how various elements of schooling in the conventional graded system may be compared with the same elements in the nongraded system. Some of the contrasts, as noted, may be debatable. Others are easily documentable.

The reader will observe that in two of the categories (curriculum goals and homework load) there is assumed to be no difference in approach. In all other categories, however, a distinct difference is claimed. What seems very likely is that in many conventional schools there has for some years been a gradual departure from the literally graded practices in some categories and a movement toward at least partial adoption of the practices associated with nongradedness. Adoption of a pupil-team learning approach, for example, would have a strong positive impact upon many of the categories, especially pupil-pupil interactions. Similarly, moving into a whole-language approach or developing interdisciplinary (and/or multigraded) curriculum units would result in some notable categorical impact, especially with reference to curriculum design and instructional methodology.

Table 4.1. Comparison of various schooling elements for graded and nongraded systems.

Category	Conventional Graded System	Nongraded System
Teacher decision-making power	Very limited; system directed	Strong; teacher-directed
Teacher freedom within curriculum	Limited	High
Teacher workload	High; enervating	High; invigorating
Adult collegiality	System discourages	System encourages
Opportunities for teacher growth	Limited	Continuous
Pupil-pupil interactions	Limited	High
Competitive atmosphere, pupils	High	Low
Relationships with parents	Grade-promotion focus: tension	Progress focus: more relaxed
Community definition of good schooling	Clear, geared to outdated assumptions	Unclear, requires constant parent education
School phobia and pupil tension	Familiar data	Notable reduction
Overall atmosphere	Some win, some lose	Every kid a winner
Expectations for pupil performance	High unrealistic	High realistic
Reporting/evaluation system	Competitive/ comparative (ABCDF)	Individualized
Pupil perceptions of academic success	Tend to follow the normal curve	Personalized and positive
Pupil achievement (actual)	Follows normal curve	Curve skews to positive side
Influence on pupil dropout pattern	Historically high	Dramatic reduction
Curriculum goals	Standard U.S.A.	Standard U.S.A.
Curriculum design	Rigid sequence	Flexible sequence
Instructional methodology	Somewhat structured	Varied and flexible
Homework load	Teacher decision	Teacher decision
Homework relevance	Fair to good	Excellent

PROCEDURES USED TO DEVELOP PRINCIPLES OF NONGRADEDNESS

The first step in the formulation of a model for nongraded schools (Pavan, 1972) was a thorough reading of the literature on nongrading. Since the search was for the assumptions under which nongrading operates, a greater emphasis was placed on the writing of the theorists.

The practical "how-we-did-it" books, case studies, and the results of survey questionnaires reported in theses and articles were reviewed for some hints or implications as to the underlying assumptions of non-grading. The major writings available in the United States describing the British informal or open educational methods were researched.

The second step, after the review of the pertinent literature on non-grading and open education, was to write and assemble the assumptions upon which these practices are based. This was done by listing the values and beliefs as mentioned in the readings and by developing theoretical statements that were implied by writings indicating common practices. In this way more than sixty-two items were formulated.

The third step was to divide the statements into categories or related groups. After the statements were classified, they were compared for redundancy and contradictions. Some items seemed to contain two or more thoughts and were rewritten into separate items. At this point, many were rewritten for clarity of meaning, some were shifted to other categories, and four of the original ten categories were finally omitted.

After the statements and the organizational headings were reviewed with an eye toward omissions, an additional section on administrative-organizational frameworks was added to clarify the confusing issue of vertical and horizontal organization. Thirty-six items and six categories were then remaining.

REACTIONS TO THE MODEL BY EDUCATORS

After the statements of principles were completed, a copy was sent to forty-eight writers and practitioners in the field* in order to provide feedback as to the clarity, validity, and comprehensiveness of the model. Thirty-nine people (81 percent) sent back useable completed forms. Three others responded, raising the percentage answering to a surprising 87 percent, but did not complete the questionnaires.

*Questionnaires were sent to the following people: William Alexander, Dwight Allen, Robert H. Anderson, John Bahner, Roger Bardwell, Juliet Beck, B. Frank Brown, Edward G. Buffie, Robert Carbone, Ruth Chadwick, Glennis Cunningham, Martha Dawson, Stuart E. Dean, Frank Dufay, Murray Fessel, Edgar Fielder, Marian Franklin, Alexander Frazier, Lillian Glogau, John I. Goodlad, William Graves, Jr., Calvin Gross, Warren Hamilton, Leslie A. Hart, Glen Heathers, Maurie Hillson, Richard Hodges, Elizabeth Howard, Eugene Howard, Virgil Howes, Madeline Hunter, Marshall Jameson, Bruce Joyce, James Lewis, Jr., William McLoughlin, Richard I. Miller, Arthur Oestreich, Henry Otto, Walter Rehwoldt, Sidney P. Rollins, Ole Sand, Harold Shane, Albert H. Shuster, Lee L. Smith, John Tewksbury, John I. Thomas, Fred Wilhelms, and Daphne Wiseman (British).

The following directions were included with each set of assumptions:

(1) Please indicate how important you feel each of the following statements is in a comprehensive definition of nongradedness by circling one letter:
- C if item is crucial
- I if item is important
- M if item is of minor importance
- N if item is not important

(2) Space is left after each item so that you may change the wording of any item to make it more suitable to you.

(3) At the end of this page, space is left so that you may add items that you feel have been omitted from the definitions. Any other comments would also be appreciated.

The responses received were overwhelmingly in agreement with the assumptions in the model. Except for one item (number 18) out of the thirty-six statements, at least 70 percent of the respondents felt each statement was either crucial or important in a comprehensive definition of nongradedness.

In general, few comments were made on the items even though ample space had been left on the questionnaire. Quite frequently, the comments were to clarify the meaning of the statements. Subsequently, five items were rewritten for that purpose.

Comments referring to the implementation difficulties did not hold weight toward revision, since a model represents the ultimate or ideal toward which one strives. It was somewhat surprising that only three additional items were suggested, and even these seemed to be somewhat adequately covered by statements already in the definition.

Five individuals (Allen, Bahner, Frazier, Otto, and Tewksbury) helped to bring to the forefront one implicit assumption: nongradedness is not just a reorganization of the graded school system, but is a total educational philosophy. It is not possible, they indicated, to describe nongradedness without giving a complete picture of what a good school should be. Actually this is a good example of the "labelling" problem in education. Those who use the term *nongradedness* in a narrow sense refer mostly to grouping and placement procedures, materials usage, and evaluation. The earlier writings on nongrading do suggest this emphasis, but as the concept has developed it has become clear that nongradedness is a philosophy of education that permeates the total school organization and program.

Later, when classroom teachers were given the list of thirty-six statements, the directions asked how important each item was in their *personal educational philosophies* rather than in "a comprehensive definition of nongradedness."

In summary, even with some of the educators (about 13 percent) electing to respond to only those items corresponding to a limited definition of nongradedness (less than half of the items on the questionnaire), each item except one received a crucial or important designation by at least 70 percent of all respondents. All but eight of the thirty-six statements were declared to be crucial or important by 80 percent or more of the respondents. In other words, there seemed to be a generally strong acceptance of the assumptions of nongradedness by writers and practitioners in education.

UPDATING THE PRINCIPLES OF NONGRADEDNESS

The thirty-six principles of nongradedness from Pavan's dissertation (1972) were published in the introduction to Goodlad and Anderson's 1987 edition of *The Nongraded Elementary School*, with minor revisions to meet the new guidelines for gender-neutral writing. Also, in the spring of 1987 these items were again sent to the earlier respondents to ascertain their thoughts about the statements at this time. Even with the difficulties of finding people fifteen years later, including such obstacles as both retirement and deaths, responses were received from twenty-three of the original respondents. Suggestions were made for some language changes (for example, substituting "cognitive" for "intelligence"), and again the issue was raised as to whether only a few items were specific to nongradedness while other items could be applied to any model for an ideal or good school. The experts reaffirmed that most of these thirty-six statements were crucial to a comprehensive definition of nongradedness.

Once again Pavan used the responses to revise the statements. This time she also realigned the categories and some of the items within the categories for a more logical flow. Two dissertations (Guarino, 1982 and Hoffmann, 1985) which had used the original list were also consulted. The resulting (1992) version has been used with large groups of teachers and administrators from a dozen different states in training sessions conducted by the authors; and these discussions have provided useful insight as to the understanding of the items by current practitioners. The present version published in this book has been submitted to several experts and has been discussed by hundreds of educators in our training sessions.

A RECOMMENDED PAUSE

We suggest that you, the reader, now pause for a moment in order to examine your own thinking about nongradedness. Turn to Supplement Two (p. S-9) which again is perforated for easy removal. Make copies as needed and respond, on the response sheet, to the items (as you did in the first chapter) before you continue reading. Responses should reflect what *you* believe an ideal school should be, not what you think others would have you believe. You are asked to indicate how important each of the thirty-six *Principles of Nongradedness* is in your personal educational philosophy by circling on the response sheet a 3 if the item is *crucial*; a 2, if it is *important*; a 1, if it is of *minor importance*; and a 0, if it is *not important*. After you have checked out your own beliefs, return to this section of the chapter.

ANALYZING THE RESPONSES

After everyone on the team or school staff has responded to these *Principles of Nongradedness*, someone could use the response sheets to provide an average group score for each item, each category, and the total. (Each person can put a secret identification mark on the response sheet in order to identify his/her own sheet after the averages are calculated.) Since there are six categories: (1) Goals of Schooling, (2) Organization, (3) Curriculum, (4) Instruction, (5) Materials, and (6) Assessment, a total score plus six subtotals may be calculated. This summary could be shared with all group members.

Total scores could range from 0 to 108, with category scores ranging from 0 to 18. Any total score of 81 or higher is at least 75 percent of the maximum possible score, as is a category score over 13. This would indicate a very high agreement with the principles of nongradedness.

Teachers actively involved in nongraded efforts (Pavan, 1972, pp. 158 and 167) had scores ranging from 73 to 104. Hoffmann (1985, p. 156) has reported average total scores of 60 to 79 from national respondent groups identified as the present members of schools that had been noted as nongraded in her literature review.

Even when there is high agreement, much time needs to be allowed to discuss items so that the group becomes aware of the issues that cause discomfort and they may pose barriers to successful implementation of a nongraded program. Issues that lead to very heated debate will obviously require further study or investigation. The leadership should remind the group of the many items with which the group is comfortable, and might suggest that those items not resolved be reviewed at a later time (such as after reading this book).

Hoffmann (1985, pp. 135–155) reported that her respondents were in greatest agreement with the following assumptions:

GOALS OF SCHOOLING
2. To maximize individual potential
3. Individuals' uniqueness
6. Positive learning environment

INSTRUCTION
20. Teacher as facilitator of learning

MATERIALS
25. Variety of learning materials
26. Range of reading levels
30. Students working at an appropriate level

On the other hand, there was the least agreement with these items:

ORGANIZATION
8. Change of child's placement at any time

CURRICULUM
13. Goals set by student with teacher
14. Individual curriculum
16. No predetermined sequence
18. Based on individual interests

INSTRUCTION
24. Improve, not compete

ASSESSMENT
33. Student involvement
36. Portfolio, not grades

NONGRADEDNESS AND OPEN EDUCATION

The major tenet of nongrading is that individuals are different, and different treatments are needed to maximize each individual's potential. Few educators, whether of graded or nongraded persuasion, would not subscribe to that first statement. Many, however, would find difficulty in accepting some of the extended principles of nongrading as envisioned in the model (examples: statements 12, 13, 18 and 23). For this reason, it has been necessary to spell out the beliefs underlying nongrading in a more detailed and precise fashion. Any assumption can be judged to be nongraded if the practices that it implies aid in development of the maximum potential of each individual.

In practice, the ideal model may never be seen. Early statements, for example in the 1950s and 1960s, equated levels with nongrading. The evolution of the nongraded concept envisions the possibility of a much more open structure with a curriculum outlined in broad strokes rather than segmented into content sequences. The teacher's role has changed from "teller" to helper. The child is an active learner, not a passive sponge.

The descriptions of nongraded schools and of open structure classrooms, by the way, have generally been almost identical. Below, for example, are excerpts from a 1972 document (see Anderson and Pavan, 1972) describing the British informal schools. A senior member of the British Schools Inspectorate confirmed at the time that it accurately described the ideal model toward which the British Primary Schools were striving. The numbers in parentheses indicate the nongraded assumption contained in the preceding sentence.

> Teachers have a high respect for the dignity of individuality and seem more able to tolerate a wide spectrum of differences than most American teachers can (3, 21). Children are expected to become truly independent and to become responsible for their own learning (1). Teachers and students are co-workers and co-learners (12). Either is able to learn from the other (12). Children's thoughts, work and ideas are taken very seriously by the teachers (3).

> Not only do teachers help children, but they help each other learn. . . . Flexible groups are formed for limited times to accomplish set tasks: skill needs, common interests, or child planned social events (9). . . .

> Classrooms are set up as workshops with space provided for a great

amount of active aesthetic expression (4). An abundant supply of varied materials are available which the children may use in different ways (25-29). Except for rules concerning breaking expensive equipment, children are free to structure the materials in their own manner (1, 29). Children select the activity or project which interests them (13). The teacher's role is one of facilitator or guide . . . [making] suggestions to the child and even [being] rather firm but not dictating to the child (2). The work process is more important than the finished product but these are not infrequently exceptional pieces of art work, original writing, or science research (23). The child may become totally immersed in work projects which are self-conceived (18).

No set curriculum has been devised with sequences to be observed, but it is assumed that all children will learn to read and compute (14, 16). The teacher's main focus is on the students *learning* rather than teachers *teaching*. Teachers prepare the environment to encourage learning (28). Opportunities for reading, writing, counting, and computing are available within almost any activity that interests a child. The teacher must become a careful observer so that the student's interests are discovered and can be capitalized upon (18). Frequent and rich communication between students is observed and teachers often chat with students about their work (33).

More than half of the nongradedness assumptions are referred to in the above short piece about open classrooms. It therefore seems safe to say that the principles as provided in this chapter describe not only the ideal nongraded school, but also the ideal British integrated day or open education school. The major premise of either label is the recognition of the need to provide for individual differences. In sum, we have found no differences between nongraded and open education in terms of underlying philosophies.

We perceive that significant agreement within the staff on these thirty-six principles will be crucial, in order for a nongraded school to develop and thrive. We recognize that any school staff attempting to move from gradedness to nongradedness will find that its collective views fall somewhere along a continuum, and the greater the agreement with the principles, the likelier will be a successful effort.

While we are suggesting that the school faculty assess their beliefs early in their progress to determine commitment to nongradedness, it would also be instructive to repeat this process at a later point in time, since changes will occur with further study and the beginning of implementation.

REFERENCES

Anderson, Robert H. and Barbara N. Pavan. "Memo to Hartford Colleagues," unpublished paper, Harvard University Graduate School of Education, January 26, 1970.

Guarino, Anthony R. 1982. "An Investigation of Achievement, Self-Concept, and School Related Anxiety in Graded and Nongraded Elementary Schools," Ed.D. dissertation, Rutgers University.

Hoffmann, Mildred S. 1985. "The Ungraded Primary Organization in the Milwaukee Public Schools," Ph.D. dissertation, Marquette University.

Pavan, Barbara N. 1972. "Moving Elementary Schools toward Nongradedness: Commitment, Assessment, and Tactics," Ed.D. dissertation, Harvard University.

CHAPTER 5
Behavioral Indicators of Nongradedness

IN order to make the theoretical model of nongradedness operational, a number of behavioral indicators have been deduced from each principle. By this linking of theory and practice it is hoped that the gap so frequently encountered will in some measure be bridged. No list of practices could encompass all possibilities; it is only possible to present a sample. Practices under each assumption are listed according to their appropriate degree of verification difficulty, with the first statements being easiest to verify and ensuing statements slightly more speculative.

We hope that the previous chapter has helped practitioners to determine their apparent affinity for nongradedness. This chapter seeks to help them to determine which of their present educational practices are compatible with this philosophy.

PROCEDURES USED TO DEVELOP
THE LIST OF NONGRADED PRACTICES

One source for these practices was the experience and background of the authors, over many years teaching and observing in classrooms, combined with ideas accumulated from reading. A systematic attempt was also made to obtain behavioral statements from the literature. Another source was classroom observational instruments. Of the ninety-two instruments listed by Simon and Boyer in *Mirrors for Behavior II: An Anthology of Observational Instruments* (1970), only sixteen were not totally dependent on teacher-pupil verbal interchange. These activity-based instruments were scrutinized, along with (1) McLoughlin's *Nongraded Primaries in Action* (1969), (2) the instruments used by the "Bank Street Study" as published in the Appendices of Minuchin et al. (1969), (3) a classroom observational schedule de-

veloped in 1946 at the University of Chicago (see Anderson, 1949) and
(4) some unpublished observational materials developed by Pavan, for
other nongraded behavioral implications.

In this way almost 260 statements of practice were formulated. The
statements were then compared for redundancy and contradictions and
were rewritten as needed for clarity of meaning. It is noted where similar practices might indicate acceptance of more than one assumption of
nongradedness. Duplicate items and those most difficult to verify were
deleted.

Even though 170 items remain, there can probably never be an all-
inclusive list of possible classroom and school practices within a truly
nongraded context. The flexibility and openness of nongradedness
negate such a possibility, and furthermore a complete list of appropriate operational behaviors might be miles long. Any such list would
also require a periodic revision, to accommodate the development of
newer or different materials, methods, and perhaps even viewpoints.

The author did, all the same, accept the responsibility to identify at
least some of the most important indicators of a legitimate nongraded
operation. After this list of 170 behavioral implications was completed,
it was submitted to several authorities in the field in both the United
States and Great Britain who maintain close contact with schools as a
content validity check. It was reassuring to learn that no item was challenged, and it was felt that the list as presented (Pavan, 1972, p. 51–63)
rather adequately cited a large variety of observable possibilities.

UPDATING THE BEHAVIORAL INDICATORS

As part of nongrading implementation training sessions the authors
have been conducting in 1990, 1991, and 1992 at various sites, educators currently engaged in developing nongraded classrooms have been
asked to brainstorm possible behavioral indicators for each nongraded
principle. In addition, principals and supervisors from Florida, Geor-
gia, Illinois, Kentucky, New York, Ohio, and Wisconsin agreed to have
groups of teachers at their school sites brainstorm additional behavioral
indicators. This collection of new indicators was added to, or used to
revise the language of, the original list of 170 behavioral indicators.
Careful attention was given to the availability of technology for instructional purposes. The revised list now consists of 204 behavioral
indicators of nongradedness, which may be evidenced through ob-

servation or through teacher or pupil interviews, or documented through artifacts such as plan books, curriculum guides, school and district policies, and examples of student work.

Once again, we urge you the reader to pause. Before proceeding further, you should attempt to develop indicators for those practices thought to be most problematic to yourself or your group. An example is given below, using the sixth principle under the "Goals of Schooling" category. This principle has been considered "crucial" by nearly all members of groups that have completed the *Principles of Nongradedness* philosophical questionnaire (see Supplement Two, p. S-9).

Principle: The school environment is designed so that children enjoy learning, experience work effort as rewarding, and develop positive self-concepts.

Indicators:

- Students and teachers appear intensely involved with their work.
- Pupils appear satisfied and busy, yet relaxed.
- The observer enjoys being in the situation.
- There is an absence of aggressive activity: grabbing, pushing, hitting, fighting.
- Pupils do not twist hair, suck thumbs, wiggle, fidget, or manipulate objects constantly and excessively.
- No child appears to be passive or withdrawn for long periods of time.

All of these are behavioral indicators that can be directly observed during classroom visits to determine the absence or presence of the six indicators. Can you or your group think of other indicators for this assumption? Before reading further, select some of the other principles and determine some behavioral indicators for them.

As an exercise to help a school faculty moving toward nongradedness, select six of the principles, one from each of the six categories. Divide the faculty into six groups and have each group develop indicators for one assumption. Then share these statements with the total faculty and compare them with the list that follows. Since the list is really only a sample of some of the possible indicators for each principle, your group would be expected to develop some indicators that are not on the list, and some with similar wording.

While a behavioral indicator may be evidence for several principles, it is only listed under one principle. The group should look critically at each indicator and ask two questions: (1) What techniques are needed to verify this indicator (observation, interviews, or artifacts)? and (2) Does this indicator provide the data needed to indicate the absence or presence of the assumption? The conversation generated during this activity should help the participants to become more acquainted with both the theory and practices of nongradedness.

THE BEHAVIORAL INDICATORS

Goals of Schooling

(1) The ultimate school goal is to develop self-directing, autonomous individuals.
  - Students chart their own progress.
  - Students are accountable and responsible for their own work, use of time, and materials.
  - Displays, exhibits, and projects are pupil planned and made.
  - Children indicate a positive attitude toward learning and being in school.
  - Students set their own goals for most of their work.
  - Teachers do not force children to learn or work.
  - Some students initiate projects off the school property, involving responsible adults other than regular teachers.

(2) The school seeks to develop individual potentialities to the maximum possible.
  - Students are observed working on many different levels of difficulty.
  - Some children are working on non-academic activities at any given time.
  - No child is waiting for others to finish before beginning another activity.
  - Pupil records show that children may work on material above that commercially labelled for their chronological age.

(3) Each individual is unique and is accorded dignity and respect. Differences in people are valued. Therefore the school strives to increase the variability of individual differences rather than to stress conformity.
  - Pupils' work displays show variety, not conformity.
  - Common assigned tasks encourage, suggest, and allow variability.

- Pupil records consist in large part of the pupil's work or narrative reports, not check lists.
- Pupils show interest in activities of others, without the need to imitate.
- Groups are not addressed as "kindergartners," "first-graders," or "five-, six-, or seven-year-olds."

(4) Development of the child is considered in many areas: aesthetic, physical, emotional, and social, as well as cognitive.
- Pupil records include space and comments referring to all five developmental areas in a balanced manner.
- Pupils are allowed to converse with their peers and teacher in an informal manner at nearly any time.
- Equipment, materials, space, encouragement, and time are provided for pupils to have art, music, dramatic, construction, or movement experiences either in the classroom or in open "workshops" within the school.

(5) Each child needs to develop the skills for productive and responsible membership and leadership in civic, social, and work groups.
- Children are assigned roles in group work that require each to use group skills.
- Teachers help groups to analyze how the group functions and to determine other needed group skills.
- Teachers encourage and model skills for helping peers to learn.
- Students evolve the rules governing their behavior in school.
- Students assume responsibility for, and are aware of, projects that need doing within the school and local community.

(6) The school environment is designed so that children enjoy learning, experience work effort as rewarding, and develop positive self-concepts.
- Students and teachers appear intensely involved with their work.
- Pupils appear satisfied and busy, yet relaxed.
- The observer enjoys being in the situation.
- There is an absence of aggressive activity: grabbing, pushing, hitting, fighting.
- Pupils do not twist hair, suck thumbs, wiggle, fidget, or manipulate objects constantly and excessively.
- No child appears to be passive or withdrawn for long periods of time.

Organization

(7) Individuals work in varied situations where there will be opportunities for maximum progress. Advancement, retention, and promotion procedures are flexible. Classes or teams of children are identified with labels free of grade-level implications.

- Rooms are designated by the team's logo, a teacher's name, a color, a number, or some other device that does not indicate a grade level or achievement level.
- There are no rules for placement such as reading levels or years in school, but each child is considered on an individual basis.
- More than a few children complete the basic program of the primary or intermediate unit in less than three years.
- Placement decisions are made by all teachers who have direct contact with the child.
- The individual child, the teacher or teachers, and the makeup of the heterogeneous, multi-age pupil group are factors considered when a pupil is placed in a "home base."

(8) A child's placement may be changed at *any time* if it is felt to be in the best interest of the child, considering all five phases of development: aesthetic, physical, cognitive, emotional, and social.

- Except in very unusual circumstances, children remain in their heterogeneous, multi-age home base group as long as they remain in the team or unit. However, each child works with a variety of different groups on any given day.
- Children are phased into the next unit for part or all of the day throughout the year.
- Regular meetings are held by the faculty so that each child's current placement is reviewed about once a month.
- Any teacher, parent, or child may suggest review of a child's current placement at the next regular review meeting.
- Although a spurt or lag in one developmental area may be the cause for a placement review, all developmental aspects are considered before a change is made.

(9) Grouping and subgrouping patterns are extremely flexible. Learners are grouped and regrouped on the basis of one specific task or interest and groups are disbanded when that objective is reached.

- There are no permanent groups that meet every day and have similar assignments.
- There are flexible furnishings that can be moved for a variety of informal groupings.
- Groups are labelled, if at all, by the specific objective to be reached (e.g., those gaining speed on math combinations, or those writing poetry).
- Cross-age groups are visible in the lunchroom, on the playground, and in most instructional groups.

(10) Each child has opportunities to work with groups of many sizes, including one-person groups, formed for different purposes.
- Groups of various sizes are observed.
- Most children participate in a two- to five-person group at least once a day.
- Most children participate in a five- to eight-person group at least once a day.
- Most children participate in a ten- to fifteen-person group at least once a day.
- At least one or more times per week, each child joins a larger group.

(11) The specific task, materials required, and student needs determine the number of students that may be profitably engaged in any given educational experience.
- An individual interest is pursued in a one-person group.
- Learning or inquiry groups contain two to five persons.
- Groups in activities that require manipulation of materials consist of five to eight persons.
- Discussion and decision-making groups contain ten to twelve members.
- Lectures, television programs, and demonstrations are limited only by the number who can comfortably hear and see what is going on and profit from it.

(12) Children and adults of varying personalities, backgrounds, abilities, interests, and ages work together in teams as co-learners in the collaborative school enterprise.
- During a week, each child will be in at least five types of groups based on such factors as:
  - homogeneity
  - heterogeneity

- interests
- mixed ages—generally two to three contiguous ages
- cross-age teaching—usually involving older teaching group and younger learners
- chronological ages
- friendships
- work-study skills
- teaching teams
- physical sizes and strengths
- teacher cycling—teacher continues with pupils for more than one year
- gender

- Teacher teams, like student home base groups, are composed of adults with varying subject matter skills, personalities, and interests. In addition, teams should have racial, gender, and age balance.
- Teachers meet together on a regular formal basis in small study groups.
- Children observe teachers teaching and planning together and work with several different team teachers each week.
- Often it is difficult to find the teacher, as the teacher's position does not dominate the room.
- Teachers encourage and accept pupil work suggestions and join pupil groups as equal co-learners.
- Teachers learn from students.

Curriculum

(13) Children formulate their own learning goals with guidance from their teachers.
- The teacher's plan book shows few activities required of all pupils. It contains ideas for individuals in response to their interests and for general educational opportunities.
- Each pupil meets with a teacher at least twice a week to assess him/herself and determine new learning objectives.
- Students verbalize and clarify their goals.
- If learning contracts are used, student involvement in writing such documents is primary.

(14) The unique needs, interests, abilities, learning rates, styles, and

patterns determine the child's individual curriculum. Conformity and rigidity are not demanded.

- The curriculum guide has a format that allows for yearly partial revisions. It is a teacher source book that increases the number of learning opportunities available, rather than mandating identical experiences for each child.
- Displays do not show rows of neat papers or drawings. Creative writing may include imperfect attempts at spelling and grammar.
- Pupils indicate that materials and time are available to help them pursue their own interests.
- Kinesthetic, visual, and auditory approaches to learning are observed in the classroom.
- Some confusion may be evidence of the diverse types of student participation.

(15) Broad thematic units integrating several subject matter disciplines are utilized, rather than presenting isolated bits of information.
- Time blocks are not labelled according to the subject matter discipline to be taught.
- Math, reading, writing, science, social studies, art, and music are often approached simultaneously, rather than being taught as isolated subjects at separate times during the school day or year.
- A theme or problem of interest to the students is used to integrate subject disciplines.
- Even though some subject matter disciplines are taught as separate subjects, there is at least one time block per day set aside for thematic learning.
- Learning to read and write is stressed, with skills of phonics, word analysis, punctuation, penmanship, and spelling taught only as needed.

(16) Sequences of learning are determined for individual students since:
   - No predetermined sequence is appropriate to all learners.
   - Individual differences in level of competence and in interest are constantly in flux.
   - There are few logical or inherently necessary sequences in the various curriculum areas.
- Pupil records do not show a series of items that must be mastered in a required order.

- No one basal textbook, workbook, or series is used by all the children.
- Most children do not have to work from "cover to cover" in a text or workbook.

(17) The curriculum is organized to develop understanding of concepts and methods of inquiry, more than retention of specific content of learning.
- Questions are more often in terms of "how" and "why," less often in terms of "where," "what," and "who."
- The district curriculum guide specifies the concepts, not the subject matter content.
- A particular item such as the Nile River is studied to show that geography influences how people live.
- Less than 50 percent of the items on a test require factual recall.

(18) Learning experiences based on the child's expressed interests will motivate the child to continue and complete a task success-fully much more frequently than will teacher-contrived tech-niques.
- No more than one-quarter of a child's day is spent on programmed learning materials, that by their very nature have preplanned adult-set goals.
- Students are able to move from one activity to another without first seeking teacher approval.
- Students choose some of their learning activities.
- Pupils are allowed to attempt mastery of material which often teachers might consider too difficult for the student.
- Children are allowed to base some of their learning experiences on topics of interest that they bring from home.

Instruction

(19) All phases of human growth: aesthetic, physical, cognitive, emo-tional, and social are considered when planning learning ex-periences for a child. Most of the following questions are answered affirmatively in considering a learning experience.
- Is beauty or creativity being fostered?
- Is there enough physical activity for comfort?
- Are emotional reactions allowed sufficient expression or encouragement?

- Are social aspects being considered in the situation?
- Is this experience cognitively challenging and yet within the child's grasp?

(20) Teachers are the facilitators of learning. They aid in children's development by helping them to formulate goals and diagnose problem areas. They suggest alternative plans of action, provide resource materials, and give encouragement or support or prodding as needed.
- Teachers ask more open-ended than closed questions.
- Teachers observe groups as they work, and assist only as needed, usually by asking questions.
- Secluded conference areas and sufficient time are provided for private teacher-pupil discussions.
- Students may explain their work tasks to the teacher, not to gain approval but to inform.
- Pupil suggestions are encouraged and accepted.

(21) Different people learn in different ways, so multiple learning alternatives should be available.
- Most of the time, students are working on different activities.
- Teachers rarely assign common tasks to the class.
- Independent activities are part of each child's daily format.
- Reading instruction is based on individual needs and therefore several options are offered or considered for each student.

(22) Successful completion of challenging experiences promotes greater confidence and motivation to learn than does fear of failure.
- Children appear deeply engrossed in their work.
- Children run excitedly to the teacher or other pupils with their work in hand, cry "Look," and explain what they learned.
- No threats of failure, of poor reports to parents, or of not being allowed to do something are made by the teacher.
- Children show pleasure in their own work without the need to share experience.
- Teachers admit their own mistakes and use them as learning experiences.

(23) The process is more important than the product. The skills of learning to learn, especially inquiry, evaluation, interpretation, synthesis, and application are stressed.

- Emphasis is on how the answer is reached, rather than on the actual answer.
- One source is not considered sufficient in any student research.
- All tests contain at least one item that consists of a new problem that the children solve by a reorganization of their present knowledge.
- Nearly all tests contain one item that asks not for an answer but requires the student to tell how to find the answer.
- Classroom materials encourage children to observe, classify, measure, and record data.
- When using manipulative materials, children's language indicates they are inferring, predicting, and formulating hypotheses.
- Some children are controlling and manipulating variables in their experimenting.

(24) Children strive to improve their performance and develop their potential, rather than to compete with others.
- Public comparisons are avoided in the room. Star charts, reading levels completed, listing the names of permanent group members, etc., are not in evidence.
- Pupil work displayed consists of dissimilar items put up for the purpose of sharing work, not comparison.
- Teacher-checked papers contain no number, letter or work grades, but offer comments that refer to pupil improvement over past work or suggest ways to improve.
- Pupils file dated items of their work for each subject area each month. They select the items and observe their growth by studying the entire folder.
- Reports to parents are in terms of accomplishments achieved and areas that need a concentration of effort.
- Pupils do not seem to be preoccupied with what page a friend is on, or how many books they have read, or asking for other comparative data.
- Students seek assistance from many sources, especially their peers.
- Extrinsic rewards are used on a very limited basis.
- Unit-culmination activities, by sharing student performances, are handled as celebrations.

Materials

(25) A wide variety of textbooks, tradebooks, supplemental materials, workbooks, and teaching aids are available and readily accessible in sufficient quantities.
- Instructional areas do not contain sets of identical books so that each child has to use the same book. Instead, five or fewer copies of any one title are used to provide a variety of sources in each curriculum area.
- There is a good-sized classroom library in use.
- Pupils may go to the school library/media center at nearly any time during the day.
- Children use the trade books and reference materials available in the classroom.
- Learning kits and learning activity packages, both commercially and locally prepared, are in use.
- Workbooks are generally cut up to provide skills sheets, rather than completed by individual pupils.
- Computers are available within each instructional area.
- Software of the interactive, not drill and practice mode is selected whenever possible.
- Newer informational sources such as CD-ROM and laser discs are provided for student use.

(26) Varied materials are available to cover a wide range of reading abilities.
- Books are available in each classroom in each subject matter area to accommodate a spread of three to five or more years in reading achievement.
- Additional materials written on very high or low reading levels are available in the library.
- Books are not labelled by difficulty, so the level of book a child reads does not become public knowledge.
- Books on audio cassettes, CD-ROM, and laser discs as well as other computer-programmed reading instruction are available on many different reading levels.

(27) Alternate methods and materials are available at any time so that the children may use the learning styles and materials most suitable to their present needs and the task at hand (including skill building, self-teaching, self-testing, and sequenced materials).

Six or more of the following well-stocked activity areas are open nearly all the time to pupils either in the room or in the school:
- math center with manipulatives
- reading center
- writing publication center
- science center with microscopes
- social studies center
- arts and crafts center
- construction center—wood and real tools
- housekeeping area
- "living room"
- store and/or bank
- painting easels
- real cooking equipment
- sand and water area
- live animal area
- theater area with costumes
- audio cassette and TV-VCR with four to six headsets
- skill development section
- clay or modelling
- blocks, Lego, Tinkertoy, erector set, Lincoln Logs
- computers—four to six with printer and software

(28) Children are not really free to learn something they have not been exposed to. Teachers are responsible for providing a broad range of experiences and materials that will stimulate many interests in the educational environment.
- Non-standard school materials are in use.
- Each week (or so) something new is presented, generally designed as an interest item.
- About once a month, a theme area is developed. Similar to the interest item, it is conceived in greater depth as a series of related items or activities.
- Outside resource people are visited by students or invited to the class on a frequent basis.

(29) Learning is the result of the student's interaction with the environment; therefore the child must be allowed to explore, to experiment, to mess around, to play, and have the freedom to err.
- Scrounged items, "stuff," and junk are put to good use.
- Nearly half of the children are manipulating materials rather than using books or paper and pencil.

- Many children appear to be playing.
- Accidents and messes happen but are cleaned up by the pupil who made the mess whenever possible. No fuss is made unless a deliberate attempt had been made to break something useful.
- Mistakes are expected and used as a positive force that indicates areas of need.
- The classroom will appear busy, noisy, and messy, yet talk is on the project at hand and students put materials away after use.

(30) Children work with materials on the level appropriate to their present attainment and move as their abilities and desires allow them.
- No time limit is imposed by the teacher for task or test completion.
- Large unscheduled time blocks dominate the day's program, so pupils can determine usage of time.
- Pre-tests or diagnostic tests precede usage of all programmed or sequential materials to determine student need.
- Students are not stopped when they reach a certain level (especially one deemed inappropriate).

Assessment

(31) Assessing and reporting must consider all five areas of the child's development: aesthetic, physical, cognitive, emotional, and social. Items for data recording include some of the following:
- physical development—movement skills, coordination, visual and auditory perception, results of physical examination
- cognitive development—diagnostic IQ tests, diagnostic achievement tests, observations recorded by teachers regarding academic progress, strategies for learning
- social development—sociometric data, teachers' and students' comments about ability to relate to peers and adults, reports from social workers or guidance counselors
- emotional development—results of psychological examinations, notes by teachers concerning how the learner perceives and reacts to a learning task, teacher comments

regarding such factors as ability to accept criticism, overdependence on peers or the teacher, expressions of hostility
- aesthetic development—samples or descriptions of dramatic activities, interests shown and/or pursued

(32) Assessment is continuous, cooperative, and comprehensive to fulfill its diagnostic purpose.
- Dates on data in pupil records indicate that information is added about once a month in each developmental area.
- Anecdotal records are made about each child.
- Teachers systematically observe each child at least once a month.
- Performance on learning activities is the focus for assessment.

(33) The child is directly involved in assessing and interpreting academic (and other) progress, and in shaping plans for future activity and growth.
- Teacher records for individual pupils are more qualitative than quantitative. These records attempt to pinpoint the exact nature of the child's learning accomplishment.
- Children record their own progress in a diary or record book. Words and/or pictures describe the important events of their day.
- Spelling lists or other lessons are derived from student writing.
- Test results are shared as learning experiences, not as threats.
- Students write a weekly/monthly report to parents on their own progress.

(34) Children's work is assessed in terms of their past achievements and their own potential, not only by comparison to group norms. Expectations differ for different children.
- Pupil records and reports show the child's attainments but no grade level standards or other norms.
- Achievement may be indicated in terms of the child's potential, especially as the child advances through school.
- The terms "slow," "average," "fast," or similar labels, grade levels, and marks tend not to be used.

(35) Teachers accept and respond to the fact that growth patterns are irregular and occur in different areas at different times.

- Pupil records indicate that a child is not required to have similar attainment in all areas at all times.
- A child may elect to associate with peers of varying chronological ages and with varying interests.
- A child may elect to work in any of many types of areas.

(36) Instead of letter or numerical grades to summarize student progress, multiple sources of documentation are utilized for reporting purposes. Sources may include the following:
- dated samples of student work including art work (portfolio)
- audio and/or video tapes of student or student projects
- student writing journal
- learning tasks completed
- item or area analysis of teacher-made or standardized tests
- classroom observational notes by teachers
- comments on monthly placement reassessment
- pupil's interests
- pupil's self-assessment
- estimate of potential revised periodically
- notes on parent conferences
- comments on all areas of child's development (aesthetic, physical, cognitive, emotional, and social)

In order to determine the nongraded practices currently being used, this list of nongraded behavioral indicators could be reviewed as a total faculty, in small groups, or by individuals. For each indicator the question is, "Is this being done?" We have no doubt that many of these practices are routine within the school and that some teachers might already be considered nongraded practitioners.

Once a school faculty has decided which principles are most important in their school philosophy, they can look at the indicators for those assumptions and develop a plan to begin immediately to strengthen these particular practices. Of course, we believe that all 36 principles and 204 behavioral indicators are essential for an ideal school. What is important for all teachers and schools is that concerted efforts are made toward *their* ideal school.

REFERENCES

Anderson, Robert H. 1949. "The Influence of a Cooperative Study on Teacher Test Behavior and Classroom Practices," unpublished doctoral dissertation, University of Chicago.

McLoughlin, William P. 1969. *Evaluation of the Nongraded Primary*. Jamaica, NY: St. John's University.

Minuchin, Patricia, Barbara Biber, Edna Shapiro and Herbert Zimiles. 1969. *The Psychological Impact of School Experience*. New York, NY: Basic Books.

Pavan, Barbara N. 1972. "Moving Elementary Schools toward Nongradedness: Commitment, Assessment, and Tactics," doctoral dissertation, Harvard University.

Simon, Anita and E. Gil Boyer, eds. 1970. *Mirrors for Behavior II: An Anthology of Observational Instruments, Volumes A and B*. Philadelphia, PA: Classroom Interaction Newsletter and Research for Better Schools.

CHAPTER 6
Structural Mechanisms

WHETHER or not a school staff is seeking to develop a nongraded program, decisions have to be made about (1) how teachers will be deployed throughout the buildings and (2) how children will be assembled or aggregated for instructional purposes. In most discussions of school organization, the upward progress (i.e., from age five to the moment of graduation) of the pupils is visualized on the vertical axis, and the horizontal axis relates to the current, day-to-day systems for assigning and grouping the pupils within the space available.

To oversimplify a bit, questions of vertical organization usually focus on the graded versus the nongraded pattern. Questions of horizontal organization focus on whether teachers will work essentially in isolation, as in the self-contained classroom, or in some form of teaming. In secondary schools, questions will also revolve around departmentalization versus multidisciplinary arrangements. Middle schools, within which a multidisciplinary (or interdisciplinary) curriculum arrangement is quite common, also have either a mostly self-contained or a mostly teamed pattern for teacher assignments. Some elementary schools, usually at the intermediate level, similarly employ one or another version of departmentalization, or teacher specialization, with self-containment or teaming as a correlated pattern.

The typical elementary school in America, whether K–5 or K–6, does not feature departmentalization or teacher specialization. In those schools where teaming of some sort is practiced, the usual but by no means exclusive pattern is for all of the teamed teachers to have instructional responsibilities for all of the so-called basic subjects: language arts, social studies, mathematics, and science. We happen to think that this is a desirable arrangement, although there is also some merit in patterns where a team of elementary teachers divides up the instructional responsibility so that each teacher can focus upon one or two of the areas.

In teams where all teachers teach all of the basic subjects, each teacher could be given the responsibility for developing expertise in one of the curriculum areas, or at least for paying special attention to that field (via readings and inservice activities), so that a process of sharing can strengthen every member's overall repertoire.

The strong bias in this volume, with reference to horizontal organization, is in favor of collaborative/cooperative patterns of staffing. The greater the extent to which teachers are co-involved in the teaching of children, the likelier it is in our view that both the teachers and the children will have productive, growth-inducing experiences. Another strong bias is in favor of multi-aging practices. These topics have already been examined to some extent in other chapters, but now it seems appropriate to address them more completely.

TEACHER TEAMING

Arguing the case for team teaching, which thirty or more years ago was regarded as heretical by many staunch supporters of the self-contained classroom, is no longer difficult or perhaps even necessary. Although the habit of working in isolation from other teachers remains very strong, and although at least three-quarters of American classrooms are still essentially self-contained, there is now a much overdue recognition of its limitations. Consequently, the self-contained classroom is one of the prime targets of the current restructuring movement. The defenders of self-containment being very hard to find, and research confirming its merits being nonexistent, it seems only a matter of time before literal self-containment (no teacher co-involvement) will have disappeared from the educational scene.

A great many school buildings built after 1957, when the Franklin Elementary School in Lexington, Massachusetts attracted worldwide attention as the first school to adopt full-fledged teaming, were designed to accommodate team teaching and featured either a number of large, open spaces without walls, or spaces with collapsible partitions so that open areas could be created at will. Some of these school buildings were used as intended with great success, and they remain unchanged and in good use in the 1990s. Others, unfortunately, were either poorly designed (e.g., from an acoustical point of view) or poorly utilized (e.g., by poorly prepared and reluctant teachers), and before long either they had been reconverted into "egg-crate" structures or the flexible partitions had become frozen into closed position. The presumed "failures" of these buildings and of the ill-fated team teaching ventures within them have caused many observers to conclude that the idea does not work.

It is true that the idea often did not work, but one may safely argue that almost every big idea, including capitalism and democracy and even Christianity, sometimes does not work. The fault, it is readily agreed, may not lie in conceptual or philosophical flaws but rather in the failures of individuals and groups to comprehend, to embrace, and to practice the concept authentically. The hundreds, perhaps thousands, of team teaching efforts that were attempted in the early days and later modified or abandoned, were unsuccessful because of the aforementioned failures: the participants were given too little information and support, a sincere commitment to making it work did not develop, and the "game plan" that was followed was simply too flawed. It was also true that many of the enthusiasts who initiated the teaming projects were simply joining the bandwagon or naively jumping into the fray without sufficient forethought or preparation. Furthermore, in the environment of those days, staff development had not yet become a respected and appreciated function within school systems, and it is likely that few school districts made a strong effort to retrain or reorient their teaching staffs so that they could better cope with the new challenge of working together.

A COMPREHENSIVE DEFINITION

At the basic level, team teaching calls for groups of teachers to work closely together in all dimensions of teaching, and to share responsibility for aggregations of children who would otherwise, under conventional circumstances, be subaggregated into so-called self-contained classrooms staffed by virtually autonomous teachers.

The dimensions of teaching include *planning, carrying out the plan*, and *assessing results*. Planning includes studying/diagnosing the needs of students; taking inventory of available instructional and other resources, including time and space; inventing, developing, or adapting activities and experiences through which learning is intended to occur; and then deciding upon the actions to be taken. Planning can be done by a single, self-contained teacher without much if any interaction with colleagues, or it can be done by groups of teachers sharing a common purpose. Many teachers, even those who do not otherwise co-involve themselves, find team planning to be a helpful, productive, and stimulating way to prepare themselves for classroom work.

Co-teaching, through which a jointly developed plan is jointly implemented, carries the concept of team teaching to another level. In some schools, teachers who are mostly self-contained will co-teach for a part of the day. Combining their class groups for specific projects or interchanging pupils so as to achieve more appropriate mixes of learners (see Joplin Plan, discussed later in this chapter) would be common examples of what might be called part-time team teaching. Full-time co-teaching, by contrast, would find teachers continuously sharing (or dividing up) tasks and dealing with the entire pupil-team population. Full-time teams usually find it convenient and desirable to have a more or less permanent subgroup of the total team assigned to each teacher (e.g., a homeroom or advisory group, with whom a somewhat more permanent and intimate "bond" is formed). Important, though, is for every child in the pupil team to have a distinct relationship with each of the teamed teachers. Ideally, when grandpa asks the child "Who is your teacher?" the child would respond, "Well, actually I have six teachers but Miss Lawrence sort of keeps me under her wing."

Assessing or evaluating results is something that teachers do in small increments almost constantly, and that periodically—as for example when report cards are due—is done more completely and formally. The self-contained teacher necessarily does this work in virtual isolation, except perhaps for consultation with specialist colleagues. In a team situation, while some of the assessment work is also done privately, there is the opportunity for pooling data, impressions, and recommendations, and as a result there is the opportunity for creating a much more comprehensive view of each child's makeup, accomplishments, needs, and overall development.

An acknowledged problem is that team pupil-assessment discussions, while extremely valuable, can also be very time-consuming. Many team members, however, cheerfully accept the extra time these discussions require, realizing that a greater understanding of the children can make future planning and teaching more successful.

While assessment is on our minds, mention should be made of the potential for peer coaching and other forms of recognizing and enhancing individual professional growth of team colleagues. Because of their constant co-involvement, teamed teachers have opportunities to observe each other at work and, given sufficient trust and mutual respect, to offer feedback and suggestions to each other. Some teams seek on a regular basis to examine and comment upon each others' specific lesson plans, as well as to consider how well the total program seems to be faring. It may be that some teachers find this type of discussion to be a bit challenging, especially in the early stages of a team's life; but for many if not most teachers, once they have learned how to give and take in a professional way, the greatest benefits of being a team member derive from thinking together about how to do the job better.

One sign of a healthy, full-fledged teaching team is the unselfish sharing of space, materials, and resources. The notion of "my classroom" changes into "our classrooms." The computers, specialized science equipment, books, and all other paraphernalia that self-contained teachers tend to protect or even to hoard become accessible to everybody. In one respect the sharing posture results in economies to the team's advantage, since it is less necessary to furnish each teacher with full sets of certain textbooks or other resources, and therefore funds become available for buying other things.

Team teaching, as briefly defined above, includes these features:

(1) Long-range as well as short-range curriculum planning, including occasional review of each teacher's specific lesson plans, is a total group responsibility.

(2) The team members, although much of their teaching is within a private or "solo" context, regularly work together (co-teach).

(3) Assessment of the overall instructional program, as well as assessment of components with which individual teachers are concerned, is a team-wide responsibility.

(4) The pupils, although connected for advisory and other purposes to one or another of the teachers, belong to and are regularly connected with all of the teaching team members.

(5) Assessment of each child's needs and progress is an activity in which all team members participate in some systematic manner.

(6) Resources are shared (co-owned) for the benefit of all teachers and students.

It might be noted that a 1964 volume on team teaching, edited by Shaplin and Olds, remains even in the 1990s a clear and useful summary of the history and the characteristics of teaming. Many more current discussions of teaming are found within books and articles examining the changing role of teachers, and the needs of teachers for collegial relationships.

Cohen's (1981) extensive review of the team teaching literature remains pertinent in the 1990s, and her conclusions have been reinforced by more recent reviews of the social organization of schools such as that by Rosenholtz (1989). Cohen found that in teaching teams, work arrangements and communications are related directly to the nature of instruction. Rosenholtz observes that such talk is geared to recognition that teaching is inherently difficult and that therefore, rather than being embarrassed by acknowledging one's professional limitations, teamed teachers consider it both legitimate and necessary to seek and offer assistance. Teaming, Cohen further noted, is a vehicle for greater instructional interaction, as teachers share and challenge each other's ideas about students and their needs, possible grouping arrangements, classroom management, and curriculum. Also determined by Cohen and again by Rosenholtz is that in collaborative contexts teachers hold greater decision-making rights and work more cooperatively with principals about those decisions.

Rosenholtz observes, in addition, that in schools where helping behaviors are valued, teachers tend to regard collaboration as a moral imperative if students are to be helped in mastering basic skills.

MULTI-AGE PUPIL GROUPING

It will be remembered that for many years all schools everywhere, as represented by the one-room "Little Red Schoolhouse," served children of many different ages in the same classroom space until the growth of cities and Horace Mann's mid-nineteenth century proposal for age-graded grouping caused a shift away from "family-type" groupings. It should also be acknowledged that in the mid-twentieth century, when pilot nongraded programs sprang up in Wisconsin, Illinois, and a few other places, children of similar ages were usually kept together. For example, a class of six-year-old children, for which the label first grade was now seen as inappropriate, would be called a primary class, with terms to suggest "junior level" or "lower level" sometimes softly added for identification purposes. Only with the appearance of the Torrance Plan in California as reported by Hamilton and Rehwoldt (1957), a book by Lane and Beauchamp (1955), and reports of several other "multigraded" programs in the late 1950s, did it become clear that age-homogeneous class groupings can be, in several respects, disadvantageous to the learners.

The original (1959) edition of the Goodlad-Anderson book, in discussing nongradedness, cited age-homogeneous examples almost entirely. Only one paragraph (pp. 68–69, which cited the Lane-Beauchamp and the Torrance references) about multi-age grouping was included. As a matter of fact, that paragraph was added to the manuscript only a month or so before the book went into production. There was also very little mention of the connection between nongradedness and teaming. One reason that Goodlad and Anderson asked their publisher to permit issuance of the 1963 revised edition was that they had come to realize how very important are connections with teaming and multi-aging if nongradedness is to succeed, and they wanted to enlarge that message in the book.

The sometimes-accidental ways in which knowledge or insight is learned are illustrated by what happened to pupil grouping in the early team teaching projects. Most of the elementary schools in which teaming was piloted had only one or two classes at each grade level, and few had three or more. Since an early conclusion was that teaching teams ought to have four to six members in order to function effectively (a conclusion that still makes sense three decades later), it was realized that multigrade teams would be not only desirable, but necessary. In Lexington, where it all began, six-teacher teams therefore worked with two adjoining grades each. Other, smaller schools opted for teams with three adjoining grades.

None of these early projects, or at least very few of them, had identified nongradedness as one of their immediate, or even long-range goals; but lo and behold, as they worked with the children for a year or two, they found themselves totally forgetting about grade labels and naturally dealing with each child on his/her own terms. Teachers would often say something like "I don't really think any more about who is a third grader and who is a fourth grader. If this is the group or activity that fits a kid's needs, that's where we put that kid!"

From this lesson learned can be derived a major generalization: *any school that wants to make nongradedness happen, can accelerate the process by adopting a teaching-team approach working with multi-age pupil groups.*

Not only through such more-or-less accidental discoveries, but also through thoughtful analysis, multi-aged grouping is gaining advocates and emerging as a powerful strategy for promoting learning. Two publications, in particular, help us to understand why this is so. One is a report by a Canadian educator, David Pratt (1986), who reviewed fifty-one references on the merits of multi-age classrooms. The other, a creative study reported by Gary Bernhard (1988), suggested, as did Pratt, that from an evolutionary perspective, age-homogeneity is not only unnatural but perhaps even destructive.

Pratt examined the findings of experimental research and also relevant evidence from ethology, anthropology, and history. His bottom line was that from the mass of evidence we may conclude that for pupils, multi-age classroom environments "are socially and psychologically healthy places" (p. 114). Looking at the historical context of age segregation, he noted that this familiar structure is neither natural nor universal. It is a relatively recent phenomenon in the human experience, and "runs counter to the pattern of upbringing of the young which previously existed for millions of years" (p. 111). He discussed studies of primates and of some 180 hunting/gathering societies that survived into the twentieth century and stated that nonpeer patterns should not have been abandoned in the nineteenth century after Horace Mann's ideas favoring age-graded classes were adopted.

Pratt in his writings also discusses children's friendships, levels of competition and aggression, and levels of harmony and nurturance in the two contrasting arrangements. In his view, multi-age situations produce better results in these areas, and also in language development, cognitive growth, social and emotional development, and altruism.

Furthermore, there is support for the conclusion that multi-age grouping is associated with better self-concept and attitude toward school.

Bernhard (1988) also discusses primate social life, emotional development, and learning. He then reviews how human societies emerged and how foraging societies provided the emotional and social contexts of learning, with interdependence, reciprocity, conversation, imitation and practice of adult skills and behavior, cooperation and sharing, individual distinction (specialization), role modelling, and role-specific formal instruction as contributing elements.

Half of the Bernhard book examines learning in contemporary society. Among other things, he notes "the triumph of self-interest over the general well-being," heightened competition, fragmented learning, age segregation, limited family involvement, limited social involvement, unnatural discipline, and too-limited exploration and cooperative activity as forces that depress opportunities for wholesome growth and learning.

From these and other recent accounts, we gain a strong impression that the much-publicized failure of American schools could well be traced at least in large measure to the unnatural conditions imposed upon children by age segregation. Until World War II or thereabouts, with homes and neighborhoods still reasonably intact and providing children with many multi-age connections, it may be that the deprivation of such connections within the school building took a less obvious toll than it seems to have taken since perhaps 1955. As family life weakens, as siblings become less and less able or inclined to cross the age barrier with each other, and as the competitive atmosphere within the school makes even the same-age connections less meaningful, many children are denied the social-intellectual-exploratory privileges that their distant ancestors and probably their great grandfathers could take for granted. It becomes difficult to put life in perspective when the only human beings with whom you have day-to-day contact are roughly in the same predicament that you are.

Multi-age grouping is a common practice in nursery schools and pre-schools, and in some respects it is strange that public schools in setting up kindergartens for only five-year-olds, first grade for only six-year-olds, and so forth, have disregarded what is naturally done in pre-kindergarten schooling. In a recent review of research and model programs, particularly with reference to young children, Webb (1992) confirms the overall conclusions in Chapter 3 of this volume and attributes the generally positive research findings about nongradedness to "components of multi-age grouping such as cooperative learning, peer tutoring, and continuity in adult/child relations from one school to the next" (p. 90). She quotes one researcher's observation: "Segregating children by sex, race, ethnic, or socioeconomic differences is against the law. Is it right to segregate by age?" She notes in particular that a pro-social orientation and a sense of social competence can result for young children from success in a multi-age, cooperative context.

Parent Reactions

Usually when a school switches from an age-segregated to a multi-age grouping pattern, this requires even more explanation or justification than does a switch from gradedness to nongradedness.

Probably all parents will have questions, but our experience shows that the adults who are most likely to doubt the value of nongraded schooling, especially where multi-age, heterogeneous pupil groupings are featured, are those whose children have been classified (officially, or in their ambitious parents' minds) as gifted. The energetic efforts of these adults to protect the graded status quo, within which their children appear to enjoy great advantages and many rewards, are understandable. One need not doubt their motivation to assure their child's future happiness and accomplishment, although it sometimes seems that certain parents of gifted children excessively enjoy and exploit their own "elite" status. But if such parents are indeed interested in helping their unusually talented children to fulfill their potential and become both productive and well-adjusted adults, they need to appreciate that the best educational route for their children is one that offers maximum rather than minimum opportunities for interactions with the full range of other children and for collaborative learning ventures.

Another potential problem is that the parents of special-education children, aware of the fact that their children have generally been in smaller-than-usual classes, may fear that their children will receive less attention in a heterogeneous classroom. Happily, such concerns are likely to disappear once the program is under way.

The research evidence on these points is very strong: when children of all ability (or achievement) levels learn collaboratively, not only do those of lower and medium ability benefit substantially, but so do those of higher ability (including the gifted). We are aware of no research in which gifted children have been shown to suffer any disadvantage whatsoever; and on the other hand there is abundant evidence to support the notion that the advantages are many. Kulik (1987) has made some claims for the gifted students that it is more beneficial for them to be in separate classes, but Slavin (1991) has disputed these claims.

The next most likely group of parents to doubt the value of multi-age, heterogeneous groupings are those whose children will be the oldest in the groups. These parents ask questions such as, "Will not the constant presence of younger, less knowledgeable and less mature children water down the program and provide less stimulation? Won't my child be spending too much time serving as a teacher or counselor of the young, and too little time on advanced studies?" Happily, the research evidence on these questions is totally reassuring: the older children thus engaged do at least as well, and often do better, in all respects, than children of their same age in other schools where multi-aging is not practiced. This we have known for at least thirty years (since the Torrance Plan data were published), and every year the data base is stronger. Undoubtedly the older children who serve as teachers benefit from re-visiting material already mastered and reorganizing it in their own mind in order to "teach it."

There is yet another benefit from multi-aging that has not been sufficiently appreciated. When elementary children go through two or more cycles of multi-aged classes on their way to secondary school, they have recurring opportunities to be for a while at the "bottom" (youngest cohort), for a while in the "middle," and for a while at the "top" (oldest cohort) and thereby to have different kinds of relationships with children older than, the same age as, and younger than themselves. In most cases this means that in their first year there will be a lot of older children helping them and serving as role models. In the second year, they'll still be with some of the older "helpers" and they will begin to serve as helpers and role models for those in the age group below. In the third year, they'll be interacting with yet another younger group and serving as the "senior citizens" of their team or group.

When the second three-year cycle begins, and they again become the youngest children, they are in fact rejoining older friends and classmates with whom they spent one or two previous years, and therefore the adjustment to being at a higher school level will be easier to make. Extending this idea to the moment when the youngster enters secondary school, again that school will be populated by many former classmates who stand ready to welcome and assist them.

Data from a number of multi-age team teaching projects over the years, including the Lexington experience, confirm that the former elementary school pupils adjust very easily and quickly not only to the social environment but to the routines and expectations that characterize a junior high or middle school operation. By contrast, pupils emerging from a self-contained single-grade classroom often face a rather awesome challenge.

There is yet another "plus" in multi-age groupings that could benefit at least a few pupils. Although the research evidence against "retaining" children is overwhelming, there may still be rare cases where a student might in fact benefit from remaining in the elementary school setting for an "extra" year. Worth noting is that when the environment is nongraded and multi-aged, remaining in the three-year unit for a fourth year might actually go relatively unnoticed by either the "retained" child or his/her classmates, since everyone's focus will be on continuous progress and academic success, rather than upon who passed, and who failed. In any case, when children are in a nongraded primary rather than a graded classroom, they are less likely to need to remain an extra year (McLoughlin, 1970).

The same argument would apply in those relatively rare cases where it makes sense to "accelerate" a pupil. Spending only two or two and one-half years in one unit before moving on to the next can be much easier, and less visible and dramatic, when the accelerated pupil has already developed academic and social relationships with the higher-level classmates.

Instructional Groupings

In the course of each school day, as children pursue their varying interests and seek to build upon their various skills, there will naturally be a great deal of movement within the space the class or team occupies. Sometimes the day begins with a total-group ceremony, during which announcements are made, happy events (such as birthdays, or Abby's return from a visit with relatives in Germany) are celebrated, the plans for the day are negotiated or confirmed, and other total-group business is transacted. Sometimes, especially if the team is involved in a large interdisciplinary unit of study, the entire group will be together for a lesson, a presentation, or an activity. Sometimes every child may be involved in a private activity, such as reading or seatwork, that calls for no interaction with other learners. Sometimes all children will be involved with one or more other children in a cooperative learning experience, or in a skill development group (e.g., reading or math), or in a task force activity of some sort. Sometimes there will be one or more discussion or decision-making activities, or planning events, that involve in each case up to twelve or fifteen students. An almost infinite number of combinations of all such pupil-grouping arrangements can be imagined.

Joplin Plan

With its name taken from the Missouri City in which the idea was originated, the Joplin Plan represents a way of distributing pupils within a building for purposes of skills instruction. Teachers who are otherwise working within a self-contained pattern but are eager to create more efficient reading (or other) groups, may agree to schedule that subject at the same time each day and then to have the children move from room to room (i.e., teacher to teacher) so that each teacher will then have a somewhat larger and presumably more homogeneous group (or two) of children with whom to work during that part of the day. According to Slavin (1988), this arrangement is most effective when it applies to cross-grade levels, as opposed to regrouping pupils from only one grade level.

The Joplin Plan was (and is) conceptually sound, and among its strengths is not only the simplification of teacher workload, but also the planning and sharing that it stimulates among teachers. For children, there are two advantages, one being the opportunity to connect with another teacher, and the other being connections with some additional children. Not incidentally, the children also have an extra chance to move around in the building, thus stretching their legs and "owning" a little more of the territory. While this might seem trivial, experience with full-fledged team teaching has led to greater awareness of the physically and psychologically stifling experience that many children have in the literally self-contained classroom. The Joplin Plan offers a welcome break in the self-contained day.

Group-Size Alternatives

It may be useful, even if somewhat repetitive, to summarize here the various arrangements for grouping pupils that might be found in a team-organized nongraded school. The numbers in Table 6.1 are intended as general guidelines only.

What might strike the reader is that the usual notion of twenty-five to thirty children in a classroom is not represented in the table, except in the "large group" range, as a workable arrangement. Research evidence and years of experience confirm that having more than fifteen pupils in a so-called "discussion" is not efficient or productive: ordinarily it is too difficult for all twenty-five or so children to make a contribution to the discussion, and so most students listen in, at best, while only a few take an active part. Teachers with twenty-five children who are eager to

Table 6.1. Grouping alternatives.

Number of Students	Learning/Instructional Activity
1	(a) When alone: independent study (b) When with a tutor or teacher: one-on-one tutorial
2–5	Cooperative learning situation (within various models)
5–8	Task force, committee, project group, or other working situation
12–15	Discussion; decision-making activity
Large group (16-plus, up to 100 or more)	Listening, viewing, attending (audience situation, e.g., lecture, video, play, reports)

sponsor a discussion would be well-advised to break up the class into two discussion groups. With reference to decision making, it has long been a part of the human experience that, on the one hand, important decisions require input from a reasonable number of persons, and on the other hand, a group much larger than a dozen or so finds it hard to reach a conclusion. It is probably not accidental that in some nations the number of persons on a jury (a decision-making group if there ever was one!) is established as twelve.

Teachers with twenty-five to thirty children can, of course, arrange for independent study or tutorial activity, can arrange for pupil team-learning groups to function, can set up committees or task forces to do their work, and can provide total-class audience situations as indicated.

Teams of three to five/six teachers with 75–125 or more pupils can also arrange for all of the group-size alternatives. It is easier for them to take advantage of large-group instruction, since only one of the team members needs to be involved while the entire pupil team is in an audience situation, and the other teachers can therefore find some extra planning time or syphon off a small number of pupils for whom the content of the large-group experience might be less helpful than would some intensive one-on-one or small-group instruction.

Total-team, or large-group, experiences can be defended so long as two criteria are met: (1) the content is sufficiently relevant to every member of the audience so that there can be for him or her a worthwhile outcome; and (2) the physical arrangements are such that every pupil can hear and see what is going on, under comfortable conditions. Total-team experiences also can be defended not only because some of the teachers can thereby have some extra moments for planning, but also because they increase the chances of the total team becoming, and regarding itself as, a family or community not only in a social/psychological sense but also intellectually. When everyone, no matter how young or old or how academically advanced, receives and owns some of the same information and perceptions everyone else has received, there is the greater prospect of dialogue and other exchanges in the hours ahead.

Working in Groups

One of the hallmarks of 1990s organizational behavior, whether in the outside world broadly defined or within education, is that people work in groups. As perhaps never before in world history, individuals are being valued for their ability to connect with other individuals and to help the groups to which they belong to be harmonious and productive. Therefore, as never before, the graduates of American schools in order to succeed in their life roles will need to possess the attitudes and skills associated with effective group participation. This represents a dramatic change from not so long ago, when there was much more emphasis upon individual accomplishment, and when the graduates of American schools were expected to be rather aggressively competitive.

We hope that elsewhere in this book we have sufficiently explained the differences between healthy and unhealthy competition. Eagerness to succeed, to become the best that one can be, to enjoy the fruits of honest labor, and to be well regarded among one's associates, remains a worthy individual goal. But such successes are more and more dependent on one's ability to work with, and help, others both as individuals and as groups. Becoming the best that one can be should not mean vanquishing others in the process. That people should value and help each other toward the achievement of worthy personal and social goals is not only an ethical/religious precept but also a guideline for creating a healthy and generative society.

The literature and the content of teacher education up to the late 1980s virtually ignored the need for teachers to be trained in the skills needed for effective (adult) group membership and participation, probably because of the assumption that teachers work mostly by themselves in self-contained classrooms and play only a small role in the "collective governance" of the school. Even the literature relating to the training of administrators and supervisors has underplayed the skills needed for working in groups and has virtually ignored the skills needed to help groups (e.g., teaching teams) to become effective.

As the business and industrial world, or at least its influential literature since the mid-1980s, has moved toward participatory decision making and a variety of networking practices, school leaders have been under pressure to abandon or soften top-down management, and there is a growing trend (see Snyder and Anderson, 1986) toward teacher co-involvements of many kinds. Among the major dimensions of the national interest in the restructuring of schools is site-based management, with attendant expectations that teachers will become active participants in work groups and task forces.

Out of the same theoretical framework that calls for adults to work together comes a strong message about children and how their school experiences should be structured. There is strong support for the deliberate shift toward more cooperative learning, on the one hand, and toward the softening of competition, on the other. Within a very short span of years, lively interaction among pupils in working groups, as distinct from the lively interaction that teachers hope for during teacher-led class discussions, has become a highly valued aspect of daily school life. For the teachers, few of whom have had training in the management and supervision of pupil groups, this poses a considerable challenge. Sad to say, many teachers have trouble adjusting to the transfer of so much responsibility from themselves to the children, and some become very nervous about the noise levels, the extra pupil movement, and the perceived lack of structure that may accompany pupil team learning. In short, the title of Tom Peters' 1987 book, *Thriving on Chaos*, is for many of them, an absurd claim.

Any effort to restructure a school, for example to develop a nongraded program within which teacher teaming and pupil team learning are integral, must therefore include inservice or staff-development activities that focus on group processes. It must also pay special attention to the needs that teacher groups will have along the way for guidance and support in resolving procedural, substantive, and interpersonal problems. Stated simply, this means that principals and other resource persons must keep a close eye on teaching teams and task forces, respond quickly and effectively to their calls for help, offer psychic and other rewards to them for problems solved, and provide general counsel as they develop necessary momentum.

Similarly, teachers both individually and in teams will need help in developing the skills that *they* need, in order to perform the same supporting, counseling, guiding role for pupil teams and groups. Fortunately, each year sees many welcome additions to a rich reservoir of books, articles, handbooks, and training programs on groups and groupwork (for example, Cohen and Benton, 1988).

Uses of Space

Some school buildings are flexible by their design, and others are inflexible. Some buildings are wonderfully equipped with specialized facilities (media center, computer lab, auditorium, playrooms, gymnasium, art studios, teachers' workroom, teachers' lounge, etc.) and others offer only the "bare bones" of classrooms. Amenities (such as pleasant decor, attractive landscaping, spacious entrance area, convenient parking) and even essentials (adequate plumbing, storage spaces, good windows and lighting, office area) will vary from building to building and, more often, from community to community. It is therefore much more pleasant and much easier to carry out a good instructional program in some schools than it is in others. It follows that introducing and maintaining a team-organized nongraded school program will likely be difficult when the physical environment does not seem adaptable to the situation.

Limitations of space, however, are not as serious a problem as may be the limited imaginations and resourcefulness of some teachers as they approach space-use decisions. All too often, regular classroom as well as specialist teachers are voluntarily locked within the boundaries of the space(s) they consider to be their own, and alternative ways of "owning" and of using space are not readily invented or accepted. Many a pilot program has run aground because one or more teachers refused to abandon, or even to share, rooms they had occupied for a number of years, even though there may have been compelling reasons for reserving the entire East Wing to the Apollo Team or moving the kindergarten to the north side of the building. Even the more general use of spaces usually occupied only a few times each week may be impossible because of strong objections from the part-time owners. Sometimes lunchrooms, gymnasia, auditoriums, music rooms, and playroom areas are empty, but custom and precedent seem to be a barrier to using them.

Every school has space, including corridor areas as well as those already suggested, that can accommodate more activities than is generally assumed. Although fire regulations and other restrictions must obviously be respected, it is possible to aggregate children in a number of places that have not customarily been well utilized. Even more likely is that small groups of children, given the freedom to hunt them out, can often find some nooks and crannies where they can work in the privacy they need while not disturbing others. Required, of course, is an element of trust on the part of teachers that children will not abuse such privileges, along with full awareness among the children of their responsibilities as well.

In buildings where walls can in fact be collapsed or rearranged, the frequent movement of individual pupils and groups/classes of pupils from space to space can be arranged quite easily. Where there are fixed walls, requiring different traffic patterns, pupil movement is not as easy to arrange. However, it should be remembered that the great majority of team teaching programs, especially in the early years, took place in buildings with fixed walls and other limitations. The teachers worked out the necessary traffic patterns; they learned how to "squeeze" larger numbers of pupils into some spaces for temporary purposes; they persuaded school officials to permit the cutting of arches or doorways in some of the walls separating adjoining classrooms; and they found ways to relocate their "work stations" (i.e., desks, files) so that classrooms were less obviously territorial and so that teachers could plan more easily together.

Perhaps most especially, these teachers adopted a positive mindset that space limitations alone would not frustrate or deter them in their effort to work closely together. Armed with such attitudes, teachers in egg-crate buildings were often able to develop full-fledged teaming by regarding all of the spaces in terms of functions rather than "teachers owners." Armed with opposite attitudes, teachers in theoretically perfect, flexible buildings have sometimes failed miserably.

REFERENCES

Bernhard, Gary. 1988. *Primates in the Classroom: An Evolutionary Perspective on Children's Education*. Amherst, MA: The University of Massachusetts Press.

Cohen, Elizabeth G. 1981. "Sociology Looks at Team Teaching," *Research in Sociology of Education and Socialization*, 2:163–193.

Cohen, Elizabeth G. and Joan Benton. 1988. "Making Groupwork Work," *American Educator*, 12(Fall):10–17, 45–46.

Gaustad, Joan. 1992. "Nongraded Education: Mixed-Age, Integrated, and Developmentally Appropriate Education for Primary Children," *Oregon School Study Council Bulletin*, 35(7):37.

Goodlad, John I. and Robert H. Anderson. 1987. *The Nongraded Elementary School*. New York, NY: Harcourt Brace and World, Inc., 1959 and 1963; Teachers College Press, 1987.

Hamilton, Warren and Walter Rehwoldt. 1957. "By Their Differences They Learn," *The National Elementary Principal*, 37(December):29.

Kulik, Chen-Lin, and James A. Kulik. 1987. "Effects of Ability Grouping on Student Achievement," *Equity and Excellence*, 23:22–30.

Lane, Howard and Mary Beauchamp. 1955. *Human Relations in Teaching*. Englewood Cliffs, NJ: Prentice-Hall, Inc., pp. 298–303; see also pp. 297–319.

McLoughlin, William P. 1970. "Continuous Pupil Progress in the Nongraded School: Hope or Hoax?" *Elementary School Journal*, 71(November):90–96.

Peters, Tom. 1987. *Thriving on Chaos: Handbook for a Management Revolution*. New York, NY: Alfred A. Knopf, 1987.

Pratt, David. 1986. "On the Merits of Multi-Age Classrooms," *Research in Rural Education*, 3(Canada):111–115.

Rehwoldt, Walter and Warren W. Hamilton. 1957. "An Analysis of Some of the Effects of Interage and Intergrade Grouping in an Elementary School," doctoral dissertation, University of Southern California.

Rosenholtz, Susan J. 1989. *Teachers' Workplace: The Social Organization of Schools*. White Plains, NY: Longman.

Shaplin, Judson T. and Henry F. Olds, Jr., eds. 1964. *Team Teaching*. New York, NY: Harper and Rowe.

Slavin, Robert E. 1988. "Synthesis of Research on Grouping in Elementary and Secondary Schools," *Educational Leadership*, 46(1):67–77.

Slavin, Robert E. 1991. "Are Cooperative Learning and 'Untracking' Harmful to the Gifted?" *Educational Leadership*, 48(March):68–71.

Snyder, Karolyn J. and Robert H. Anderson. 1986. *Managing Productive Schools: Toward an Ecology*. Orlando, FL: Academic Press, Inc.

Webb, Tamsen Banks. 1992. "Multi-Age Grouping in the Early Years: Building upon Children's Developmental Strengths," *Kappa Delta Pi Record*, 28(3):90–92.

CHAPTER 7

Curriculum Approaches and Learning Modes Compatible with Nongradedness

NEARLY all children come to their beginning school years wanting to learn and believing that they are capable of learning. Yet within a few years this eagerness seems to have disappeared for all but a small group of children. How can this be possible? The curriculum in the early years stresses the attainment of the basic skills of reading and computing, and teachers during these years frequently spend nearly the entire school day providing direct instruction in skills acquisition. Teachers have received training that emphasizes this approach, both in their own preservice and inservice training and from the teaching manuals provided with the textbooks they use. Teachers work very hard to make the system work, and yet a significant number of children are not learning under this method (witness the high early years' retention rates), and many children "drop out" while still in school as their attention wanders off the teacher-prescribed tasks.

How can this happen? As Farnham-Diggory (1990) and others have observed, children learn some of their most difficult tasks outside of school and before they come to school: talking, walking, eating, climbing stairs, riding a tricycle, throwing a ball. They learn these things with no formal instruction and within their own time frame. These tasks are not programmed into small bits and put into a scope-and-sequence chart, but are attempted in a holistic manner by the child. Some children even learn to walk without learning to crawl. Yet if walking were to be a school learning task, undoubtedly children would be required to demonstrate mastery of crawling before moving to the unit on walking!

Due to the continuing rapid expansion of knowledge, emphasis must be placed on the skills of learning to learn, rather than on content learning, especially in the early years. Reading is viewed as a skill with subsets of skills such as decoding and comprehension. A child reads in order to learn. Reading should not be a separate subject, as the whole language advocates are now suggesting and as the language experience and literature-based reading advocates have suggested in the past.

What is needed is the integration of both subject matter content and learning skills acquisition under broad themes that reflect issues and problems of significance and interest to the children. Note that the word *relevance* was not used, since we observe that even young children have concerns such as preserving the ecology which are not in the selfish realm that relevance seems to imply. Hidi (1990) reviews recent research on reading and states that "individuals interested in a task or activity have been shown to pay more attention, persist for longer periods of time, and acquire more and qualitatively different knowledge than individuals without such interest" (p. 554). She acknowledges Dewey's early awareness of this fact when his book, *Interest and Effort in Education*, was published in 1913.

BRAIN RESEARCH

Caine and Caine (1991) have reviewed brain research as it relates to learning and we have adapted their major points as follows:

(1) The human brain performs many operations including parts and wholes simultaneously.

(2) Learning engages the entire physiology.

(3) The search for meaning is automatic and occurs through patterning.

(4) Emotions and cognition cannot be separated.

(5) Learning involves both focused attention and peripheral perception.

(6) Learning always involves conscious and unconscious processes.

(7) Isolated facts and skills require more effort to learn since they are unrelated, but learning related to past experiences allows usage of spatial memory, which is more efficient.

(8) Learning is enhanced by challenge and inhibited by threat.

(9) Each brain is unique (pp. 79–87).

Caine and Caine suggest that brain-based schooling would use thematic units in which the teachers are models of "relaxed alertness" (p. 126) "orchestrating immersion" (p. 107) of students in their activities to then be followed by student reflections. Essential to the process are the connections or wholeness of the learning experiences.

Teachers under Della Neve's direction in East Windsor, New Jersey provide "brain compatible" instruction by using the following focal points to design instruction:

(1) Create a nonthreatening climate.

(2) Provide a huge amount of input so students can extract patterns.

(3) Emphasize genuine comprehension.

(4) Provide for much manipulation.

(5) Emphasize reality rather than work sheets.

(6) Address learning activities to active productive uses.

(7) Respect natural thinking (Della Neve, Hart, and Thomas, 1986).

In an earlier book Hart (1969) provides a model of how such a school might operate. The stress is not on the learning of content or factual information, but on the understanding of concepts. An individual can have a vast store of isolated information and yet not be truly educated if an understanding of key concepts is missing (see Figure 7.1).

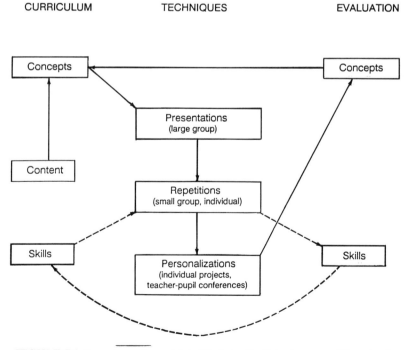

FIGURE 7.1 Our schematic model to illustrate Hart's brain-compatible school.

Hart suggests a three-part work cycle: presentation, repetition, and personalization. About one-third of the students' time would be spent with 125 to 140 students of varying ages in a large theater. Content from different subject areas would be used as a vehicle for development of concepts. The concepts would be presented and represented in varying ways with differing materials in new contexts. Good presentations would be revised and/or repeated. Rather than each teacher making many ill-prepared presentations in each classroom, teams or team members would prepare talks using multimedia which would then be seen by many children. Fewer presentations would be made by each teacher, and therefore more time would be available to work in areas for which the teacher has greater competency. A concept such as change might be developed in a presentation on automobiles, archeology, and again in a unit on cities. The materials would determine the length of the presentations. Students would not be required either to participate during the presentation or be tested afterwards.

The balance of the day is spent in repetition or personalization activities. Computers, language labs, programmed materials, skills sheets, and other interesting drill materials are located in "drill rooms."

Projects and activities are the stuff of personalization when students use the knowledge in their own way. Pupil-teacher conferences are frequent, with the teacher being allowed time enough to hold private, unpressured conferences.

The Key Elementary School in the Indianapolis Public School System was founded by eight teachers using Howard Gardner's theory of multiple intelligences: linguistic, musical, logical-mathematical, spatial, kinesthetic, interpersonal, and intrapersonal. Gardner's book *Frames of Mind* (1983), suggests that student involvement in self-selected activities such as puzzles, games, and challenging materials would indicate their interests and provide a personal profile of mental strengths. Each student at the Key School spends three forty-minute periods per week in the Flow Activities Room (FAR), which is equipped with many challenging games, art materials, and construction supplies. The teacher in charge of FAR records which activity each student pursues, and students review their interests. Each activity is noted as to the intelligence(s) it taps: Othello, to spatial; Scrabble, to linguistic; Twister, to kinesthetic; and My Home and Places, to interpersonal. The term *flow* is taken from Csikszentmihalyi, *Flow: The Psychology of Optimal Experience* (1990), who writes of experiencing flow when one becomes so absorbed in what is being done, that one is unaware of anything else. Even children who have difficulty in other school areas become totally involved in some of the most challenging activities in FAR. Students learn to make choices and discover that problem solving and direction following is rewarding in itself (D. Cohen, 1991).

Even though the Key School is quite unusual, we believe that these ideas are especially compatible with nongradedness and might be modified for more general use.

CURRICULUM INTEGRATION

Unifying themes, especially when developed by children's own questions, which have a high level of interest for children, lead to very high involvement and high effort on the part of the students. In addition, themes where teachers are collaborating foster teacher interest and development. Not only the children, but also the teachers are able to increase their professional capacity in terms of both content and skills. Teachers working as a team are able to divide their preparation in such a way that they too will have the opportunity to work in depth on some aspect of the topic.

Elementary teachers, like their secondary cohorts, may be able to prepare in depth and present to the entire team of children—or repeat to each group within the team—a set of presentations that are polished to near perfection, as other teachers have responsibilities for other lesson planning areas. Because elementary teachers generally are with the same group of students for all but lunch, recess, and one period per day, they must prepare many more lessons than secondary teachers. Due to this lack of repetition, elementary teachers are required to prepare up to twice as many lessons as secondary teachers, which may result in an overreliance on textbook material.

Thematic units provide for integration of both content and skills usage in more realistic situations than is possible with the traditional subject matter curriculum. In addition to high involvement by students and teachers with thematic units, students have the opportunity to learn and use the skills of learning to learn. Students have more time for trial and error, as they perfect their performances, than in the drill and practice mode of more traditional lessons.

What if teachers have never worked in teams and are just starting to nongrade their program? To these teachers, implementing the ideal curriculum model of thematic units may appear to be an impossible goal. So how can a principal facilitate this collaboration?

A principal in Florida circulated to her staff an article on thematic teaching, and asked for volunteers who would like to do this for one day. Several teachers on different grade levels (this was a traditional graded school at the time) volunteered, including one teacher the principal never would have anticipated. Each teacher picked a theme (such as butterflies, dinosaurs, running, and quilts) and each child was allowed to select the topic of his/her first, second, and third choice. Nearly all the children participated in their desired activity and the school was alive with activity. The final result? The kids had a great time, teachers became interested in what their colleagues were doing (even those who had not participated), new teacher talent was discovered, and plans were soon in the making for more teacher-student multi-age collaboration.

Mini courses were used at the Franklin School in Lexington, Massachusetts to provide enrichment, to allow students to participate in multi-age groups involving all students in the school from five- to twelve-year-olds, and to add a "spark" to a time when students were getting restless. First, students in the school were asked to write or draw, to let teachers know what they wanted to learn about. Lists were compiled and the students' papers were hung in the cafeteria so that parents could see them during a Parent-Teacher Association meeting. A request was sent via the school newsletter for parents who would be willing to work with small groups of eight to twelve students each from 2 to 3 P.M. on the five Fridays in January. A small catalogue was produced, with course descriptions and instructors' names. Courses were offered such as film making, newspaper production, portraiture, watercolors (which Pavan, as principal, taught), constructing a trail for the blind, medicine (a different doctor each week with a different speciality), yoga, sewing, first aid, and baby sitting training, which involved the preschoolers of parents running mini courses.

Each child indicated a first, second, and third choice on a form. A group of parents sorted out the requests to form the student groups. Those who were presenting mini courses could call the principal to discuss their presentations and/or to request needed materials.

Several lessons were learned after the first go-round: (1) teachers need to review the student groups so that no group consists of only major behavior problems, and so all groups are balanced by gender and age level; (2) a number of teachers need to be available as "floaters" to find materials or assist any presenter experiencing difficulty; and (3) the best lesson was that those parents who presented mini courses gained enormous respect for all the teachers.

Parents worked all week on their one-hour lesson for twelve students and could not fathom how a teacher could plan so many hours for so many students.

Teachers, especially those who taught older students, saw their own students in a different light, as they observed the older ones assisting the younger ones, and some of them were surprised that younger children often generated ideas as interesting and as useful as the older students. The mini courses were so successful for students, parents, and teachers that they became a twice yearly tradition in January and May.

Educational Leadership in October 1991 (Brandt), published a theme issue entitled "Integrating the Curriculum." This issue, and many other recent publications on curriculum integration, will help teachers who want to use thematic or problem-based teaching, but feel nervous about the emphasis on accountability manifested by reliance on standardized tests, and the move toward national standards and testing. Most districts have grade level curriculums for each subject that teachers are responsible to teach. Mastery Learning and Outcome-Based Education, note Spady and Marshall (1991), have unfortunately been seen in rather narrow curriculum-based objective terms for each unit or segment of the instructional process, rather than as the exit competencies needed by school graduates. Educators need to work backwards from this view of the future citizen.

Districts can develop competencies in a broad manner such as the Aurora, Colorado Public Schools' set of five role-based outcomes: collaborative worker, quality producer, self-directed learner, complex thinker, and community contributor. The district guide for the elementary schools (Shoemaker, 1991) has six concepts: communities, change, power, interactions, form, and systems. These are explored in three strands: human societies, the earth and the universe, and the individual. Thematic units have been listed at the intersection of each strand and concept. Teachers work together to develop instructional units following an eight-step process in which they have received training (Shoemaker, 1991):

(1) Select themes and concepts, then brainstorm topics.

(2) Generate questions that students will use as focus.

(3) Decide on specifics, partially determined by available materials.

(4) Identify prerequisite skills and those to be taught.

(5) Develop daily plans. Unit is to start from the "big picture" and use active learning strategies.

(6) Identify student products and assessment strategies.

(7) Teach the unit.

(8) Evaluate student progress and revise unit for district publication.

Jacobs (1989, 1991) suggests that the starting point for curriculum integration is for each teacher in the school to indicate on a monthly outline the units of study that he or she now teaches. These are then transferred to a total school calendar and clustered by teams. This enables teachers to eliminate repetition and to build collaborative units. To move from discipline-based content design to the next step, parallel disciplines, requires only that teachers reschedule already-planned units in order to dovetail, say, a literature selection with the appropriate historical period. A multidisciplinary unit would have several disciplines (art, literature, and science) investigate one theme, such as color. Jacobs defines interdisciplinary units as those in which all the disciplines in the school's curriculum are included in one unit, while the integrated day model of the British Infant School movement requires total integration for the full day. We would expect that a nongraded program might include at least one multidisciplinary or interdisciplinary unit along with some single-discipline teaching segments.

Many readers, especially those teachers with many years of experience, may wonder what all the fuss is about integrated curriculum, since to them it is not a new idea. Terms such as core or activity curriculum have been used since the early days of the Dewey School at the University of Chicago between 1896 and 1904 (Squire, 1972). A fascinating primary unit of study on boats that was developed at the Lincoln School in New York City in the 1920s (reproduced by Cremin, 1961, pp. 204–285) would provide an excellent example of a multidisciplinary unit. Vars (1991) notes that students in core interdisciplinary team teaching programs performed as well or better on standardized achievement tests than students enrolled in the usual separate subjects (p. 15).

Any school seriously contemplating beginning a nongraded primary program should have as resources (in addition to this book and Goodlad and Anderson's *The Nongraded Elementary School*) two documents developed in British Columbia, where all schools are organized in this fashion. The nongraded-continuous progress program is carefully explained as to its rationale and its objectives in each of four major curriculum areas:

(1) Fine Arts—Dance, Drama, Music, Visual Arts

(2) Humanities—Language Arts, Learning for Living (personal needs including health and safety), Social Studies

(3) Practical Arts—Physical Education, Career Education, Home Economics, and Business Education

(4) Sciences—Math and Science

Change as part of the implementation process, setting up learning centers, schedules, special needs students, parents, assessment, evaluation, and reporting are described in detail. Forms that may be reproduced are especially useful for observing student behavior and reporting to parents. In order to demonstrate the meaning of integrated studies, theme units on winter, water, the forest, spiders, and self understanding detail the learning expected and the actual activities including computer usage. We are not aware of any more useful materials and suggest you order *The Primary Program Foundation Program* (1990) CG079 and *The Primary Program Resource Document* (1990) RB008, from Crown Publications, 546 Yates Street, Victoria, B.C., V8W 1KB.

COOPERATIVE LEARNING

This term, and several variants thereof, refers to approaches at both elementary and secondary levels to pupil learning in groups of two or more. There are many models in place, some more formalized than others. It would seem almost unimaginable to have a successful nongraded program without pupil team learning as a major feature.

The origins of cooperative learning as a deliberate instructional strategy go back at least a half century, although it is obvious that for hundreds if not thousands of years teachers encouraged or at least permitted their pupils to study and work together. Quintilian in A.D. 93 observed that the new learner is the best teacher, and it has long been understood that the explanations/responses/questions offered by a fellow learner are sometimes more "educative" than what one hears from a much more knowledgeable person such as the teacher. When a child tries to explain something to another child, it becomes necessary to organize his/her thought in ways that will communicate ideas effectively; such "cognitive elaboration" enhances his/her own understanding of the idea, and therefore there is intellectual growth in both directions. Teachers have known about this for a long time. Therefore, to contend that cognitive learning is a new discovery would be at least naive, and at worst presumptuous. That recent work has helped it to become a well-organized and productive activity, however, is to be gratefully acknowledged.

Dewey insisted that learning should be active, with students participating in a variety of activities . . . "requiring natural divisions of labor, selection of leaders and followers, mutual co-operation and emulation." He described students working together preparing food, a learning experience in which the measure of success lies in working together, not in individuals "getting ahead of others, in storing up, in accumulating, the maximum of information." This interaction should lead to "the development of a spirit of social co-operation and community" (Dewey, *School and Society*, pp. 14–16). Dewey's focus was on a learning community, more so than on teams of students learning together.

Early systematic work on the topic was begun in the late 1950s at Boston University, with funds provided by the U.S. Office of Education. Professor Donald D. Durrell was the director of a larger research project in which pupil team learning was a major construct to be developed. The public schools of Dedham, Massachusetts provided the site for the study, in which intermediate-grade teams of two or three pupils of approximately equal ability were permitted to progress in arithmetic, spelling, and other subjects as rapidly as they could (all) demonstrate mastery. Of interest is that some of the content turned out to be "thin" (Durrell's word) for at least the upper third of the pupils, and it proved possible to complete the work of two or more grades in a single year. Study guides appropriate to the level of the pupils in the class were made available to the pupil teams in the content areas.

Another feature of the Dedham program was the use of heterogeneous five-pupil team discussions following whole-class presentations, with one pupil acting as the recorder who later read a summary to the whole class. This method gave all children ample opportunity to participate and contribute to the discussion, whereas in a whole-class discussion such opportunities are limited.

The project also provided for individual learning activities, as well as whole-class enrichment activities. Among the findings (see Durrell, December 1959) were that the teachers improved in techniques of adapting instruction to the varying needs of children; the program worked better in the skills subjects than in the content areas; there were significant achievement gains in grades five and six (no change in grade four); and arithmetic achievement, especially in problem solving, as well as spelling and geography improved significantly. Also reported were a number of other mostly mixed results, including a statement by the Dedham superintendent (Harvey Scribner) that the most encouraging single factor of the experiment was that a much higher percentage of pupils made a full year or more of growth. Noting that there were both positive findings and disappointments in the study, Durrell and Scribner in a concluding chapter stated that few teachers would willingly depart from the team learning program, that many important research questions had surfaced, and that inservice programs are urgently needed for improving the individualization of instruction.

Increasingly clear is the need that teachers and administrators have for developing strategies to promote higher-level cognitive behavior through cooperative learning situations. Sad to say, many teachers are still having trouble accepting the fact that when children are actively learning together, the noise level in the classroom will inevitably increase. Equally difficult for many teachers will be the switch from being the manager of a competitive environment to being the manager of a cooperative environment.

Slavin at Johns Hopkins University has synthesized the comparative research studies, as indicated in Table 7.1.

All variants of cooperative learning employ deliberate heterogeneous teams, but many other aspects differ, especially with respect to the cooperative or competitive elements. The major models developed at

Table 7.1. Highlights of research on cooperative learning.

In cooperative learning, students work in small groups to help one another master academic material. There are many quite different forms of cooperative learning, and the effectiveness of cooperative learning (particularly for achievement outcomes) depends on the particular approach used.

- For enhancing student achievement, the most successful approaches have incorporated two key elements: group goals and individual accountability. That is, groups are rewarded based on the individual learning of all group members.
- When group goals and individual accountability are used, achievement effects of cooperative learning are consistently positive; thirty-seven of forty-four experimental/control comparisons of at least four weeks' duration have found significantly positive effects, and none have favored traditional methods.
- Achievement effects of cooperative learning have been found to be about the same degree at all grade levels (two to twelve), in all major subjects, and in urban, rural, and suburban schools. Effects are equally positive for high, average, and low achievers.
- Positive effects of cooperative learning have been consistently found on such diverse outcomes as self-esteem, intergroup relations, acceptance of academically handicapped students, attitudes toward school, and ability to work cooperatively.

Source: Slavin, 1991, p. 71.

Johns Hopkins (Slavin, Madden, and Stevens, December 1989) are Team Assisted Individualization-Mathematics (TAI) and Cooperative Integrated Reading and Composition (CIRC) for students from eight to twelve years old. The programs are quite detailed and structured, with printed materials available for the math program. Even though students work in pairs and groups, the major focus is on academic achievement, not on social skills. A team score consists of the individual achievement scores of each member of the team.

By contrast, Johnson and Johnson (December 1989), acknowledging the pioneering work in social interdependence by Morton Deutsch, require that the students be taught specific social skills, and it is the demonstration of these skills that gives the groups their points. Unlike TAI and CIRC, this is not the total math or reading program, but an instructional strategy that might be used with any subject matter.

Kagan (December 1989, p. 14) has described a number of what he calls team structures, which we might call instructional strategies or techniques, that are curriculum-free. These have catchy names such as "corners," "numbered heads together," "think-pair-share," and "inside-outside circle," which teachers can easily learn and immediately use in their classrooms without any revisions in curriculum. Teachers as a team might want to try some of these strategies with their students as an introduction to cooperative learning.

Elizabeth Cohen (October 1990, p. 134) indicates that while cooperative learning leads to increased academic achievement "in academically, linguistically, and culturally diverse classrooms" especially in the inner city, extreme caution must be taken so that high-status students do not dominate the team. Such dominance actually decreases the learning of low-status students because interaction and participation is necessary for learning. Her book, *Designing Groupwork* (1986), provides the techniques needed for effective teams. Each cooperative task must be a complex one rather than a routine, right-answer task, as groups faced with completing a computational worksheet quickly learn that the most efficient way to handle this task is to have one student complete the sheet. Each student must turn out a product, but may use the resources of the group. Students are prepared for cooperation by learning new behavioral norms, such as "You have the duty to assist anyone who asks for help" (Cohen and Benton, 1988, p. 17).

The teacher assigns managerial roles such as facilitator, checker, or reporter to each group member. Roles are then rotated. The teacher's role changes in group work from direct supervision to a supportive role. Teachers observe, ask questions, and remind students of their role responsibilities rather than answering questions and helping them to do their tasks. Cohen suggests that teachers observe each other and provide feedback as they practice their own new roles and prepare new cooperative learning units.

Ideally, themes should be stated as problems so that the efforts of the students are engaged in problem solving, and thereby the theme becomes a vehicle for developing problem-solving skills. Teachers should resist the temptation to plan each theme unit in minute detail, but should involve the children in the planning. Sharan and Sharan (1989) have updated Thelen's (1960) group investigation model, which we have modified as follows:

(1) Identify the topic and form student groups for various subtopics.

(2) Student groups plan their investigation strategy.

(3) Students investigate as previously determined.

(4) Groups prepare final report.

(5) Groups present final report.

(6) Students and teachers evaluate the investigation.

Most observers would view this as one format for cooperative learning. Use of different variants of cooperative learning helps to resolve some of the dilemmas teachers believe are raised by multi-age, multi-ability grouping.

"AT-RISK" STUDENTS

Unfortunately, a policy of segregation has generally been used, albeit with good intentions, to help children of poverty (all too frequently black), children not born in the U.S.A., and children with special needs. Federal regulations for Chapter 1, bilingual or English for Speakers of Other Languages programs, and special education have generally required "pull out" programs that remove these students from the mainstream. In addition, the curriculum for these students has often consisted of repetitive, rote teaching until mastery of the "basic" skills is achieved. In general, this strategy has not been successful, as too many children have not achieved sufficiently to move out of these special programs. What is needed is a rich instructional program beginning early on, with problem-solving skills and mixed ability grouping. Knapp and Turnbull (1991, p. 332) are writing about children of poverty in Table 7.2, but their chart could be applied to all types of at-risk students.

"Success for All" is a Johns Hopkins University program developed for urban elementary schools (Slavin et al., 1989) with heterogeneous age-grouped classes for all, except during the daily reading period with performance level groups across grades one, two, and three. A class size of fifteen is obtained by using certified teachers who also tutor on a one-to-one basis those children in difficulty. The objective is to avoid remediation and special education placement and to have most students on grade level by the end of grade three. Students are not retained during this three-year period. All eligible students are to attend a half-day preschool and a full-day kindergarten. Even with the extra costs of a full-time program facilitator and a family support team, the direct extra costs of this program are said to be offset by the savings from the elimination of student retentions. This program helps illustrate our convic-

Table 7.2. Schooling for children of poverty.

Conventional Wisdom	Alternatives
1. *View of disadvantaged learners:* An emphasis on learners' deficits—that is, what the students lack in terms of knowledge, intellectual facility, or experience	• An emphasis on the knowledge students do bring to school • Explicit teaching of how to function in the "culture" of the school
2. *Curriculum organization:* Curriculum that teaches discrete skills in a fixed sequence from "basic" to "higher-order" skills	• Early emphasis on appropriate "higher-order" tasks • Extensive opportunities to learn and apply skills in context • An emphasis on meaning and understanding in all academic instruction
3. *Instructional approach:* Exclusive or heavy reliance on teacher-directed instruction	• A combination of teacher-directed and learner-directed instruction
4. *Classroom management:* Classroom management principles uniformly applied across the school day so as to forestall disorder in the classroom	• Variation in classroom management approaches depending on the kind of academic work being done
5. *Arrangement of instructional groups:* Long-term grouping of students by achievement or ability	• Some use of grouping arrangements that mix ability levels • More flexibility in grouping arrangements

Source: Knapp and Turnbull, 1991, p. 332.

tion that schools need to be reconstructed (nongraded) in such a manner that students do not fail but are placed in situations where it is possible to achieve success.

"Reading Recovery," another early intervention program, was established by Marie Clay in New Zealand for at-risk first graders (DeFord, Lyons, and Pinnell, 1990). Early in the year each "first grader" in the bottom 20 percent of the class receives daily, individual, thirty-minute lessons and continues in the program until the average level of the class is reached, which usually is within fifteen weeks. Reading Recovery teachers are trained in a process that stresses the reading of a new whole story each day using a problem-solving text approach with teacher prompts and minimal reading interruptions. Books are re-read and skills are taught as needed.

The Accelerated Schools Project (ASP) was established at Stanford University in 1986 after an extensive review by Harry Levin of the minimal progress made by at-risk students over the previous twenty years. He suggests (see Rothman, 1991) that disadvantaged children should be instructed in the same way that gifted students are, in a rich environment with active, hands-on learning using a problem-solving focus. Lessons should be organized around themes, and teachers should have high expectations for all students. Three principles guide the program: (1) unity of purpose in which a vision is developed so that all teachers and all activities focus on bringing students into the mainstream; (2) school-site empowerment so that decisions are made by the key participants, both teachers and parents; and (3) building on the strengths of the students, the school staff, parents, and communities (Levin and Hopfenberg, 1991).

To become an ASP school, 75 percent of the staff must agree. Stanford provides one week of training to help schools develop a vision, adapt a participatory governance structure, and learn an inquiry model for school research. The Daniel Webster School in San Francisco, which became an ASP school in 1987, made the largest gains on standardized tests in the district during the 1990–1991 year. In order to provide time for teachers to do the committee work needed, the principal has scheduled a daily schoolwide aerobics class.

We are now beginning to realize that for the benefit of both the individual and society, schooling opportunities must not be limited. Dewey first published this idea in 1900, "What the best and wisest parent wants for his [her] own child, that must the community want for all of its children. . . . Only by being true to the full growth of all the individuals who make it up, can society by any chance be true to itself" (Dewey, 1956, *The School and Society*, p. 7).

LITERACY INSTRUCTION

Our preference for reading instruction would be for teachers to work with their own multi-aged advisory group in an individualized manner using trade books. This would not mean that students would be working alone, as there would be partners reading to each other; small groups discussing both their reading and writing; story dictation (language experience approach) by individuals and by the total class; the teacher reading aloud to the class; and small groups working on specific decoding and comprehension skills. Yet each child would have selected his/her own reading text.

In our preferred model, the teacher would conference with each child once or twice a week in order to note needed skill instruction, to work on the construction of meaning, and to keep track of the child's general literacy program. This is a private, personal time for student and teacher, and it grows in importance over the years since a child will remain with the same home base teacher for two or three years.

Each child has a reading notebook. The teacher suggests activities, especially in the area of needed skills acquisition (a commercial skills sheet might even be stapled in the notebook). The student records when books are started and completed, and describes or lists the book project that celebrates each book completion. At the Franklin School, there was developed a list of seventy-one different book projects. Students would orally present their book projects to the class. Teachers would have a separate recording sheet for each child, indicating what transpired during each conference, and would note student errors in reading aloud—not to come up with a score, as in "running records" (Davidson, 1991, pp. 56–58), but to determine instructional needs through reading miscue analysis. Specific skills groups might be taught across the entire team to reduce the amount of preparation for each teacher.

Many experienced teachers will recognize that what we are advocating resembles the literature-based reading program described in detail by Leland Jacobs, Jeanette Veatch, and others in Miel (1958) and by Moffett (1973) who describes some of the practices at the Franklin School at that time.

In *What's Whole in Whole Language?* Kenneth Goodman (1986) notes the strong connection between reading and writing, and indicates that a literacy program should focus on the meaning of language in authentic events, rather than by slicing language into isolated skills to be mastered before children actually read and write. While Weaver (1990, pp. 27–29), denies that whole language is the same as language experience or open education, we believe that the philosophy of whole language encompasses both. The whole language philosophy (Monson and Pahl, 1991) requires a major shift from teacher-centered to student-centered instruction and from passive to active student learning. As such, whole language is very compatible with nongradedness. However, we do agree with Weaver that you cannot buy an authentic Whole Language or individualized reading program in a package, with a teachers' manual that spells out a step-by-step method for the teacher to follow. It would be helpful if textbook publishers would abandon the leveled basal reader and instead produce collections of literature in attractive paperback editions such as those that have been produced by the Scholastic Press for many years.

In our ideal school, writing would be part of the reading "period," and journal writing would be a daily activity for the home base group. A separate notebook (or folder) is needed for each student. It is essential that students form the habit of dating their own work, so that they can observe their progress, and that they use the writing process to improve their writing. Writing, of course, would not be limited to this time block, but would occur whenever there was a need.

From the very beginning, children should be encouraged to illustrate their writing. Often a child will develop a story while doing an easel painting and then dictate the story to another student or the teacher, since oral language usually precedes the needed reading and writing skills. There are many examples of this method of instruction for disadvantaged children in the classic book *Teacher*, by Sylvia Ashton Warner (1963), in the very beautiful book by Sybil Marshall, *An Experiment in Education* (1966), and in Elwyn Richardson's *In the Early World* (1969).

When discussing how to teach writing to learning-disabled students, Graves (1985) suggests four components necessary for a writing-process program: sufficient time to write, writing topic chosen by the child, teacher-student dialogues about the child's writing, and a classroom atmosphere that fosters writing. Graves believes that for thirty minutes at least four times a week, students need to write in a studio atmosphere where children work and help each other with beginning drafts and final editing for school publication. Writing "motivators" or "story starters" are not needed because ideas come from the student's daily journal or other written thoughts and opinions.

During the writing portion, Graves wants the teacher to move from student to student, reading, asking questions, rarely giving general praise, but referring to the specifics of the student's work and in the student's own words. Work is kept in each child's folder so progress can be noted, and each writer is encouraged to develop an area of expertise. Several children share their pieces at the end of each writing period. As the need for certain writing skills becomes evident, the teacher will have the entire class learn the same procedure together.

In addition to classroom publishing, children may make books to be placed in the school library. The school may establish a publishing center with parental labor and financial assistance to laminate books written by the students or to publish schoolwide anthologies. At Franklin, the principal (Pavan) requested that children submit their best work directly to her, by placing it in a box outside the office. Writing accompanied by art work was especially encouraged, as selected pieces were placed on the bulletin board outside the office and some were then placed in a book to be given to a sister school in London.

SCHEDULES

The development of schedules that foster nongraded practices and teacher teaming is an important task for the principal. Teachers should provide extensive input in the developing of the school policy for scheduling. The teachers should indicate what items have their highest priority, and then the principal and/or any teacher who enjoys this exercise must develop the best schedule possible. Several actual schedules will be given in the following tables as examples. The first, in Table 7.3, is a primary unit schedule for a teacher team of five with 125 children from ages six to eight.

In this example, each teacher has a home base advisory group consisting of one-third of each age group, all of whom remain with the teacher for their three years in the team. This means that each September the oldest third is replaced by a younger third consisting of only eight or nine new faces, whom the "old hands" quickly orient to the team. The reading block is spent together if the team is using a literature-based reading program as previously described. However, a school just moving into a nongraded program may choose to retain the basal readers with which teachers are familiar. If so, the students are divided among all five teachers with each teacher handling two non-contiguous levels. The basal readers are used mainly to develop comprehension skills, with emphasis on contextual clues.

During the reading group time, teachers use an individual card for each student to record the miscue analysis, which provides the basis for forming decoding skills groups across the entire team. While students have reading groups and partner reading with one teacher (possibly not their home base teacher), their daily skill group may meet with another teacher. During the reading block all Chapter 1 aides, special education teachers, and tutors are available to reduce group size. In addition, art, music, and physical education teachers may be used to assist during the reading block.

In order to accommodate a district-mandated math levels program, this team has divided the children according to present achievement on the various levels, and each of four teachers handles two noncontiguous levels as for reading. One team teacher has developed, and supervises, the math lab, which contains a variety of manipulatives, problem-solving tasks or job cards, and the needed materials. Students are

Table 7.3. Primary unit block schedule.

8.30	Home Base Advisory
8:45	Reading Block—Decoding
	—Comprehension
	—Partner Reading
10:15	Recess
10:30	Math Block—Skills Groups
	—Math Lab
11:30	Lunch—Recess
12:15	Unit Project Theme Block
	Social Studies or Science
	Language Arts
2:15	Students—Music, Physical Education,
	Art, Library, Crafts
	Teachers—Group Planning
3:15	Home Base Advisory

rotated in and out of the math lab in various ways, depending on individual and team needs. If the math lab is conducted by a teacher and an aide, larger groups may be handled so that the instructional group size may be reduced.

The two-hour after-lunch block may sometimes be handled with integrated themes as described before. However, at times science might be taught as separate units incorporating language and mathematics skills as feasible. Each teacher on the team may select one of the pre-packaged commercial units or units available from a local science museum, and, using a discovery approach, plan a week-long unit. This teacher may then teach the same unit to each multi-age home base advisory group. If each group is cycled through each unit, five weeks of intensive science activity thereby becomes available with much less teacher preparation. Alternatively, each teacher may offer a science unit and students could choose their preferred topic. A program such as this assumes that problem solving is more important than specific content retention.

For social studies, an umbrella theme is usually selected and is opened with a teacher(s) presentation as noted previously. Often teachers then divide the topic into subtopics such as history, geography, economy, governance, and architecture/art if studying a country. Again the heterogeneous home base groups spend one week with each teacher. Groupings might also be based on student choice of projects or interest areas. A whole team culmination project would conclude and celebrate the unit. Very often the art, music, and physical education teachers work with the team on a social studies theme.

In order to provide the teachers with team planning time during each school day, the art, music, library, and physical education teachers, along with a classroom teacher aide skilled in crafts, would plan for the entire student team. As long as district guidelines are met, the specialist team can divide the children into hour or half-hour segments to facilitate their program. The specialists consider themselves as a team in the same way that team teachers do.

This primary block schedule is approximately the same as one followed by the Alpha Team at the Franklin School. Actually only six- and seven-year-olds were on that team. Beta had eight- and nine-year-olds, and the Omega Team had ten- and eleven-year-olds. A schoolwide recess provided for all teachers to interact, since aides handle all recess, lunch, and bus duties. In the Franklin School schedule (Table 7.4), each team requested that both reading and math be taught at dif-

Table 7.4. Franklin team schedules.

Time	School Beginners Age 5	Alpha Ages 6-7	Beta Ages 8-9	Omega Ages 10-11	Specialists Schedule
8:45		Home Base	Home Base	Home Base	Team Planning
9:00 9:30		Language Arts	Block 1	Language Arts	Mon., Wed. w/A and B
10:00	Special Group 1	RECESS	RECESS	RECESS	School Begin. 1
10:30		Math	Block 2	Art French Music Library Physical Ed.	Omega
11:00					
11:30	Teachers' Lunch	LUNCH RECESS	Art French Music Library Physical Ed.	Math	Beta
12:00					
12:30		Theme	LUNCH	RECESS	Lunch
1:00	Special Group 2	Social Studies	RECESS	LUNCH	School Begin. 2
1:30	Special Group 3	Science	Block 3	Theme	School Begin. 3
2:00		Arts Crafts Music Library Physical Ed.		Social Studies	Alpha
2:30				Science	
3:00		Home Base	Home Base	Home Base	
	60 Students 1.5 Teachers	125 Students 5 Teachers	125 Students 5 Teachers	125 Students 5 Teachers	4.5 Teachers

ferent times so that the math specialist and the extra reading people would be available for each team.

Beginning in September 1991, all seven grade-level teachers at the Southeast School moved to the one long hallway and arranged themselves into three clusters with each teacher, in each cluster, having a home base group of two ages. Since they had recently developed a Whole Language approach, they decided to have a two-and-one-half-hour language arts block for all students in the morning. During this time, each teacher instructs two noncontiguous groups. There are seven math groups across all age levels, one for each teacher. Students will be moved between math and language groups whenever needed. Themes are being developed for science and social studies to be taught to home base groups. Art, music, library, and physical education are scheduled during the long language arts block to enable teachers in the same cluster to plan (see Table 7.5).

All teachers agreed to meet ten minutes before school each day to keep communications channels open, and they also met every Tuesday after school. The principal of this school is responsible for two schools. There are too few lunch and recess aides, so the specialist teachers have been scheduled to help cover a schoolwide recess so that

Table 7.5. Southeast School.

Red Cluster has three teachers and sixty-two children ages six to seven.
Blue Cluster has two teachers and forty-seven children ages eight to nine.
Yellow Cluster has two teachers and fifty-two children ages ten to eleven.

8.45	Home Base Group
9:05	Language Arts
	Reading
	Block
11:45	Lunch, ages eight to eleven
12:10	RECESS—schoolwide
12:35	Lunch, ages six to seven
1:00	Math
2:00	Social Studies/Science/Health
	Theme
3:00	Home Base

Art, Music, Library, and Physical Education are scheduled during the Language Arts blocks by cluster:
    Red every day but Tuesday between 10:35 A.M. to 12:10 P.M.
    Blue every day but Tuesday from 9:50 A.M. to 10:35 A.M.
    Yellow every day but Wednesday from 9:05 A.M. to 9:50 A.M.

the majority of the teachers will have a fifty-minute lunch and preparation period daily.

Each of these schedules depends on the school resources, both material and personnel, and on the readiness of the staff to handle change. Each schedule represents a compromise, and each schedule will change or has been changed as the staff experiments with other ideas. These examples, we hope, will stimulate teachers in other situations to invent their own best arrangements.

TUTORING

An ERIC search done in 1991 by the authors, using cross-age tutoring as the reference indicator, yielded sixty-two items. From the items located, some general descriptions of current practice could be generated. Tutors usually work with younger tutees, sometimes from the same elementary school, but sometimes junior or senior high students will tutor. Quite often the tutor is a handicapped student (learning disabled, emotionally disturbed, or mentally retarded) who might tutor a regular or special education student in subjects such as math, reading, spelling, or language development.

In most studies where benefits were researched, both the tutee and the tutor improved their academic achievement, and the tutor's level of self-esteem rose (see also *Harvard Education Letter*, March 1989 and Cohen, Kulik, and Kulik, 1982). Several studies noted that students experiencing academic problems are able to deal with lower-level materials without embarrassment when they have the "excuse" of tutoring someone younger. Peer tutoring may cause some discomfort if it makes it more evident that some students are experiencing great difficulty and their tutors are not. This problem is removed in a multi-age classroom, where different ages work together on a regular basis. The act of tutoring or teaching helps a child to better understand the social skills needed by the learner. Tropani and Gettinger (1989, p. 7) report that an eleven-year-old learning disabled boy, after tutoring a seven-year-old boy in spelling, said, "I didn't like it when I couldn't give a sticker because he didn't pay attention. I wonder if Mr. W feels that way about me? You know, if you're nice to them, they are nice to you back."

Training for tutors is essential for an effective program. Tutors need to know both what they are to teach and how to respond to their tutees.

Tutors need fairly structured activities, especially in the beginning, so that to have a productive situation one of the adults must work with the tutors on a regular basis. It is possible for a teacher aide to direct the program if the tutoring materials are clearly structured and the aide has received training. Monitoring the progress of the program (including the tutors' attendance) is required regardless of whether the tutors are children or adults.

Levin and Meister (1986) have estimated student achievement gains in math and reading per $100 spent per pupil and for five educational interventions, with results from highest to lowest in the following order: student tutoring, class size reduction, computer assisted instruction, adult tutoring, and increasing instructional time.

TECHNOLOGY

In the early 1970s a classroom equipped with an audio center holding six headsets that could be attached to either a phonograph or a cassette player was considered technologically advanced. In addition, a rolling cart with a film projector, a filmstrip projector, a slide projector, and an overhead projector would be available for each teaching team. At that time, most schools still relied on a ditto or mimeograph machine for copying in quantity. A very fortunate school would have one television, one video recorder, and possibly a black and white video camera.

Many schools are still struggling to obtain even the primitive hardware mentioned above. A well-equipped school in the early 1990s, however, has at least one copier machine that can reduce or enlarge material in addition to collating. Each classroom should have a video center with a color television, VCR, and six headsets, arranged so that others are not distracted by the picture. An Audio Center and overhead projector should be available in each classroom, as well as a rolling A-V cart for each team. But this is just the start.

Less than 20 percent of the public schools in the United States had a student/computer ratio of 15/1 or better, according to a fall 1990 study. Only 14.5 percent of the schools had at least one modem; 3.2 percent, one laser disc player; 1.4 percent, one integrated learning system; 3.9 percent, one CD-ROM; and 23 percent were in districts with satellite dishes ("High-Tech Have-Nots," *Business Week*, 1990, p. 98ED). All of this hardware is needed for a school to be up to date on technology, and requirements change at least annually. Industry has been using these systems to train employees for a number of years. Of course, without a sufficient quantity of quality software, the hardware is useless.

Ryan (1991) was able to find forty research studies attainable from ERIC or *Dissertation Abstracts* between 1984 and 1989 which had quantitative academic achievement obtained by comparing elementary students using microcomputers as an instructional resource to those who didn't for a duration of eight or more weeks. The mean of the fifty-eight effect sizes in this meta-analysis of forty documents was .309, which indicates that the average student in the computer usage groups exceeded the performance of 62 percent of the students not using computers. Another way to express this difference is that those students with computers had a one-third greater gain or approximately three months additional gain. If the computer instruction continued for three years with the same magnitude of effort, students using computers would advance in academic achievement the equivalent of four years.

Teacher training was reported in twenty-three studies and was the only implementation variable where a reliable significant result was attained. In those studies where teachers had five hours or less of training, the mean achievement was less than the average of all studies; but in those where teachers received more than five hours of training, computer students exceeded the meta-analysis average.

Teachers need to receive extensive training in order to utilize the programs to their full educational advantage. Also teachers, with leadership from those most knowledgeable, need to be involved in the selection process. When equipment lies unused, it was often purchased by well-meaning home-school organizations before teachers had decided what was needed and how it would be used. Equipment compatibility remains a problem that needs to be resolved, much like the phonograph record speeds and VCR types were in days past.

School staffs also must decide whether the equipment is to be placed in classrooms, a computer lab, or the instructional materials center (IMC). If the school is small and has limited resources, placement in the IMC might be best, especially if one staff member could then service all the information sources. Security for this equipment is a major factor, especially in urban schools, and there is also a need for a trained staffer to maintain the equipment in working order. Unattended computer labs where teachers bring groups of children invariably have too much equipment not working.

Imagine the learning possibilities when students (and teachers) have access to optical memory devices (CD-ROM) which can store up to 2.5 million pages of information on a single disc, and laser video disc technology where one disc can hold over 1,000,000 pictures that can be accessed within one second (Van Horn, 1991, p. 530)! Interactive instruction is possible when microcomputers are used to control the systems.

Newer forms of software utilize artificial intelligence to analyze computation error patterns, check English grammar, and analyze reading difficulties. The software then provides a computer-assisted instructional program based on a student's specific difficulty, which is like having a teacher instantly available. While an integrated learning system (ILS) is estimated to cost as much as $60,000 per year, the ILS lessons are matched to the school district objectives, so Van Horn suggests that dropout reduction and a slight increase in class size would cover the costs.

Bell (in Miller, 1991) estimates that the cost for transforming a 525-student elementary school into a high-technology facility with a computer for every three students and an electronic teaching center in each classroom would be $480,000. Gifford (1991) reports that students at the Corona Avenue School in Los Angeles, who are predominantly Hispanic, made tremendous gains in communication skills after receiving computer and video equipment from the Model Technology Schools project.

Rural schools are able to provide a wider range of instruction using distance learning received by satellite dishes. In 1987 the Kentucky Legislature provided $11.4 million for a closed-circuit satellite system connected to each of the 1,300 public schools in the state. Some of these schools are using a key pad to allow student interaction with the distance teacher (Teltsch, 1991). Computer instruction has also been used for special education students and is often incorporated as part of the tutoring projects noted previously. Computers are the key to cultural diversity integration in the heterogeneous classroom, according to DeVillar and Faltis (1991).

Computer and video games motivate students by the challenge of accomplishment. The pace is controlled by the student. "Where in the World is Carmen Sandiego?" is such a compelling computer program that PBS has made it into a television program with a game show format. Software that is more than "drill and practice" is needed across the curriculum.

In sum, schools must move into the technology era. The obstacles are money, staff training, appropriate selection and integration of technology into the instructional program, and the creation of quality software.

CURRICULUM PLANNING

Any consideration of the curriculum might use the following list, which contains seven principles for curriculum that we believe are compatible with nongradedness from the 1992 *ASCD Curriculum Handbook*:

Does your curriculum:

(1) Provide a balanced core of common learning?
(2) Focus on results with multiple assessments?
(3) Integrate subject areas?
(4) Involve students in learning?
(5) Recognize and respect student diversity?
(6) Avoid tracking plans?
(7) Develop students' thinking skills?

We would add to this list one item:

(8) What is the hidden curriculum in your school?

If your school has adopted goals such as those given in Chapter 4, which stress pupil self-direction, uniqueness, individual differences, and group interaction skills, then control and containment of students would not be a dominating factor. English (1988) suggests that walking throughout a school with a camera, taking over 100 pictures in an hour without a flash and without planning ahead or allowing students to pose, would give a good basis for making such a determination. Photos showing lists of school rules and the placement of student desks in isolation from each other would illustrate control and containment of students as the hidden curriculum.

CLASSROOM MANAGEMENT

Classroom management problems will be significantly reduced when children are actively engaged in a program of learning that is based on a relevant problem-oriented curriculum, such as has been previously discussed. In addition, the physical space and the materials within can be organized in such a way as to reduce management problems. If the teacher or the team teachers track the movement of students as they go to get needed materials, congested areas are easily noted. Often, moving the pencil sharpener may reduce previous difficulties. Some sections should be designated for quieter, less messy work while others are planned for noisy and messy collaborative student construction projects. Materials needed by students should be available to students on shelves readily accessible to them. Teachers should demonstrate how students are to obtain and put away materials. While students may rotate the responsibility for care of materials in different areas, the expectation for all is that each is to return materials in good condition to the appropriate storage area. Maria Montessori has shown us that even very young preschool children are capable of doing this, where the classroom has been carefully organized and prepared.

As should be clear from the previous paragraph, the emphasis is on preventative measures to ensure a classroom environment where all can learn rather than devising a system of rewards and punishments. Teachers need to believe that all students want to learn and want to act in a manner that is acceptable. Some teachers need to rethink the need for absolute quiet in a classroom, as a project-based curriculum requires student movement and a higher noise level than the traditional workbook-textbook model of instruction. As noted by Kounin (1970) teachers need to develop "withitness," or awareness of all the different people and activities happening at the same time, and "overlappingness," or the ability to do several things at the same time. Such teachers always position themselves so that they can see everything in the class and make frequent visual sweeps of the room. They anticipate when a group or individual is experiencing difficulty and signal either visually or by moving to the situation in order to assist *before* anything gets too far advanced.

The reader will note that the schedules presented in Tables 7.3, 7.4 and 7.5 include recess periods. The schools from which these schedules were obtained all had recess on outdoor playgrounds except on rainy days. We believe that vigorous outdoor physical exercise several times a day will enable children to concentrate during academic periods. Stevensen and Stigler (1992) have found that the longer days and longer year in Japanese schools are spent in frequent and long recess and lunch periods or in extracurricular activities, not in academic classrooms. They also note that class instruction involves work-

Slavin, Robert E., Nancy A. Madden and Robert J. Stevens. 1989/1990. "Cooperative Learning Models for the 3 R's," *Educational Leadership,* 47(December/January):22–28.

Slavin, Robert E. et al. 1989. "Can Every Child Learn? An Evaluation of 'Success for All' in an Urban Elementary School," *Journal of Negro Education,* 53(3):357–366.

Spady, William G. and Kit J. Marshall. 1991. "Beyond Traditional Outcome-Based Education," *Educational Leadership,* 49(October):67–72.

Squire, James R., ed. 1972. *A New Look at Progressive Education.* Washington, DC: ASCD Yearbook, Association for Supervision and Curriculum Development.

Stevenson, Harold W. and James W. Stigler. 1992. *The Learning Gap: Why Our Schools are Failing and What We Can Learn from Japanese and Chinese Education.* New York, NY: Summit Books.

Teltsch, Kathleen. 1991. "To Teach Distant Pupils Educators in Kentucky Turn on Interactive TV," *New York Times* (October 30):B7.

Thelen, Herbert. 1960. *Education and the Human Quest.* New York, NY: Harper and Row.

Trapani, Catherine and Maribeth Gettinger. 1989. "Effects of Skills Training and Cross-Age Tutoring on Academic Achievement and Social Behaviors of Boys with Learning Disabilities," *Journal of Research and Development in Education,* 22(Summer):1–9.

Van Horn, Royal. 1991. "Educational Power Tools: New Instructional Delivery Systems," *Phi Delta Kappan,* 72(March):527–533.

Vars, Gordon F. 1991. "Integrated Curriculum in Historical Perspective," *Educational Leadership,* 49(October):14–15.

Weaver, Constance. 1990. *Understanding Whole Language: From Principles to Practice.* Portsmouth, NH: Heinemann.

CHAPTER 8

Assessment and Reporting Practices

IN 1978, Richard Curwin said "If there were a governing body that watched school practices as carefully as the FDA watches food and drugs, grades would be removed by law as a dangerous substance." This is advice that must still be heeded by Americans in the 1990s. By the term "grades" Curwin referred to "all evaluation systems that use symbols — letters, numbers, blue-birds, and so on — to indicate achievement or the lack of it" (p. 60). His argument, which is even more valid now, was that grades fail to report accurate and useful information and to stimulate learning; they are neither valid nor reliable, and they are not predictable. They are highly subjective, although they purport to be objective. They tend to "account only for the more insignificant aspects of learning; it is impossible to consider values, feelings, creativity, intuition, judgment, high levels of cognition, or any other qualities that truly influence the lives of students. Thus, students who wish to receive good grades must ignore or separate those aspects from their work in school and concentrate on the aspects that are rewarded" (p. 61).

Curwin's remarks were not contained within a discussion of gradedness-versus-nongradedness, although it seems likely that the lockstep organizational structure with which symbolic marking systems are intimately connected would also have been repugnant to him and others of like mind. Educators who reject competitive ABCDF report cards tend also to reject such concepts as first grade and fourth grade. We think it would be great if the pedagogical equivalent of the FDA were to join forces with them!

Except for the effort necessary to make the transition, we believe that working in a nongraded school is not more difficult, and may in many ways be easier than working in a graded one. Similarly, we believe that abandoning symbol-based evaluation systems and adopting more appropriate assessment policies and procedures lead to a reduction rather than an increase in instructional and reporting problems. We believe that classroom management has long been rendered very difficult by the tensions and other dysfunctional behaviors that are triggered in children when teachers use conventional marking systems. We believe, further, that the teacher-pupil relationship has also been needlessly poisoned by symbolic reporting within a competitive context, and the building of a healthy partnership with parents has been similarly injured. By suggesting that "there ought to be a law" against it, Curwin set the stage for this chapter in a helpful way.

The label often used for chapters and articles about this topic is "reporting pupil progress." No one has ever tried to use a different label, such as "reporting pupil failure." Yet the overwhelming message that is delivered by the usual "report card" is a negative one for most children; and even for those whose report cards are loaded with As, or numbers in the high nineties, the message is less about progress than it is about the child's position on an academic totem pole. Only rarely does the reporting system identify the academic content recently mastered, or the various academic, personal, and social skills that have been recently honed or modified, or the particular contributions recently made by the child to the school and its members, or the overall gains that have been made since the last time that the child's status and/or needs were reviewed. There is, in short, little if any substance in the written reports parents receive, and unfortunately the focus upon the child's competitive standing reinforces parental addiction to the win-lose thinking that characterizes graded schooling.

ASSESSMENT AND TESTS: SOME BRIEF OBSERVATIONS

Before we turn to the topic of reporting, it seems important to offer a few observations about the larger, and more fundamental, problem of academic assessment. A full treatment must be left to other volumes; but it may be helpful, before we approach questions about reporting, to alert the reader to some background issues, especially about the unfortunate impact of standardized tests upon reporting processes. We believe that with regard to broad assessment questions, the almost total dependency of researchers, educational administrators, and politicians upon standardized tests and other dangerously narrow (and irrelevant) measures has made it very difficult to examine in sufficient manner the needs and the academic progress of individual pupils. In this chapter, we have elected to deal only briefly with broader policy matters and to concentrate primarily upon the gathering and the sharing of evidence about each child's growth and well-being as influenced by school experiences.

In Chapter 3, reviewing the research, we had little choice but to report those studies in which standardized tests represent virtually the only data base for estimating program success or failure. Further, we are aware that most of our readers who elect to implement nongradedness will at some point have little choice but to examine standardized test scores and share their findings with local school officials and the general public. In light of the overwhelming message in the available research, we are confident that this will not prove to be embarrassing for them.

Unfortunately, neither will the test results be enlightening or, for that matter, useful. Other data, especially when related to well-defined goals and outcomes toward which the school or school district has determined to move, will be far more valuable in the effort to determine whether the nongraded program is successful. From the standpoint of each separate family, given its stake in the successful forward movement of their own children, evidence that illuminates the child's progress is by far the most important thing they need. Test scores, we hold, are non-illuminative, and may in fact be cruelly misleading.

A succinct paragraph from the Foundation Document issued by the British Columbia Ministry of Education (1990) serves admirably to express our own views about standardized tests:

> The use of standardized achievement and ability tests designed for and administered to groups is inappropriate for use with primary children. This kind of testing brings with it problems of reliability, validity and standardization. Standardized achievement and ability tests evaluate learner achievement in highly abstract ways. They do not match the way children learn or the curriculum which serves as a basis of instruction. (p. 29)

The document goes on to concede that for a very few children, about whom questions cannot be answered in any other way, individual diagnostic assessment may be useful. Such assessment, however, must be conducted by an appropriately trained professional, and the results should be used primarily to make recommendations about instruction and support services.

In recent years, rather than recognizing their limitations, federal officials and others have been urging that tests assume even greater importance as tools of assessment and control. In November 1991, *Phi Delta Kappan* published a special section on national testing, with articles derived from a special meeting called by the American Educational Research Association earlier that year "to build bridges between researchers and policy makers." In response to political efforts to establish a national testing policy, researchers raised serious questions about standardized tests regarding not only their failure to produce positive effects, but also their "unintended negative consequences for the quality of American schooling and for the equitable allocation of school opportunities" (Lieberman, 1991).

In the same *Kappan* issue, Darling-Hammond observes bluntly that testing in the United States is primarily controlled by commercial publishers and nonschool agencies that produce norm-referenced multiple-choice instruments designed to rank students cheaply and efficiently (p. 220). She goes on to say that test instruments "were initially created to make tracking and sorting of students more efficient; they are not intended to support or embrace instruction . . . they ignore a great many types of performance that we expect from students, and they place test-takers in a passive, inactive role, rather than engage their capacities to structure tasks, generate ideas, and solve problems." Nor do they measure students' higher-order cognitive abilities or support their capacities to perform real-world tasks (pp. 220, 221).

In her paper, Darling-Hammond further confirms that testing policies and related practices of teaching and grade-retention have had a debilitating effect not only on many children but also upon society. She calls for the creation of more authentic assessment systems (which will require much time and enormous effort) and also for major national investment in the instructional capacities of the schools and in the welfare of the students they serve.

We perceive the effort to establish nongradedness as one aspect of the "major national investment" to which Darling-Hammond refers. We also perceive that within each school making such an effort, significant progress can be made toward identifying goals and outcomes that make sense, toward developing measures and procedures for determining progress toward these goals, and toward helping each child to enjoy a sense of enthusiasm and fulfillment. In the best of all worlds, we would hope that the child develops this sense within a progress-reporting framework that offers to him/her and to the family much more, and much more relevant, information than test scores, competitive grades, and other disreputable mechanisms can provide.

INFORMATION THAT PARENTS NEED (AND DESERVE)

Having criticized the tendency of school people to communicate totem-pole rather than specific-progress information to parents, we now have an obligation to set forth a more legitimate alternative. We will start by asking a basic question: What kinds of information is it the school's responsibility to provide to parents concerning their child's performance, broadly defined, in the environment that is under the educator's control? We believe that the adults (parents, grandparents, guardians, and/or others) who bear the responsibility for "raising" each child, and who entrust that child to the school's care for about 180 days of each year, are entitled to receive at least four kinds of information:

(1) A complete and accurate picture of the child's potential, especially in the cognitive/academic and personal/social domains
(2) The extent to which his/her growth and performance in the school setting measures up to that potential
(3) Approximate information about the child's relative status or standing within his/her own class or team and the school
(4) Approximate information about the child's relative status or standing within the larger American society

It is our contention that by far (repeat: *by far*) the most important of these four categories are the first two, and that therefore the schools' reporting system should be geared almost exclusively to descriptions of progress being made toward best-possible achievements. However, we recognize that parents not only expect, but in fact deserve, to receive information about how the child "fits in" to the daily school environment and how in a broader sense he/she "fits in" to the national scene.

This may seem to contradict what we said earlier about the totem pole approach, but what we are arguing for is keeping the four questions in a proper relationship to each other. Information about Question 4 is almost totally irrelevant in the child's early school experience, but through the years it becomes increasingly useful for both the child and his/her parents to acquire a realistic perception of the larger world in which the (former) child hopes to participate and compete as an adult. If, for example, the early evidence suggests that the child has some extraordinary capabilities, talents, or inclinations that could lead to some very special adult role or roles, this can be taken into account as the family makes its own plans (e.g., building up a college fund) during the next decade or so. If, on the other hand, there is some strong evidence that the child has limitations or handicaps likely to persist over the years, again such information would be helpful to the child and the family as they contemplate and make plans for the future.

We offer the foregoing comments about limited-ability children with some caution, however, because more and more we realize, along with Bloom (1976), that the potential for extraordinary adult achievement resides in a far greater proportion of American children than has been generally assumed. The more stories we hear about children once classified in the schools as below average (or worse) who have become very successful adults, the less we are willing to encourage the delivery of pessimistic messages to them or their parents. In fact, the more we think about the depressing effect on some so-called "average" children of being identified (e.g., with "C" report cards, or at-grade-level scores) as less than wonderful, the more anxious we are to destroy the "C" mentality and the grade-norm mindset. Given the probability that the literally graded atmosphere in many schools has actually caused huge numbers of capable children to lower their sights and abandon the effort to "become somebody," we urge that teachers in tomorrow's nongraded schools think long and hard about making premature less-than-optimistic predictions about any child's intellectual/academic future.

Question 3, about the child's relative standing in the immediate school environment, poses a somewhat different and more sensitive challenge. Whereas Question 4 deals with the long-range future and can generally be sidestepped as appropriate, Question 3 has daily importance. For thousands of years, parents have wanted their children to fare well within the group and have taken note of how the talents and achievements of other children in that group compare with those of their own. Furthermore, there is often a healthy and stimulating dimension to the competition that takes place in human groups, and one of the important functions of parents is to respond to their children's victories and defeats in appropriate ways.

It is therefore natural for parents to wonder about their children's status within school groups, and teachers should recognize and welcome their obligation to provide parents with information that will be constructively useful to them. Such information, however, ought always to be phrased with care and connected to specific contexts (e.g., current level of reading skill, or artistic tendencies) rather than to the global classroom scene. Children invariably develop on a "broken front," with higher achievements in some subjects or activities and lower achievements in others. This means that the same child could be among the best achievers within his/her (approximate) age group in some respects, and among the least achievers in other respects. For a teacher to mentally average it out and simply inform the parent in global terms that the child is above, at, or below average is not only a lazy approach but also a disservice.

One of the worst features of the traditional report card, offering up a mixture of As, Bs, and Cs every reporting period, is the redundancy involved. Not only does it focus on the wrong questions, but except for minor up-and-down fluctuations it usually repeats the same oversimplified message (within this class she's a top student, she's a bit above average, she's average, she's a bit below average, she's a loser) month after month and even year after year. We suspect that if we could collect all the report cards in America and feed their data into the Great Computer in the Sky, we would discover that for most kids there is hardly ever a Big Surprise awaiting them down the road. Translated into parental terms, this means that once parents have been led to think that their child is in the middle (or the top, or the bottom) of the pack, subsequent report cards rarely tell a different story. Why, then, do schools put so much effort into reconfirming already-established (and probably not accurate) impressions about Question 3, and so little effort into answering Questions 1 and 2?

It is in the effort to answer Questions 1 and 2, after all, that non-gradedness becomes a wonderful and powerful force. Knowing that their child's recent progress within the school is equal to or less than the teachers' optimistic expectations is a thousand times more useful to a parent than being reminded, perhaps for the thousandth time, that the child moves around a particular position on the class totem pole.

X TO Y: A SIMPLE CONSTRUCT

An oversimplified, but perhaps useful, way to look at the pupil-progress picture is illustrated in Figure 8.1. In the illustration, we use two letters of the alphabet: X (to stand for current status) and Y (to represent a desired and attainable future). Presumably at each contact point (reporting period), the teachers and the parents reach an understanding of where Juan is *now*. If his current status is well beyond what it was at the last contact point, we have good reason to celebrate. If he has been mostly treading water, or even losing momentum, we have a problem with which to deal.

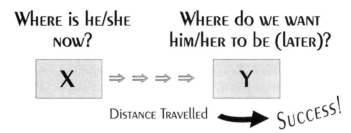

FIGURE 8.1 X to Y: A simple construct.

On the other hand, whether Juan has been doing well, or less than well, during the past six to ten weeks is something in which his parents have a vital and continuing interest. They can't do much about pupil well-being in Topeka or San Diego, or about the forty other kids on the school bus, but they have a tremendous interest in Juan's happiness, Juan's growth and success, and Juan's future. Tell them what they must know, from your perspective as his teacher, so that together you and they can make that future as bright as possible. The news about "X," with its supporting data, provides a basis for identifying "Y": where we hope he will be when we have our next contact.

The "X" for each child will of course be different. There probably has never been a school in history, whether graded or ungraded, in which every pupil was at exactly the same stage of growth and development across the board. This is even more true if we recognize that X can stand for not only academic status, but also physical/social/emotional and attitudinal status. The myth that supports gradedness is "X as a common denominator," and like many myths it has done much more than ordinary mischief within society.

Therefore we welcome the fact that every child's current status (X) is unique. In the same spirit, we welcome that the anticipated/predicted distance between X (now) and Y (future) will not be the same, either qualitatively or quantitatively, for any two children in the same class or team (or for that matter, the world). We also urge that when the next contact point arrives, and a discernible distance has in fact been travelled by the child, the flavor of the discussion about it will be celebrative. There is ample reason to believe that a child who feels respected and appreciated for gains made will be all the more eager to keep travelling. Conversely, mountains of evidence confirm that children who feel punishment (or its equivalent) for minimal mileage between X and Y, will likely try to find ways of abandoning the journey.

WHAT, NO COMPETITION?

Before we delve further into policies and procedures for reporting, let us deal head-on with the view held by perhaps a majority of parents and citizens, and probably a very large number of school people as well. ABCDF report cards could not have survived as long as they have, were it not for a deep-seated national faith in competition, with its attendant symbolic rewards, as a strong motivating factor in the school environment.

The big academic reward, according to competition-oriented doctrine, is to be promoted to the next grade. Conversely, the big punishment is to be retained. Day after day, continues the doctrine, the prizes for good academic effort are As and Bs, and the punishments are lesser grades or, horrors, the F. The teacher, omnipotent dispenser of the rewards/punishments and the annual scorekeeper as well, hopes that the prizes will spur productive behavior and that the prospect of punishment will deter unproductive behavior. At the same time, the teacher manages the classroom and choreographs test situations in ways that pit children against each other in the contest for prizes, and that discourage or inhibit the sharing and collaboration that, we now know, is much more natural to children and much more evocative of productive behavior.

In the ideal nongraded classroom, however, there would not be a total absence of competition. In fact, it would be impossible as well as pedagogically impractical to try to eliminate the competitive spirit that is natural to human beings. With the reader's permission, we will simply use the label "healthy competition," of which the healthiest version is competition-with-self, for those attitudes and activities that are seen as acceptable and even desirable. We have no quarrel with healthy competition in schools. We expect, in fact, that children from nongraded schools will turn out to be very successful (and ethical) competitors in those dimensions of adult life where competition makes good sense. Wanting to be "the best that one can be" is a healthy and fulfilling trait, and eagerness to succeed at a high level is a great quality whether the frame of reference is being a parent, or being (as we are) a writer of books, or whatever. What we object to is the unfortunate and premature emphasis in most schools, and their communities, upon what is obviously *unhealthy* competition.

Stated another way, healthy competition is both fair and discriminate; unhealthy competition is both unfair and indiscriminate. In the adult world, there are plenty of examples of each type, but on the healthy side of it, professionals (such as lawyers, doctors, architects) tend in a sense to compete only with each other, and presumably the most skillful of them become the most well known and well paid. This is a fair competition because the competitors, at the starting line, have essentially equal histories and credentials. Within the occupational trades, the same tends to be true: carpenters, plumbers, metalworkers, and other workers bring essentially equal histories and credentials into the competition for household clients. Similarly, musicians, actors, and dancers bring their bodily resources and their training into the competition for performing roles, and again the competition may be regarded as essentially healthy.

In the elementary school, by contrast, the competition is often very unfair and very indiscriminate. Future physicists, future plumbers, future singers, future lawyers, future metalworkers, future butchers or health workers or designers or retailers, all are often found, as children, reading the same textbooks and taking the same tests and doing the same experiments, even though they may bring very different histories and credentials to each of these tasks. The unevenness of the competition is exacerbated by differences in the linguistic backgrounds, socioeconomic situations, family contexts, health histories, and other variables that cause some children, at this moment in time, to be far more or far less ready for each school experience. To pretend, as many teachers do, that for this test (or recitation) they are, or should be, equally prepared is an egregious error. Subsequently, to hand out a mixture of As, Bs, Cs, Ds, and Fs on the assumption that each mark tells a true story, is mischievous folly.

In summary of the above, we have tried to say that the forms of unhealthy, unfair, and indiscriminate competition that are still found in many schools must be eliminated. On the other hand, we have acknowledged that there remains a place for "healthy" competition. Aware that for many parents the elimination of symbol-oriented report cards will be one of the hardest adjustments for them to make, let us reinforce this section with material from a "neutral" observer whose conclusions can be shared with hard-to-sell parents.

For parents (and for that matter, professional colleagues) who cling to the idea that a competitive environment is a necessary stimulant to academic effort, perhaps the most persuasive counter-arguments have been written by Alfie Kohn. Essentially a writer (and a very good one!) rather than an educator or researcher in the familiar sense, Kohn has done a masterful job reviewing a broad range of literature and discussing/arguing the topic with countless groups or individuals. As summarized in his 1986 book, *No Contest: The Case against Competition*, the ingrained and traditional view of competition is inherently destructive. Whether within the classroom, the family, the sports world, or business and industry, gaining success by making others fail is unproductive and also poisonous to the relationships on which a healthy society depends.

Kohn's book disputes the myth that competition is an inevitable part of human nature. In effect, he observes, families and schools put a lot of misguided energy into transforming children from the helping, cooperative creatures they prefer to be into selfish and win-oriented adults. He describes schools as sometimes being "a carefully designed laboratory of competition" (p. 26), in which "cooperation" means obedience to the teacher and following instructions, rather than working within a framework of mutual assistance (often described as "cheating" by the teacher).

As early as 1900, John Dewey in *The School and Society* lamented the use of competitive measures of success in schools, which created an atmosphere within which "for one child to help another in his task has become a school crime" (pp. 15, 16). "Mutual assistance," he noted, "instead of being the most natural form of co-operation and association, becomes a clandestine effort to relieve one's neighbor of his proper duties." By contrast, in schools where active work is going on, "helping others, instead of being a form of charity which impoverishes the recipient, is simply an aid in setting free the powers and furthering the impulse of the one helped." Dewey's views are consistent with these of Kohn, who, in similar spirit, laments the prevalence of schools in which there are winners and losers, and where there is emphasis on "triumphing over others." Messages sent to the home (report cards) focus upon that dimension of success (or failure) rather than upon the personal progress and accomplishments that deserve to be noted and celebrated.

Typically, Americans believe that competition enhances success and productivity and also "brings out the best in us." Quoting Elliot Aronson, Kohn notes that the American mind has, regrettably, been trained to equate success with victory, to equate doing well with beating someone. He notes the difference between goal-seeking in such a way that it prevents others from reaching *their* goals, and goal-seeking that is personally satisfying for its own sake and can include sharing the tasks and

the satisfactions with others. His descriptions of a cooperative classroom, in which such satisfactions predominate, are in marked contrast
to the descriptions of actual classrooms, such as Goodlad and Sizer
have reported.

In another more recent statement, Kohn (1991) observes that American society's infatuation with the word "competitiveness" has leached
into discussions of education and has encouraged "a confusion between
two very different ideas: excellence, and the desperate quest to triumph
over other people." He laments widespread flaws of character, reflected
in teenage pregnancy, drug use, and rampant selfishness and competitiveness among young people:

> At a tender age, children learn not to be tender. A dozen years of school-
> ing often do nothing to promote generosity or a commitment to the wel-
> fare of others. To the contrary, students are graduated who think that be-
> ing smart means looking out for number one. (p. 498)

Kohn's observations are consistent with a growing view, even in the
presumably ferocious world of business, that competition and collaboration need to be placed in better perspective. No less an industrial
guru than W. Edwards Deming, the American largely responsible for
the revolution in Japanese management practices, has taken a strong
position in favor of reducing competitive strategies in education.
Schools, he says, should abolish such approaches as traditional grading
and merit pay. He states as his greatest concern that "there should be
joy in learning" (AASA, 1991, p. 1). These and similar views should be
helpful as school people deal with those skeptical parents who regard
the reduction of competition in the schools as "somehow un-American."

The reduction of unhealthy person-against-person competition in the
schools ought to be accompanied, in our view, with increased opportunities for *group* competition within which children's energies can be
channeled "into positive and cooperative behaviors that receive rein-
forcement" (Benson, 1987, p. 116). The typically aggressive selfish behaviors in very young (age three to five) children, Benson notes, are ac-
tivated less by a need to outperform their peers than by a yearning to
attain an object or goal. After age six, children are likelier to make
social comparisons and see outperforming their peers as a social value.
However, their engagement in "spontaneous competition" tends to be
characterized by shared decision making and shared power. Self-confi-
dence thereby develops in a safe, nonjudgmental context, one's contributions to the groups influence acceptance, "maturity and interdepen-

dence are promoted, and winning is less important than belonging and participation" (Benson, p. 113).

Adult-controlled children's contests (e.g., Little League baseball and Pop Warner football), by contrast, "can be psychologically and physically damaging to children," even those who are successful. Emphasis on external rewards may undermine intrinsic motivation, and children may choose to withdraw or, worse, become confused about the win-lose ratio as it relates to their self-worth.

Benson reviews studies in academic settings in which individual competition has positively influenced performance and achievement. However, this finding is restricted to what we have called "discriminate" competitive situations, where the competitors are similar in ability and rewards are clearly related to individual effort. All the same, even more important benefits, such as greater social behavior and feelings of belonging, accrue from increased cooperative endeavors. Apparently, she observes, "the most beneficial situations for optimal learning are those that combine individual competition with group cooperation so as to foster both achievement, performance, and prosocial behavior. Such situations lessen ability discrepancies and promote involvement and willingness to participate on the part of less able students" (p. 113).

Damon (1991) offers some good suggestions for helping children to work more effectively with others. These include the creation of buddy systems and partnerships, helping students to know and appreciate their own and others' different learning and performance styles, using cooperative learning techniques in the classroom, scheduling activities and games that are not competitive; holding events or assemblies in which cooperative achievements are celebrated, and creating as many situations as possible that permit students to work and play with others of the same and different ages. He also urges the elimination of potentially harmful practices related to student placement, test scores, athletic events, and achievement rewards. He proposes emphasizing cooperation in every arena and level of interaction with one another.

REPORTING: CONSIDERING THE OPTIONS

One of the most comprehensive discussions of reporting pupil progress in the literature of nongraded schooling is provided in Chapter 6 of the text by Goodlad and Anderson (1987). Our hope is that many readers of this (Anderson-Pavan) volume will also refer on occasion to the 1987 book, and this is particularly recommended with respect to reporting. Some of the following material draws upon that chapter.

In the Goodlad-Anderson (1987) chapter on reporting, there is an italicized sentence that summarizes best-informed opinion about how reporting can/should best be accomplished: *the parent-teacher conference is the approach most universally advocated in the current literature of reporting and is probably the most fruitful and effective single means available* (p. 123). With this conclusion we are in strong agreement, although we are mindful of the fact that 1990s conditions are apparently worsening the prospects of having parents visit with teachers during schooltime hours. How to counteract this trend and make face-to-face conferences possible represents a challenge to be met.

There are, of course, some available options or alternatives to direct conferencing, such as written messages to the home, use of media materials, telephone contacts, and variants of the report card. Inasmuch as conferences are much to be preferred, however, the material in this chapter will focus especially on that option.

One of the questions most often raised, when conferencing is advocated as the preferred reporting approach, has to do with the ability or the willingness of parents to visit the school several times each year. Another question, easier to solve (by use of substitute teachers and/or adjusted work schedules), has to do with freeing the teacher not only for the conferencing but also for the preparatory and follow-up work that is required. Unless these two questions can be successfully addressed, conferencing will not seem to be a viable option.

When the problem of getting parents to come to the school relates to their daytime employment, some schools have responded by scheduling conferences for late afternoons, evenings, or Saturdays. Providing substitutes for the teachers so that they can therefore have compensatory "free" time may be necessary or helpful in such cases. Looking at the problem from the other side, however, it may be that parents can also seek flexibility in their schedules. There is much talk these days about "partnerships" between the schools and the business community. One of the contributions that could be made by that community would be for employers to allow paid time off for those employees who need to confer with their child's teachers. This suggestion might well be called to the attention of local service clubs (Kiwanis, Rotary, Lions, Chamber of Commerce), and announcements at PTAs or through the local newspapers might help to create a friendly employer response.

When the problem of getting parents into the school is related to other factors, such as difficult family situations or reluctance on the part of the parents/guardians/caretakers to set foot into what they perceive as dangerous or alien territory, then school people need to develop other means for establishing a comfortable and productive relationship with the home. When launching a conferencing system, school people and community representatives will need to "brainstorm" this problem and come up with some approaches and guidelines.

On the assumption that the aforementioned problems can be addressed in reasonable ways, let us next turn to one way of viewing the sequence of events in a conferencing cycle.

A PROPOSED CONFERENCING CYCLE

Figure 8.2 depicts a five-stage reporting cycle that approaches an ideal ("potentially perfect") sequence of events. The sequence, explained as follows, brings together the ideas of all those persons, within the home as well as the school, who have a stake in the child's academic (and other) well-being. Included are four conversations/conferences plus a final event that completes the loop and sets the stage for a subsequent cycle in the next several months.

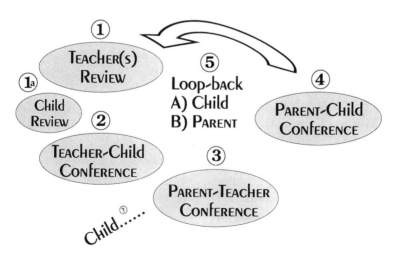

FIGURE 8.2 Reporting cycle.

The purposes of the cycle, beyond the familiar obligation of the school to keep the parents informed, include:

(1) Formalizing and insuring conversations that enable teachers to share insights and information about the child with each other. In most school situations, such conversations happen more by chance than by design, and one teacher often has little if any sense of how other teachers react to, and deal with, a given child.

(2) Providing the child with opportunities for self-assessment followed by in-depth discussions with the teacher(s), on the one hand, and the parent(s) on the other. In most school situations the child is not actively involved in the reporting process; furthermore, all the child receives in the school is the report card, delivered to the child without much comment, or knowledge that the parent is scheduled for a parent-teacher conference on Thursday at 3:15 P.M. In the home, if there is conversation about the report card or the conference data, it tends to be one-sided since the child has had little opportunity or encouragement to prepare for it.

(3) Establishing a true trilateral partnership. The child, the parent(s), and the teacher(s) have a contributing role to play and a shared stake in positive educational outcomes.

(4) Maintaining focus on the positive dimensions of the child's school experiences and efforts. All too often the time for report cards and/or conferences is an unpleasant one for the child, if not for the adults as well. While the several conferences in the cycle should not gloss over problems that exist, it is important at all stages for progress of many sorts to be highlighted and celebrated. Evidence of welcome growth, when featured in the successive conversations, provides a much greater stimulant to further growth than does evidence of a negative sort.

(5) Establishing that both the home and the school represent potentially nurturant environments. It seems doubtful that receipt of a report card, regardless of the "good" or "bad" message it delivers, provides either the parent or the child with much guidance as to future behaviors. Preparation of the report card, similarly, has very little impact on the teacher's perception of next steps to take. Out of the sharing sessions, by contrast, come many insights into how the school environment could be made more supportive of

the child's efforts and how the atmosphere/activities in the home could be similarly improved.

Formalizing the involvement of the child at several stages in the cycle seems especially desirable in light of the greater attention now being paid to developing independence, responsibility, and autonomy in children. Probably John Dewey, who emphasized the child's role in program planning and evaluation, would applaud the idea of inviting the child to engage periodically in a personal assessment. In a recent statement by the Ontario Ministry of Education, as quoted in British Columbia document GO279 (1990), it was indicated that

> Self-assessment helps children to develop a sense of responsibility for their own learning. It encourages children to reflect on their growth and learning, giving them a sense of where they have been, where they are, and where they are going.

Presumably self-assessment also helps children to acquire a stronger overall sense of satisfaction with themselves and their school experience.

Looking back at Figure 8.2, we see that the five-stage sequence might "play out" as follows:

- *Stage 1—Teacher(s) Review*—All teachers/professionals who work with the child convene to share impressions and information. The "home base" teacher chairs the session and takes responsibility for summing it up, and preparing the material for subsequent conferences with child/parent. Sometimes this procedure can be streamlined by the circulation/sharing of written materials, checklists, anecdotes, and so forth.
- *Stage 1a—Child-Assessment*—Especially for older children, a personal stocktaking by the child helps to prepare him/her for the upcoming conferences. This may be facilitated by reference to notes from previous reporting cycles in which "growth agenda" for the child were identified.
- *Stage 2—Teacher-Child Conference*—The teacher shares progress information with the child. The child also shares information and perceptions with the teacher. Agreement is reached on things to celebrate, and things to do next. The child might be responsible for assembling and organizing a portfolio of work for the teacher and later the parents to view. Following this conference, the child feels well prepared for his/her conversations in the home (Stage 4).

- *Stage 3—Parent-Teacher Conference*—The teacher shares information with the parent(s). The parent, in turn, shares information with the teacher. Agreement is reached on things to celebrate, things to do next. Optional possibility: the child also participates.
- *Stage 4—Parent(s)-Child Conference*—In the home, there is discussion, celebration, and preparation for "next steps." Both parties have had equal access to the progress-information base.
- *Stage 5—Loop-Back to the School*—The child and the parent, either separately or together, provide feedback to the teacher(s) in terms of matters celebrated, problems or needs identified, and the agenda established for the future. This might be done via a note (or message form) sent to the school, or by a telephone call.

From the teacher's point of view, it might be noted that of the events in this cycle, Stage 2 is in some respect the least familiar. In a research study funded by the Ford Foundation in a Massachusetts school district some years ago, one of the authors of this book (Anderson) discovered that teachers felt much more comfortable about conferring with parents than they did about conferring (in depth) with pupils. Probing for an explanation for this seemingly anomalous view, the researchers found that discussing a third party (the child) is less "sensitive" than dealing directly with that party. In the Massachusetts project, therefore, an effort was made to provide training for the teachers in adult-child conferencing strategies.

In the same study, it was learned from the children that they had very little real conceptual understanding of the ABCDF marking system. What they perceived was that it is either "good" or "bad" to receive the various grades; and it was felt to be more important for them to be "approved" by the teacher than to receive a particular grade for its own sake. The researchers were surprised to learn that the children, although aware of their "standing" with the teacher, were generally unable to tell how the teachers felt about the marks they were giving out. Stated another way, even the "A" students seemed unsure whether the teacher really respected their achievements, and many of the "C" students perceived only disapproval/disrespect even though their teachers when probed often interpreted the Cs as a compliment for good progress recently made.

We perceive that the usual brevity or even the absence of explanations to the child, in connection with marks or grades, is at the root of most such confusion. We perceive further that making the effort within each cycle to communicate progress information to the child, in rich detail, can be one of the most productive and progress-inducing activities in which teachers can engage. In situations with which the authors are familiar, the teachers held such teacher-child conferences regularly, and found that the students usually were very motivated, even eager, to devise strategies to help themselves improve.

As a postscript to our earlier discussion about difficulties in getting parents to visit the school, we recommend that even if Stage 3 (the Parent-Teacher Conference) proves impossible to schedule, teachers should proceed with Stage 1 (Teacher Review) and Stage 2 (Teacher-Child Conference), and then try to make the Conference Report information known to the parent in some other way. A telephone interview is one possibility. Another is to prepare a letter or equivalent written summary, for mailing or delivery to the home. It may then be possible to encourage the parent and the child to proceed to Stage 4 (Parent-Child Conference in the home), and it might then be possible for the loop-back (Stage 5) to occur. While compromises of this sort obviously can dilute the overall experience, they may accomplish at least some of the purposes of the total cycle. Furthermore, there is good reason to feel that full-fledged attention to Stage 1 and Stage 2 will in itself reap rich dividends: far, far more than the dividends (such as they are) from the use of traditional ABCDF report cards.

SO WHAT ABOUT REPORT CARDS?

In our view, progress-related messages delivered on paper are much less useful or understandable than messages delivered through face-to-face conversation. However, it would be unrealistic for us to propose that the former be entirely proscribed or avoided. What we do propose, however, is that efforts to communicate pupil progress in letter or other written form should, insofar as it is possible, respect the concept of "X to Y" as introduced earlier. Nearly all traditional-style report cards violate that concept, and make few (if any) references to the specific events and accomplishments that have marked the child's school experience since "the last time around." In addition to ignoring the substance of gains made, they also deliver a competitive-status message — making report cards an altogether unsuitable form of communication.

RECORD KEEPING

In order to provide the multiple sources of data needed for the authentic assessment of individual students, extensive records must be kept. A system needs to be devised which, while comprehensive, does not overburden teachers (or students) and thereby reduce teaching-learning time. We are convinced that much of the testing conducted in classrooms, especially that mandated by school districts and state departments of education, is not useful for diagnostic purposes, nor are the results available in timely fashion. Large-scale standardized testing, useful mainly for comparing individual children to their local classmates or to national norms, would be sufficient if conducted at three major points: age nine (grade four), age thirteen (grade eight), and about age seventeen (grade twelve).

Assessment should be conducted in order to better understand the needs of the learner and to determine the direction of instruction. Authentic evidence should include observing the child in the classroom, looking at the student's work (audio and video tapes may be evidence here, in addition to work on paper), reviewing skills achievement records, and talking with the child. Artificial demonstrations of learning, as manifested in contrived testing situations, may not represent the child's learning as accurately. The stress on observing children as they work is new in the United States, although child study was common in the 1930s.

Parents and teachers in school districts that have developed very detailed grade level objectives for major curriculum areas generally express concern as to how they will know if children are progressing satisfactorily when the school decides to go nongraded while the other district schools remain graded. The Lexington, Massachusetts School Committee adopted such specific objectives for reading and mathematics long after nongradedness was in place at several of the schools so materials were developed for tracking students during a summer workshop and were published (Pavan et al., 1973). These will be described so that teachers may take their district (or state) curriculum objectives and develop similar recording devices.

First, look at the organizational framework for the subject matter objectives. Reading had been organized under three major headings: phonetic analysis, vocabulary, and comprehension, with items clustered in four subtopics by each grade level under each heading. Since the schools were using two multi-age teams, the material was reorganized

so that items in Phase A would be appropriate for most students between the ages of five and seven (kindergarten, grades one and two).
Phase B covers ages eight and nine or grades three and four. Phase C
contains items for children ten and eleven years old (fifth and sixth
grades). See Figure 8.3 for an illustration. (Note that the words are
deliberately blurred since it is the *format* we are trying to illustrate.)

An 8-1/2 " by 11 " sheet was divided into four rows (for the subtopics)
and seven columns. After lines are drawn, there are twenty-eight
boxes. The first column of four boxes lists the four subtopics, and
learning objectives are entered in the row for that subtopic. All the objectives for Phase A are entered first and then empty spaces are left so
that all Phase B objectives begin in the same column. The same procedure is used to complete Phase B and begin Phase C.

Objectives are abbreviated so that room remains in each cell for the
teacher to make dated notations of the student's progress and mastery
of that objective. The number in each cell does not indicate sequential
teaching order, but is the reference number from the district's scope
and sequence plan. Since each of the three topics is detailed on two
pages, the entire elementary reading program is covered in six pages.
These six sheets are stapled into an oaktag file folder for each student.
In addition, a sheet of lined paper is stapled into the folder to list the

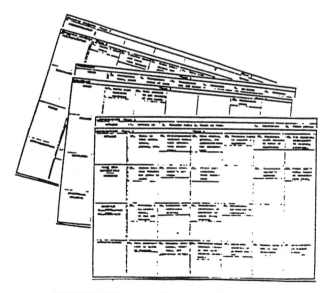

FIGURE 8.3 A recording system for reading.

books read, with beginning and completion dates. When this page is filled, another blank sheet is added to list books read. This folder follows the child throughout the entire elementary school program and is available during parent-teacher conferences.

The same type of folder should be developed for mathematics. The major math headings at that time in Lexington were Number, Operations, and Applications. Nine pages were needed to include all the various objectives, even when review items were omitted and others were combined. As was noted above for reading, sheets indicating books and materials that were used by the student should be stapled to the folder.

Additional papers could also be included in each folder, although in Lexington each student had a third folder, this one with two pockets in which various samples of work from many subjects were collected over the year. This folder might be kept by the student or be in a place accessible to the student. Students should be encouraged to keep samples of their best work so they may view their progress. Art work should also be in this portfolio. These three folders should provide much of the documentation needed to assess student progress.

To facilitate the collection of data for the reading and math skills charts and for team decisions about skills groups, teachers would have a 5″ × 8″ file card for each student on which they make dated entries during class, group, or individual conferencing sessions. These cards could be clipped together according to groups, and having individual cards makes it easy to move the student record from group to group or even from teacher to teacher. These cards were considered informal records for teachers and were generally not shared with parents, but used when teachers met to review students and to make entries in the skills folders.

These large file cards are used for data on specific skills acquisition, and smaller 3″ × 5″ cards are used to record observations of children and child-to-child interactions. By observing children at work, much can be learned about each child's interests, learning styles, and different needs. Some teachers write brief anecdotal incidents on large labels, including the date and initials of the child observed. These labels are then placed on a separate sheet for each child. Anecdotal records are most useful when reviewing a child prior to parent conferences.

Forms to assist parents in observation of their own children are provided in the *Primary Program Resource Document* (British Columbia,

1990) and teachers will find useful guidance for their own observations in the *Primary Program Foundation Document* (British Columbia, 1990) (see again Chapter 7).

REFERENCES

AASA. 1991. "Collaboration for Students Focus of Sessions on Quality," American Association of School Administrators, *Leadership News*, 92(December 15):1.

Benson, Doris J. 1987. "Children and Competition," in *Children's Needs: Psychological Perspectives*, Alex Thomas and Jeff Grimes, eds., Washington, DC: National Association of School Psychologists.

Bloom, Benjamin. 1976. *Human Characteristics and School Learning*. New York, NY: McGraw-Hill.

British Columbia. 1990. *Primary Program Foundation Document G0279*. Victoria, British Columbia: Ministry of Education.

British Columbia. 1990. *Primary Program Resource Document RB0008*. Victoria, British Columbia: Ministry of Education.

Curwin, Richard. 1978. "The Grades of Wrath: Some Alternatives," *Learning* 6(February):60–63.

Damon, Parker. 1991. "Competition Doesn't Belong in Public Schools," *Principal*, 70(4):14–15.

Darling-Hammond, Linda. 1991. "The Implications of Testing Policy for Quality and Equality," *Phi Delta Kappan*, 73(3):220–225.

Dewey, John. 1900. "The School and Society," reprinted in *The Child and the Curriculum and The School and Society*, combined edition, with introduction by Leonard Carmichael. 1956. Chicago, IL: University of Chicago Press.

Kohn, Alfie. 1986. *No Contest: The Case against Competition*. Boston, MA: Houghton Mifflin Company.

Kohn, Alfie. 1991. "Caring Kids: The Role of the Schools," *Phi Delta Kappan*, 72(7):496–506.

Lieberman, Ann. 1991. "Accountability as a Reform Strategy," *Phi Delta Kappan*, 73(3):219–220.

Pavan, Barbara N. et al. 1973. *Record Keeping in the Elementary Classroom*. Lexington, MA: Lexington Public Schools.

CHAPTER 9

School-Community Relationships and Nongradedness

VERY little will be said in this chapter that wouldn't apply to any school, especially a school attempting to implement an innovative program. All personnel in the school, not only the teachers, must develop and maintain good relationships with the public in general and parents in particular. Their impact on the perceptions held within the community about the school is extremely important; yet the prime responsibility for positive feelings about the school rests squarely on the principal's shoulders. An overarching principle of openness and honesty/integrity shall guide all information-sharing regardless of the group: professionals, parents, or community or business groups. The need for a positive perception of the school and involvement in the school by all the various publics is essential for the nongraded school to survive.

Even though the principal and the school should be shown in a positive light in order to increase the public's confidence in public education in general and this school specifically, this should never be at the expense of integrity. Honesty and openness should be the policy guidelines for information sharing, limited only by the need to protect the confidentiality of student records and some professional personnel matters. What is so frequently lacking in letters or newsletters sent from the principal's office is an explanation as to why this particular decision has been made by the principal and the staff. Parents are much more likely to accept a decision they do not favor if an attempt has been made to give a background of the issue and the reasoning that influenced the recommendation. All decisions, especially the unpopular ones, must be explained to all school members: the students, the teachers, the custodians, the secretaries, the cafeteria workers, the aides, and even affected volunteer workers in addition to the parent and school community. On controversial issues the principal is wise to keep the central office informed even if no guidance was sought during the decision process.

PARENTAL INVOLVEMENT

Epstein (Brandt, 1989) has been researching the topic of parent involvement and has developed a model showing the five various types:
basic obligations of parents, basic obligations of schools, parent involvement at school, parent involvement in learning at home, and
parent involvement in governance and advocacy. In order to emphasize
the school's obligation to assist parents in all these roles and to show
more clearly the required and voluntary levels of parental involvement,
we are adapting her framework as follows:

(1) Basic needs of children
(2) Home learning activities
(3) School volunteer activities
(4) School governance and child advocacy

All children need to be fed, clothed, housed, safe, and healthy. In addition, they need love and discipline, and they need to learn self-care
and social skills. Most parents have little difficulty with these child-
rearing practices, but some need a great deal of assistance, and every
parent may benefit from parenting education. The school should alert
parents to available social services and must contact the appropriate
agency if child abuse is suspected. One school used the films ordered
for a student unit on child developmental stages with the parents, in
sessions facilitated by the guidance counselor to help parents develop
more age-appropriate expectations for their children's behavior. Providing daycare or inviting toddlers to these sessions may be necessary
if the parent is to attend, and these practices will also provide the opportunity for educators to model interactive behaviors with the infants
and toddlers. Print or video materials might also be sent home.

Parents welcome ideas for home learning activities. These should be
discussed at any open house and should be included in newsletters or
classroom activity sheets. Parents need to understand the homework requirements and the roles they should/should not play. Teachers frequently suggest that the parent should read to the child, but in homes
where parents do not read, young children should be encouraged to
bring home books so the pictures can be discussed. Rosow (1991) notes
that homework can be designed to foster family literacy if it is based on
enrichment activities such as pressing flowers, making puppets, and
having the children read stories or books already read at school to their

parents. Epstein has developed math and science materials called TIPS, Teachers Involve Parents in Schoolwork, which are available from the Center for Research on Elementary and Middle Schools at Johns Hopkins University. Parents must be kept well informed about their child's progress through parent-teacher conferences, as discussed in Chapter 8. An understanding of the school program is fostered at open houses and through print communications from the school.

Nothing is better to develop an understanding of the school and the teacher's job than having parent volunteers. The school should develop a list of needed activities and survey all parents. Include in the list activities that need to be done outside of school hours so that working parents will have some opportunity to participate. Some parents might volunteer to provide child care while others are working in classrooms. Involvement of parents in teaching mini courses has been described in Chapter 7, and parents who participated became very strong teacher advocates. Clear expectations, training, and a school coordinator are needed for the school volunteers.

Only a small percentage of parents are able to volunteer to work in the school, and even fewer will be able to be active in the PTA/PTO or school advisory council. The principal should recruit all segments of the parent and community population for such roles, in order that these groups be truly representative and not dominated by one group. Many principals will need training in group facilitation techniques so that these groups are enabled to provide the school with their perspectives. Both teachers and parents will need to change their role behaviors as they work collaboratively for school improvement.

The school advisory committee, composed of parents, teachers, a member of the mental health team, and the principal, is a key component in Comer's School Development Program (1986), which significantly raised the academic achievement in an inner city elementary school. This committee is responsible for developing a master plan consisting of three parts: improvement of the school climate, academics, and school staff development. The other key component is a mental health team consisting of a psychiatrist, a social worker, a psychologist, and a special education teacher. This team meets with the principal, the classroom teacher, and the parents to plan programs for individual students. Its major focus is to help teachers as a group to understand that children's behaviors can be modified by actions of the teachers and the school. As such, there is a school focus on the affective domain—the relationships between people.

Comer believes that a caring atmosphere is essential to improving the cognitive functioning of the students. All aides in the school (who work ten hours per week) are parents or guardians of students in the building. In this way, children see teachers interacting with community parents who share the school's values. Both the aides and teachers teach the children the social skills they need to be successful in school. In order to forge this community-school link, parents are being brought into school for good times (not just when their child is in trouble) and a school social calendar is planned by the aides and the School Advisory Committee. Events such as pot luck suppers, fashion shows, book fairs, and workshops for both teachers and parents are sponsored. Comer's plan as described requires funding for aides and the mental health team, and control of school staff development budget. However, many schools have considerable expertise in the existing staff on child development and ability to provide their own staff development. Involvement of parents is more dependent on the will of the staff and the principal than on funds.

Parents (and their children) feel more welcome in a school where all adults reach out in a friendly fashion. For the safety of the children, any unknown adult without a school badge obtained in the office should be approached by a staff member. A smile and "May I help you?" indicates a very different environment than "What are you doing here?" Guidelines for interacting with the public need to be discussed in meetings that include all building workers. Close attention should be paid to the office and the hallway leading to it. Are visitors guided to the office and welcomed at the same time? Are there attractive displays of student work and also symbols that indicate what this school stands for? Of course, the outside of the building and the grounds should indicate that this is a special place that is well cared for. Unfortunately, this is a near impossible task for some inner city schools, but constant attention (monitored daily by the principal) often reaps results undreamed of as the neighborhood joins in.

Every school needs a school handbook, which gives basic school information in such a way that it is easy to locate. Besides the usual data including school hours, rules, calendar, list of staff and parent association board members, map, building floor plan, and district information, a nongraded school might want to include information on its philosophy and organization. One such handbook section began with a historical note, then included two paragraphs under each of the following questions: *Why team teaching? Why nongradedness?* and *What about open education?* Another page was devoted to specific description of how children were grouped in home base, language arts and reading, social studies, science, and mathematics along with some indication as to how these subjects are taught. These pages along with the staff list and building floor plan were used as a handout for school visitors.

Newsletters may be sent home on a regular schedule or published as needed. They need to be written with the parents' interests in mind and in a language(s) understood by the parents. Parents want to know what is happening in the school, and each issue should include something about each team or unit. One section might include some child development information or tips for parents. Be careful about merely copying commercial material since it may or may not be relevant to your particular school. Individual student art work, stories, or poetry might also be featured. Some schools or teams publish a special edition containing only student work. A student publication should truly be the work of students, and it is possible for students with access to computers to do all the work associated with publication. At the beginning of each month a calendar might be sent home with school events and the school lunches indicated. The first day of school, each team could send home a letter introducing the teachers, and giving some personal information about each one of them.

Parents are most likely to come to school when they know they will be able to see their child's own work or see a student performance. Some schools hold performances or celebrations during both the day and early evening to accommodate parents with a variety of working hours. If programs are short (as they should be) siblings of nearly any age are also welcome. The halls outside each classroom should display student work, and if possible classrooms might be open for a period before or after the performance with students' portfolios on their desks.

School meetings at one school always included slides taken in each school unit, with the principal or teachers describing the activity and its relation to learning. Explanations for play-like activities helped parents to better understand the school program and philosophy. A theme of interest to both parents and teachers was selected for each meeting and no time was spent on correspondence reading or other organizational matters.

Parents and teachers can work side by side, making learning games for both home and school. This is the popular "make it, take it" form of inservice that teachers have always enjoyed. One school that had assembled many problem-solving activities for its math lab sessions invited parents to become the students, and a student was in charge of each activity. What a boost to the students to "teach" their parents! Actually it may be best to do this before the "make it" session so parents discover how valuable teacher (or parent) made materials can be.

Participation activities should be sought that will involve as many parents as possible. One parent project known to us involved building elaborate playground equipment. While a landscape designer made the plan, the actual fabrication would not have been possible without the equipment and skill of the construction worker parents. Other parents obtained gifts of building supplies and some fed the crews on the weekends of the actual labor. The children helped also, which may be one reason that the climbing structures and the multi-level decks were never vandalized.

Teachers may be reluctant to involve parents in curriculum matters. One team had developed a unit on human growth and development that included sex education. All the parents were invited to a meeting to learn about the plan and to see the media materials to be used. Three teachers on the team were planning to teach the unit to the older students on the team, while the other teachers were involving the rest of the students in a unit on the circulatory and respiratory systems. This would give parents the opportunity to have their children opt out of the sex education unit without embarrassment to the child. Parents had been informed that students would be included unless parents made a request in writing. No parent made such a request. Probably because the teachers were willing to share the instructional materials and strategies to be used with their children, parents gained the confidence to allow every eligible child to participate.

Schools, especially nongraded ones, should involve parents before their children even enter the school. This is the optimum time to provide parenting skills and information to young parents. These sessions should also include medical and health information provided by the school nurse or local medical clinics. The importance of maternal and prenatal care should be stressed, and pregnant teenagers should be encouraged to join the group. If an annual census is conducted, this may be used to determine households that have very young children; or children presently in school can be enlisted to deliver informational flyers to the neighbors. These parents of preschool-age children should be invited to all school events, especially ones such as the child development films mentioned earlier. In addition, parents might be invited to bring their infant or toddler to visit a class on a monthly basis so that children may learn about growth and how child care needs change at the various stages. It is easy to see how these visits could be coordinated with the curriculum unit referred to previously. This interaction will foster the positive relationship with the school, which will benefit the children.

Single parents or families where both parents work face enormous problems in finding suitable daycare for their children before and after school, during school vacations, and during inservice time. Some public schools are providing daycare on-site, usually at cost but sometimes financed by grants, the school district, or other social agencies. Most common is after-school daycare, where students are given a snack, assisted with their homework, and supervised in games and crafts activities. It is essential that this time be different from school time, more relaxed and with the provision of self-selected noisy and quiet activities. Younger children probably need a place to rest. Early childhood experts express some concerns that these children may be spending too much time in adult-organized activities, with too little time to explore and "mess around." This extended day may add considerably to the overburdened principal's responsibilities. However, this is a marvelous opportunity for parent participation on a paid basis.

In many school districts, the local YMCA provides all the needed daycare services for parents, with payment on a sliding scale based on ability to pay. Parents may drop their children off at the Y on their way to work, the children are bused to school by the Y and picked up after school by the Y, and then the parent picks up the child at the Y on the way home from work. Additional programs are then scheduled for the summer and for all weekdays when school is not in session. Since the YMCA provides more daycare than any other organization, it is essential that schools communicate their needs to this and all other agencies.

Schools need to communicate, not only to outside agencies, but also within the district. The more that the nongraded program is misunderstood by other school district people, the more likely it is that parents and the general public will question the program. The principal, the guidance counselor, and teachers of the oldest children in the nongraded school need to meet with their counterparts in the receiving middle or junior high school. These exchanges should provide information on both the sending and receiving schools' expectations and programs. Students and faculty should visit each other's schools and consider periodic exchanges of teachers or students for specific curriculum objectives. The principal should invite central office people to the school as frequently as possible in order to demonstrate the viability of the program.

Some schools have sought to use recorded messages for their parents, and districts have set up homework hotlines. However, these practices do entail additional expenses in both labor and equipment and do not reach the vast non-parent public now estimated to be up to 75 percent of the taxpayers. Members of the general public learn about their community school by word of mouth, the local newspaper, and television or radio. Unless the district produces a program for the local cable channel, the individual school has limited access to broadcast media. Most local newspapers are willing to publish stories and photographs from the local schools if school personnel write the story, take the photographs in black and white, and deliver it in a timely manner following the guidelines established by the paper. While principals may need to assume this responsibility or to oversee this task, the enhancement of the school reputation is well worth the effort. Regardless, the most powerful public relations vehicles are satisfied parents and happy children. Every effort to involve and inform parents about the school and the program leads to a more positive perception of the school by the general public.

Bringing people into the school in ways that provide satisfaction and pride of accomplishment to the adult will also serve to enhance the school image. Volunteers need not only be parents, but anyone who lives or works in the school community. Students of other public schools and colleges find working with people younger than themselves to be rewarding. In order for a school volunteer program to be successful, the needs of both the school and the volunteer must be considered. Someone who will follow through on all details must coordinate the program. All volunteers need some training, depending on the activity that they will carry out, and expectations on both sides must be spelled out. Teachers need to understand exactly what the volunteers will and will not do. Few volunteers will return if all they do is clean paint brushes, but many return willingly week after week for one to three hours if they are working with specific assigned students or on a specific task such as assisting younger children with journal writing. If volunteers are expected to tutor students in certain skills, they need precise instruction as to how that is to be accomplished. At least once a year there should be public acknowledgment of the work of the tutors, possibly at a pot luck supper organized as a social event.

SCHOOL AND BUSINESS PARTNERSHIPS

Even though business-school partnerships have received much media attention, the actual involvement of business at the elementary school level has been minimal. Large urban school districts have been more successful in developing these relationships. As the result of a school-business collaboration in Philadelphia, every school has been adopted by a local business at official ceremonies complete with certificates posted in the school and district offices. Fast food places have donated free coupons for the schools to use as rewards, sailors from a ship in port have visited a school with lots of equipment to explain their jobs, ties were donated for boys to wear as part of their school uniforms, paper printed on one side has been made available to schools, students are being tutored, mentoring programs have commenced, money has been contributed for teacher travel and inservice to improve instruction, students have toured various business facilities, ice skating lessons have been provided along with tickets to a number of sporting and cultural events, additional telephone lines and computers have been purchased. Often a phone call from the school to the business partner asking how to obtain a given item (such as forty-five clipboards) at a good price will result in such a donation.

Much time was spent by the principal, an intern principal, or a teacher in order to make these arrangements, yet very few of the partnerships yielded more than a pleasant but brief activity. Both the schools and the businesses experienced difficulties in meeting the expectations of the other organization, probably because the relationships were not specified in writing and were not seen as central to either organization. This has been typical of most school-business partnerships.

Those that have been more satisfying to both parties involved the use of released time for business persons to work in the school on a regular basis, where the school worked with and placed those volunteers appropriately. Donations of supplies and equipment that enhance the school program and for which needed training is provided are always welcomed, especially in budget-crunching times. Mini-grants of two to five hundred dollars to teachers for new classroom projects have been a real morale booster for them. Businesses are better able to feel that they are getting a return on their investment (MacDowell, 1989) if the partnership involves a topic related to the company such as the joint sponsorship of an Earth Day by a local environmental company. The outcome of this project was clear to the company as the students moved throughout the area on a massive cleanup recycle effort. The company was able to supply teachers with much needed information on the subject.

Perhaps the closest school-business collaboration has been the worksite school satellites program, set up in Dade County, Florida when Joseph Fernandez was superintendent. These satellites house only primary students with the employer providing security, maintenance, and the building, and the school district providing everything else as specified in a formal contract. Hoffman (1990) reports that parents are delighted to be so close to their children and that before- and after-school programs are available to cover the parents' longer working day.

The public relations efforts of nongraded schools need to be based on openness and sharing and should include sincere invitations for others to join in the efforts of the schools. While the children's best interests are always primary, school people who wish to involve other adults in the school mission must also consider the needs of these volunteers.

REFERENCES

Brandt, Ronald. 1989. "On Parents and Schools: A Conversation with Joyce Epstein," *Educational Leadership*, 47(October):24–27.

Comer, James P. 1986. "Parent Participation in the Schools," *Phi Delta Kappan*, 67(6):442–446.

Hoffman, Ellen. 1990. "The Worksite School," *American Educator*, 14(2):33–36, 45.

MacDowell, Michael A. 1989. "Partnerships: Getting a Return on the Investment," *Educational Leadership*, 47(2):8–11.

Rosow, La Vergne. 1991. "How Schools Perpetuate Illiteracy," *Educational Leadership*, 49(1):41–44.

CHAPTER 10

Administrative Dimensions

ALTHOUGH by far the most important actors in the nongraded drama are the teachers, there are others who also play important roles, without whose strong support the effort can seem to teachers to be an uphill battle. In this chapter we take the optimistic position that with administrative (and other) support the effort can, by wholesome contrast, be very successful as well as satisfying.

These days, almost every discussion of school improvement is geared to the premise that changes take place school by school, not district by district or even state by state. Related to that premise is the realization, amply supported in research data, that the leadership of the principal is a particularly powerful force. Many school staffs, for example, find it difficult to pursue needed changes when their principal is either unwilling or unable to embrace and facilitate those changes. At the opposite side of this truism, school staffs who are themselves unwilling to embrace such changes may find themselves in an awkward position if the principal makes a strong and visible commitment. Ideally, of course, the principal's leadership combined with staff enthusiasm can move mountains. We will therefore open the discussion with some comments about the qualities that are needed in the principalship. Then we will examine the roles that other leaders and agencies can and must play.

Among the other persons or groups whose commitment and enthusiasm can help bring about changes such as nongradedness are the Superintendent of Schools; the Board of Education; the various administrators and support personnel who are based in the school district office; county and/or state agencies with regulatory, financial, and other responsibilities for public education; and the colleges and universities whose role is to provide not only the professional preparation of educational workers but also (broadly defined) consultative services and research information to guide program evaluation and development.

To this list we might also add funded research/service laboratories, regional or state service agencies, teacher unions, and organizations serving the needs of various professional subgroups (e.g., administrators, supervisors, principals, teachers in various disciplines) at state and national levels. Increasingly the latter groups, particularly through their publications and the conferences, workshops, and institutes they sponsor throughout the year, provide educators with up-to-date information as well as skills training that can serve as a foundation for successful change efforts. It would seem that in a very high percentage of such efforts, representatives of the school or the school district were inspired and informed by attending in-depth sessions sponsored by Phi Delta Kappa, ASCD, AASA, NASSP, NAESP, and other membership associations. In addition, there are a growing number of for-profit organizations providing useful training on topics of current interest.

THE PRINCIPAL

Let us begin with brief observations about the person usually identified as the key to school programs. Given the confirmed importance of the principal's leadership, it becomes especially necessary to have intelligent, well-educated, highly committed, thoroughly informed, and skillful people occupying that role. In most of America's educational history, until quite recently, the principalship was often more a maintenance-and-oversight role than it was a change-agent role. The selection of principals was often a politically contaminated process, and such factors as cronyism and personal networking were all too influential in many school systems. While many good educators nonetheless found their way into principalships, it seems probable that needed changes were thwarted in many schools over the years by principals whose limited qualifications, authoritarian orientation to the role, and conservative views of educational practice made it difficult for new concepts and ideas to get past their doors.

The educational climate in the 1990s is so charged with the expectation that changes must be made, and the art of personnel recruitment and selection is so much more advanced than it has been, that the typical newly appointed principal is in fact a better bet for getting changes underway than was his/her predecessor. In state after state that we have visited recently, we perceive that local school leadership is now a positive rather than a negative force for implementing such organizational changes as nongrading and teaming, and for promoting corollary changes in the instructional program. Our earnest hope is that this perception is shared by the readers of this volume, and that the term "principal" in their immediate experience brings smiles of appreciation to their faces rather than frowns of frustration.

Speaking directly to the prospects for nongradedness in a given school, or for that matter any "new" idea being put to the test, we consider it essential for the principal to satisfy three requirements:

(1) To be at least as well informed (knowledgeable) about nongradedness as anyone else on the staff or in the community. This is not to expect total erudition on the principal's part, but rather to emphasize that the principal must understand nongradedness, conceptually and operationally, so well that he/she can deal capably and confidently with questions that arise, and serve as an able informant on philosophic as well as practical issues.

(2) To be manifestly and energetically supportive of the nongraded effort. Again, this is not to expect impassioned behavior on the principal's part, but rather to emphasize that the leader's obvious enthusiasm for nongradedness, and his/her clear commitment to its success, can go a long way toward reducing parental and staff resistance and toward building the positive climate within which the challenging tasks of implementation can best proceed.

(3) To be a skillful engineer of the implementation process. The principal is not the only person who must understand the mechanics and strategies of the change process, but he/she should have a particularly strong grasp of the overall plan, good instincts about what to do (and not do) at each next stage or as problems arise, and effective communication skills so that all participants feel comfortable and well informed. We would, as an example, expect the principal to be capable of implementing, and/or inventing alternatives to, the suggestions presented in the final chapter of this volume.

COMMUNITIES AND BOARDS OF EDUCATION

The Community

Even in places like Kentucky, where a state law became the prime force behind the introduction of nongradedness, the community served by a given school or school district will inevitably play an important role when such an innovation comes under discussion. The community posture will of course be greatly influenced by the information (and sometimes misinformation) that becomes available through documents, through the media (notably local stations and local newspapers), and through both formal and informal efforts by school people to explain and advocate the "new" arrangement.

Communities can be either highly advocative of a change, or highly opposed to it. Much more often, communities are either apathetic or passively supportive. In the history of educational innovation, "by far the most prevalent case is that school boards and communities do not initiate or have any major role in deciding about innovative programs; that is, administrators and teachers develop or make recommendations about most new programs, or governments legislate new policies" (Fullan, 1991, p. 243). Communities can, however, force a sometimes-abrupt end to innovative programs about which they were not sufficiently consulted/informed in advance, and/or whose features they do not consider to be appropriate or well conceived.

In a recent study, Dansberger et al. (1987) concluded that local school boards are often overlooked in reform initiatives, are rarely prepared or trained for their jobs, and generally do not have in place any process for monitoring and evaluating their role in bringing about and assessing change. When school boards are successful, note LaRocque and Coleman (1989), they are knowledgeable about district programs and practices, they have a clear set of goals related to firmly held values and beliefs, and they have been actively engaged in activities whereby they could articulate these values and beliefs. They also work actively and interactively with superintendents and the district administration.

We therefore turn briefly to the Board of Education as a group whose needs and whose potential contribution to success of a nongraded program must be well understood.

The Board of Education

The lay citizens who serve on local school boards have not only unique responsibilities for directing a major societal endeavor, but also unique opportunities for influencing the quality of life in their communities. Beyond carrying out their legal obligations, school board members often contribute substantially (sometimes for better, occasionally for worse) to the morale and esprit of the educational workforce and to the populace at large. When they are divided or in conflict as a group, their impact on the schooling situation can be negative and even disastrous. When they work well together and respond intelligently to the problems they face, their impact can be very positive indeed. It is especially clear that their posture toward proposed school improvements, only one example being nongradedness, can often be the determining factor in their success or downfall.

Within the latitude permitted by federal and state laws and related mandates and regulations, school boards have more opportunities than they usually exercise to break away from conventional policies and procedures and to create a particular and special environment in their districts. Most boards, unfortunately, have a very conservative or conventional orientation with respect to educational policies and practices, and for many members it is primarily the political, economic, and management dimensions of being on the school board that interests them. It seems reasonable to state that "accountability" for most board members generally means remaining above suspicion with respect to fiscal management and legal compliance, on the one hand, and on the other, making sure that pupil academic progress (translate: standardized test scores) is up to community expectations.

Board members also strive to keep reasonable peace with the increasingly numerous pressure groups or constituencies that present either grievances or special requests that must be addressed.

It is partially within this context that we consider the role that can be played by the board, and to some extent by its members as individuals, in the effort to introduce and support organizational changes. Since most such changes involve important policy matters and can generate a great deal of public curiosity (friendly and otherwise), it is very important for the board to receive, to examine and discuss, and then to act upon the recommendations of the professional staff.

The skill, and the apparent conviction, with which the superintendent and colleagues present to the board the case for nongradedness, multi-aged classes, teaming, and other elements of a proposed new organization will of course be a critical factor in the board's ability to comprehend the plan and make a commitment to it. But it needs to be recognized that comprehension and commitment come more easily to an open mind than to a closed mind. Each board member has a special obligation to set aside some of the perceptions that derive mainly from habit and familiarity rather than from a considered rationale or data base. The "new" is of course not automatically better than the "old," but willingness at least to review a new idea is a necessary first step if progress is to be made.

From various polls that have invited lay opinions over the years, from the literature that board members consult (such as their national journal) and from the experience of nearly all communities in which nongradedness and related arrangements have been introduced over nearly forty years, it seems safe to claim that most American adults want their children to be educated within a humane environment that responds to individual differences and seeks to help children to fulfill their potential. This being so, the concepts and the philosophy of nongradedness, once sufficiently understood, are not difficult to embrace. The efficacy of nongradedness, however, needs to be "proved" to the average citizen, as does the abandonment or softening of promotion/retention policies, competitive marking systems, and the familiar unit-age self-contained classroom. Of all lay groups, it is most of all the Board of Education whose understanding and support on these matters must be cultivated by district and school leaders.

While our view on this point may seem a bit extreme, we would say that in order for nongradedness to succeed, board members no less than district officials should be both able and willing to answer all of the general, broad questions about the program that might come to them by telephone, or in social situations, or in whatever meeting they attend. Many a school "reform" has foundered when a school board member, confronted by a skeptic in the supermarket or in a church gathering or during a sporting event, appeared to be neither knowledgeable nor enthusiastic. In such situations, taxpayers are moved to say, "Hey, if even the school board is not sure about it, why should *I* be?"

Making sure that board members do not provide fuel for a negative public reaction is a challenge for the school leaders who work with them. Not only is an excellent orientation necessary at the outset, but complete progress reports along the way can help to keep board support at a high level. Especially, school people need to feed success stories to the board (with, hopefully, an alert press taking notes). They also need to be altogether "up front" about problems being encountered and measures being taken to handle them. Research updates, whether locally generated or taken from sources such as we have reviewed in

Chapter 3 of this volume, can help to keep interest and support levels high.

THE SUPERINTENDENT OF SCHOOLS

Although the national trend is toward viewing the individual school as the unit of change, and although the local school principal is more and more identified as the key player, nonetheless it is the Superintendent of Schools who has the greatest visibility and who has the most opportunities for providing the overall support for educational changes and for dealing with the broad general public. It is within the total school district that each drama unfolds, and as overseer and leader of the total district the superintendent has a unique role to play in facilitating (or, sad to say, squelching) the efforts at each site.

School districts come in many different sizes, of course, and the larger the district the more likely it is that what we are saying here about the superintendent's role is applicable to associate, assistant, or area superintendents. Whoever is perceived by the local school people as "the boss," and as the provider/supporter/enabler to whom they are essentially accountable, is the person whose actions and decisions can often make or break a change effort.

We might point out that decisions about personnel, unless (as is rarely the case) there is a great deal of school-level control over recruiting and staff mobility, will be among the most important ways that support for the program can be either granted or withheld by the superintendent. Providing a graceful "out" for teachers who are unable or unwilling to join in the change effort, and assigning supportive new personnel to the school, can greatly improve the chances for success. Providing funds and other resources as needed, particularly with respect to staff development, can also make a positive difference. Making frequent appearances at staff meetings, at parent meetings, and other activities where there may be lay discussions of the new program, can also be a valuable form of "boss-level" support.

Superintendents also sometimes function in a sense as troubleshooters for the district, moving into situations where a policy or an action has aroused public concern, and sometimes it is in the heat of such events that misunderstandings and even hostility can surface. It is possible, for example, that parents from a school that is *not* moving toward nongradedness will sense that the district is providing favorable treatment for the "experimental" schools, and they will vent that feeling in one way or another. In the past, some superintendents have been known to lose their ardor for the experimental program if it seems to be causing district-wide negative reverberations. A far more admirable response would be to make it clear that every school deserves to have some "wiggle-room" with respect to innovations, and that the district as a whole can only benefit as it learns what works best for various pupil populations in various contexts. Districts that have already established "magnet schools" or "charter schools," incidentally, are less likely to encounter such parental skepticism; and in the current national climate the idea of "choice" (even though these authors are wary of the federal proposal) is becoming somewhat familiar and attractive to the citizenry.

District-wide specialists are more and more seen as a resource on which local schools can and should draw, and in a healthy school district the various specialists ought to view pilot programs and innovative efforts as being especially deserving of assistance and approbation. It seems likely, for example, that schools breaking out of the conventional paradigm will become much more restless much more quickly than conventional schools, about gaps and anomalies in various areas of the curriculum. Curriculum specialists, presumably eager to see new content and strategies in their field put to test, might profitably regard the adventuresome schools as "laboratories" or pilot centers and do all that they can to acquaint the teachers with the "new" materials and approaches. Similarly, media people might find that the adventuresome school staffs respond gratefully to training and/or guidance that will help them to put technology in the service of the (nongraded) effort. Countless other possibilities could be imagined.

What seems certain is that the imaginative and promising ideas that are, in the best school districts, tossed around in central-office staff discussions and in the various staff-development sessions that happen each term, may well find a welcome testing ground in those schools we have described as "adventuresome." The prospect of a mutually beneficial partnership between the district's designated specialists and the front-line teaching staff is, or could be, an exciting one.

THE CONCEPT OF WAIVERS

Within each school district, and within county and state jurisdictions, many policies and practices tend to become deeply entrenched over a period of time. The perceived need to achieve uniformity, admirable as that may be when it comes to insuring equal and fair treatment of citizens and their children, sometimes becomes an end in itself. At the state level, the need for statistical and other evidence of compliance with well-intended laws and regulations also can degenerate into a static process that stifles efforts to accomplish the (legal) intentions in other and conceivably superior or more economical ways.

When bureaucratic processes remain static and unyielding over too long a period of time, mindless repetition may cause means (such as collecting data) to become sacred and ends (such as seeking to find better ways) to be forgotten. The bureaucracy that keeps the static system in place tends to become lethargic and oversized, with some units literally pursuing obsolete objectives and others mostly spinning their wheels. Worse, sometimes agencies become the havens of patronage, on the one hand, or of persons discarded by the regular system, on the other.

What we have just said about schooling may also be true about the military, about huge corporations (General Motors comes to mind), about the ecclesiastical world, and of course about state and national governments. It also seems likely that the tendency for organizations to ossify was first discovered in prehistoric times and has persisted in the human experience over millennia. We need not feel that American schools have suffered from institutional rigidity in some unique and unfair fashion. We do, however, need to perceive that escape from the hardening cement is necessary to our survival.

What is greatly needed is for state departments of education and equivalent agencies to adopt a friendly posture toward schools and school districts that want to introduce and develop unconventional programs. They should, for example, provide the "wiggle-room" mentioned earlier, with respect to mandates relating to clock hours, or curriculum guidelines, or testing procedures, or statistical reporting. Although it might be a slight inconvenience for state auditors, why not permit schools to report enrollment/attendance figures within blocs of time (e.g., Primary Unit, Intermediate Unit), rather than grade by grade? To know that 304 children of several ages are enrolled in the Primary Unit is no less useful than knowing that 101 "First Graders," 99 "Second Graders," and 104 "Third Graders" attend that unit. Similarly, reports on "retained" children and statistics on so-called dropouts need not be provided in ways that conflict with the ungraded effort. Waivers of regulations that force districts to provide inappropriate statistics or to follow inappropriate schedules would be a real signal from the state that innovations and creative efforts improving schooling are welcome.

Similarly, at the local district level, the concept of policy/practice waivers should be implemented. The school board, for example, should make it possible through waivers for a would-be nongraded school within the district to develop reporting forms, record-keeping systems, and any other policy/procedure arrangements that are unique and appropriate. If we are serious about empowering each school staff to find the best ways to serve its children, some freedom from district-wide requirements will be needed. Also needed, however, are signals of facilitating leadership at the district level.

In a study by Hill and Bonan (1991), supported by the MacArthur Foundation and the Rand Institute for Education and Training, it was concluded (among other things) that although site-based management (SBM) focuses on individual schools, in fact it involves the entire school system:

> Schools cannot change their established modes of operation if all of the expectations and controls of a centralized system remain intact. School boards, superintendents and central office staffs must commit themselves to long-term decentralization and enable the schools to use their interdependence for the benefit of students. (p. v)

SBM will lead to real changes at the school level, they note, "only if it is a school system's basic reform strategy, not just one of several reform projects" (p. vi). Among the implications of such an approach is that community leaders must understand that SBM is a profound change, and one that will not always produce quick results or work smoothly. The teachers' union (or its equivalent) must collaborate with the superintendent's office in preparing teachers to accept greater responsibility and in helping to resolve conflicts. Traditional control mechanisms must be relaxed; school personnel must pay more attention to issues of climate, curriculum, and pedagogy fitted to the needs of the students; and a new "culture of accountability" must be created wherein teachers and principals "take the initiative to inform parents and the general public about what they intend to provide students and how they will ensure that students succeed" (p. vii). This, it seems to us, is excellent advice.

THE NEED FOR CHANGES IN TEACHER PREPARATION

Next we turn to the role that can, and should, be played by colleges and universities in the support of educational improvement and reform.

At the most basic level, of course, higher education institutions carry major responsibility for exploring the frontiers of knowledge and serving in many ways as the brain of society. Among the functions of universities is to examine, to expand, to reconfigure, and to invent new applications for what is known. Relative to schooling, this implies perennial (re)thinking about what children in a democratic society need to know, feel, and act upon if they are to lead fulfilling lives and if the society is to become and remain a healthy one. It further implies that human growth and development must be a special focus of university-based research and inquiry, along with implications for policies and practices in those institutions, especially including schools, that seek to nurture and fulfill the capacities of human beings.

Within the purview of this particular volume, such an argument clearly implies that universities must examine new options, and help educators to make intelligent choices among the various ways that educational services can be delivered or provided.

It also clearly implies that university-sponsored programs for preparing teachers and other educational workers must be carefully fitted to the conceptions of "best practice" that derive from such efforts.

Speaking of university-sponsored teacher-education programs, the sad fact is that these are almost invariably insufficient, both quantitatively and qualitatively, to provide assuredly competent teachers for the schools. Most of the reasons for this lamentable situation are out of the control of educators themselves, and they derive largely from the desire of the power structure (in the universities, and in the larger society itself) to keep the costs of public education at the lowest possible level. Preparation programs for teaching have never had the depth and breadth that is characteristic of, say, medical or engineering education. New teachers arrive at the school with sketchy knowledge, at best, of (among other things) human growth and learning, effective classroom management, curriculum, and group dynamics. On the job, they generally receive very little help from colleagues, insufficient supervision, and (until recently) few meaningful inservice training opportunities. They survive mostly by resorting to traditional management practices, by relying heavily on conventional textbooks, and by staying with procedures that help them to "keep their heads above water." The four walls of their self-contained classroom provide a protective cover, but also deny them opportunities for sharing discoveries, successes, and problems with each other.

That the entire population of university professors tends to function within similarly obsolete structures could also be argued, but the major differences between public school teachers and university teachers are that, for the latter, (1) they almost invariably have the advantage of terminal (i.e., the highest possible) degrees in the field within which they work; (2) the rewards and incentives for research and scholarship are much more influential in their lives than the rewards for expert teaching; (3) the adult student population whose needs they must meet is far, far more homogeneous, especially in the sense of readiness and willingness to learn, than are the populations in public schools; and (4) the traditions of didactic, "frontal," delivery-oriented teaching remain rather securely in place in the university and in fact are generally taken for granted. The public school teacher, by comparison, has too little knowledge to draw upon, virtually no opportunity for research, an overwhelming variety of students to deal with, and little chance for success when relying on a didactic repertoire.

It is probable that the foregoing depiction of professors is somewhat unfair or inaccurate, since many departments and individuals are striving to improve their instructional approaches and are implementing strategies geared to the realities of learning. But it remains true that awareness of the extreme complexity of public school teaching, and therefore of the need to expand and enrich teacher education programs, is in very short supply on most campuses. It also remains true that on most university campuses the College of Education is the most undersupported academic unit. In fact, it may well be that across the entire country, university presidents and their Vice Presidents for Academic Affairs who have a highly supportive posture toward their COEs are so few that they could all travel together in the same school bus.

While the struggle to strengthen teacher education programs will probably go on for a long time, efforts to help refocus attention within the universities toward substantive and procedural reforms may prove to be more successful. Arts and Sciences faculty no less than Education professors (and their public school allies) have a legitimate interest in curriculum reform. The K–12 curriculum is in almost desperate need of streamlining and reform. The question "What should be taught?" and the even more relevant question "What must be learned?" deserve top priority on every campus.

Related questions about optimum delivery systems and appropriate learning environments also deserve a high priority. From the standpoint of this volume, we see as especially important the identification of "best" ways both to organize the school and its staff and to provide for the continuous educational progress of its clients (the students). Our readers will realize by now that we think university researchers and teacher educators should be paying considerable attention to questions about gradedness, unit-age grouping, and self-containment. Unfortunately, these questions have, more often than not, been ignored.

Teacher education programs in most colleges and universities are still geared to obsolescent organizational and instructional patterns, the most obvious of which is the self-contained classroom. In a spring 1991 survey of professors of educational administration as reported by Gies, there was widespread concern among the respondents about how many of their colleagues "continue to prepare teachers in self-contained classrooms and to prepare administrators to administer schools batched that way" (p. 19). It is possible to speculate that this derives in particular from the professors' own experience with, and therefore unthinking loyalty to, the practice of working alone, both in their public school careers and within the relatively non-collegial atmosphere in most universities.

Similar deficits in the professorial outlook can be identified with respect to gradedness, which again represents the typical prior experience of professors, and with respect to multi-age pupil groupings.

Although multigrade classrooms have existed, especially in smaller communities, for a long time, teacher education institutions have tended to ignore them. Gayfer (1991) notes that many universities actually avoid placing their student teachers in multigraded classrooms, and pay little attention to the management of such classrooms in courses that are offered. To make matters worse, only rarely in university courses does one encounter published material (such as Cushman, 1990, and Cohen, 1986) about managing mixed-age and heterogeneous classes, or how to adapt or modify the curriculum/course of study to fit multigraded situations.

It would therefore seem that researchers and curriculum developers in the universities (and also in state agencies and local school districts) need to put a great deal of time and energy into designing multigrade curricula and related materials. At the same time, heroic effort must be made through staff development programs to provide the existing cadre of classroom teachers with the training in teaching strategies and the materials they will need in order to succeed in the nongraded, multi-age classrooms in which they are being encouraged, or required, to work.

Other categories within which preservice and inservice training should provide guidance are curriculum integration, grouping students for various purposes, pupil cooperative learning and mentoring, learning centers, independent study, drill and practice activities, activity-based education, evaluating student progress, record keeping, and rotating/alternating the "regular" grade-oriented curricula. On the current scene, attention to the whole language concept is also highly desirable.

REFERENCES

Cohen, Elizabeth G. 1986. *Designing Groundwork: Strategies for the Heterogeneous Classroom*. New York, NY: Teachers College Press.

Cushman, Kathleen. 1990. "The Whys and Hows of the Multi-Age Primary Classroom," *American Educator*, 14(2):28–37, 39.

Dansberger, Jacqueline P., Lila M. Carol, Luvern Cunningham, Michael Kirst, Barbara A. McCloud and Michael D. Usdan. 1987. "School Boards: The Forgotten Players on the Education Team," *Phi Delta Kappan*, 69(September):53–59.

Fullan, Michael G. with Susan Stiegelbauer. 1991. *The New Meaning of Educational Change, Second Edition*. New York, NY: Teachers College Press.

Gaustad, Joan. 1992. "Nongraded Education: Mixed-Age, Integrated, and Developmentally Appropriate Education for Primary Children," *Oregon School Study Council Bulletin*, 35(7):37.

Gayfer, Margaret. 1991. *The Multi-Grade Classroom: Myth and Reality*. A Canadian study, extracted from research by Joel Gajadharsingh, Toronto: Canadian Education Association.

Gies, Frederick J. 1991. "Perspectives on Leadership: Queries from the Benches and Trenches," *The AASA Professor*, 13(Spring):8–11.

Hill, Paul T. and Josephine Bonan. 1991. *Decentralization and Accountability in Public Education*. Santa Monica, CA: Rand.

LaRocque, L. and P. Coleman. 1989. "Quality Control: School Accountability and District Ethos," in *Educational Policy for Effective Schools*, M. Homes, K. Leitewood and D. Musella, eds., Toronto: OISE Press, pp. 168–191.

LaRocque, L. and P. Coleman. 1989. "The Politics of Excellence: Trustee Leadership and School District Ethos," paper presented at *The Annual Meeting of the American Educational Research Association*.

CHAPTER 11

How to Get Started

PERHAPS the title of this chapter should be expanded to include "How to Keep It Going" or "How to Move to More Advanced Stages," since many readers may already have spent one or more years in developing their nongraded programs. We trust that those who are veteran protagonists will find both affirmation and some fresh insights in the procedural suggestions below. For those who are beginners in the most literal sense, we hope that following those same suggestions will make the effort seem less daunting. We hope all readers will realize that each school situation is inevitably so unique that some of our ideas may not seem workable or appropriate, while others may be especially relevant and even in need of considerable elaboration or expansion. There are few absolutes on our list, and doubtless we have unintentionally overlooked some great ideas that need to be added to it. It is a wonderful learning experience that lies ahead for all of us.

THE GENERAL PLAN

There are four basic strategies or concepts that undergird our recommendations:

(1) It is crucial, at the outset, for the entire school community to acquire a working understanding of nongradedness. While this includes especially the teachers, administrators, and other professionals who will carry out the program, it should also include the nonprofessional staff (e.g., secretaries, custodians, lunchroom workers, bus drivers), as well as parent representatives, aides and volunteers, substitute teachers, civic officials, and leaders of the business community. Pupils and their parents/guardians represent the ultimate audience for such information, and by the time the program is launched they must also have a thorough understanding of the concept.

(2) Within the professional staff, augmented as feasible by the other groups mentioned, a group consensus must be developed on the basic principles and values to which they subscribe. Beyond the working understanding noted above, there must emerge a strong and universal loyalty to the beliefs on which nongradedness is based. For example, if the nongraded program seeks to abandon all use of a competitive (ABCDF) marking system, but some teachers continue to feel that assigning grades is a useful motivational device (or weapon), the program will face a rocky road ahead. Even though the process may take time, thoughtful discussions and debate about fundamental questions and practices is an essential prerequisite to a "safe launch."

(3) To accomplish all of the preparatory as well as ongoing work that needs to be done, it is essential to organize the school community (again see above, regarding its potential membership) into a number of committees or task forces, each focusing on one or more parts of the job. Not only do "many hands make light work," but the greater the opportunity for active involvement the likelier that both enthusiasm and awareness will emerge. Relying on only a few persons, such as the administrative team, to carry the entire planning responsibility puts not only the workload but also the sense of "ownership" into too few hands.

(4) Under the direction of a designated steering committee, a comprehensive action plan including committee/task force responsibilities, resources, and target dates should be developed and monitored. A good idea is for the action plan to be set down on a large bulletin board (or its equivalent) that is prominently posted so that everyone involved can keep track of work accomplished as well as tasks that lie ahead.

CREATING AWARENESS

In order to pursue the first of the strategies listed above, the members of the school community need to locate, share, and discuss all possible sources of information about nongradedness. This will include books, journal articles, research summaries, notes from university classes, notes and handouts from professional workshops/conferences/institutes, materials collected from other school districts or state agencies, recollections of conversations with other professionals, and probably dozens of other references. The steering committee might at the outset create an "Awareness Task Force" whose responsibility it will be (1) to oversee the collection of all reference materials, (2) to put them in a convenient location, (3) to sponsor the various seminars/meetings/"coffee sessions" during which they can be discussed, and (4) to pursue ways of helping the staff to develop greater awareness of commonly held beliefs, areas of disagreement or concern, and matters about which more information is needed.

At this early stage, or later if it seems more appropriate, it might be helpful to view a videotape that provides a general overview of non-gradedness. The tape was created by Phi Delta Kappa in 1991, and cassettes became available for purchase in early 1992 through the Agency for Instructional Technology. In the tape, the authors (Anderson and Pavan) were interviewed about various dimensions of the topic. School people might find this to be a helpful introduction to the topic, and the tape might also be of much interest to parents and community groups.**

One of the best ways to promote the aforementioned discussions and interactions is to sponsor a retreat, or a series of retreats, during which people can relax together in a comfortable environment, share their thoughts and convictions, struggle with puzzling questions, and search for consensus on matters of importance.

Visiting Schools

We have observed that when teachers and administrators are trying to learn as much as possible about a presumably new and at least an un-familiar idea or procedure, they are eager to see the idea or procedure in action. We are constantly being asked to identify schools around the country in which an authentic nongraded program is already underway, and we have mixed feelings about providing such information. For one thing, most of the schools we might mention are still in the early stages of development, which means that (1) an "authentic" program may not yet be observable, and (2) having visitors can be for them a serious distraction and interruption. Another problem is that nongradedness is not an easily observable condition, and visitors might not notice some of the very subtle differences that exist between a graded and a nongraded program. They would, of course, see no graded labels on classroom doors, nor should they hear teachers using graded language or symbols in their work with children. When they see groups of children working together, they might not realize the spread of ages and levels of skill unless the host teachers point such things out to them.

All the same, we heartily recommend that school-team visits be

**See The Agency for Instructional Technology. 1991. *The Nongraded School*, a video-tape with Robert H. Anderson and Barbara Pavan. No. 2 in the *Phi Delta Kappan* series, *School of Thought*. Box A, Bloomington, IN 47402. Unit price: $125.

made to other schools, whether nongraded or not, in the course of creating awareness. Schools in your own neighborhood or district may be easy to get to, and to negotiate with. Just getting out of your own school environment can be a liberating experience, making it possible to observe other professionals as they go about their work lives. It will be important to agree as a group, in advance, on the questions you want to ask and the topics you want to focus on, such as: (1) Why do you . . . ? (2) How do the kids respond to . . . ? (3) What do you wish you could do more of, or less of, or modify in some way? (4) What do you feel best about? (5) How does policy restrain or support your efforts to do a better job for kids? (6) To which practices do the kids respond most enthusiastically? least enthusiastically? (7) What are the most important lessons you have learned?

When groups of teachers visit another school, they will find it easy to collect information about routines, schedules, space layouts, and other logistical matters. They can also get some idea of the support system that is (or is not) in place for the teachers; some sense of pupil enthusiasm about the school's progress; some sense of how teachers work together toward common purposes; and some sense of the problem solving (by adults and children) that typically goes on in the school. The sharing of impressions about such matters, following the visit, can be a rich and eye-opening experience for the visitors, and it can help them to think about similar or different conditions that they hope to create in their own school.

Visitors must always remember that what they have seen is only part of what really is. They must realize that what can (and cannot) be observed at a given moment has a contextual history, and what seems to be working, or not working, in context X may or may not work in context Y or context Z. What is to be hoped is that reflecting upon the observed situation, whether it seemed to be inspiring or not, will serve to reinforce those good instincts and aspirations that prompted the visit in the first place.

Some Warm-Ups

Sometimes when a group of teachers is coming together for the first time, or at the opening of a new school year, it is helpful to introduce some ice-breaking, warm-up activities that provide for a few laughs, help people to get (better) acquainted with each other, and ease the group into the more serious business on the agenda. Probably every administrator and teacher has a few such trust-building, tension-reducing games or exercises in his/her repertoire, so it should not be difficult to get the ball rolling.

"Brainstorming" games are often useful for this purpose—for example, breaking the group into three or four groups and seeing how many ideas each group can come up with in, say, ninety seconds on a given challenge. For example, in how many different ways could we make use of six carloads of hula hoops that the manufacturer has discarded as surplus? Or, how many different words or phrases could a teacher use to tell a child that his/her homework assignment was done very well, indeed?

At a more serious level, the groups could be invited to describe, in a series of words or phrases, an "ideal" working environment for elementary school teachers. After a few minutes of brainstorming, the groups could share their descriptions, and discussion would follow.

Scenarios

Getting down to children and their educational well-being, the groups of teachers (and also groups of parents) might be invited to think together about the following three scenarios.

Scenario A

The Event: A child (or youth) is visiting friends or relatives in another city. The conversation turns to schooling, and in a burst of enthusiasm the child exclaims: "I am really lucky. My school is the most wonderful school in the world!"

Possible Explanations: Let us assume that a random sample of children/youth from that school would volunteer equally positive statements about the school. Using a "brainstorming" approach, generate a list of factors/conditions/practices/policies/attitudes (etc.) that might be characteristic of that school. Then try to cluster some of the similar ideas together, to come up with a briefer list of "explanations."

Scenario B

The Event: We are now talking with a child (or youth) in a different city, and when invited to comment about his/her school the child replies: "I have to work very hard in my school, but I really learn a lot."

Possible Explanations: Again assuming that other children/youth from that school would comment in similar fashion, "brainstorm" a list of things that are probably true about the school. Again, cluster the explanations.

Scenario C

The Event: A child/youth reveals that he/she hates going to school and can hardly wait for each school year to end.

Possible Explanations: Brainstorm reasons for the child's unhappiness. Cluster and label.

Scenario Follow-Up

If there is a small subgroup of community members in the retreat or seminar session, it might make sense to invite the group to react to all three of the scenarios, either in A-B-C order or in some other sequence. If the group is large (e.g., thirty persons or more), it might make sense to break it up into three groups, one brainstorming each scenario. If time is limited, the retreat purpose would perhaps be better served by brainstorming just one of the scenarios (A, B, or C).

If A and B are brainstormed, either in sequence by the same adult group or concomitantly by two groups, a good follow-up activity could be to examine the two lists and see how (if at all) they compare. When the "wonderful" school is contrasted with the "hard work/productive" school, in what ways are they similar and in what ways are they different? If the differences are many, what are the implications for school staff seeking to create an environment for pupils that is *both* productive and satisfying? If the differences are few, does it tell us something about the compatibility of high expectations with a nurturant climate?

Other Awareness Resources

Two instruments, developed by the authors, are recommended as resources that may be profitably used in a retreat or similar situation. These are the Inventory of Educational Beliefs and Ideas, as presented in Chapter 2, and Basic Principles of Nongradedness, as presented in Chapter 4. The former provides a global overview of school practices, within which aspects of nongradedness are included. The authors' opinions concerning the appropriate (true or false) response to each question might provoke some respondents and reinforce others. Asking participants to identify the statements about which they have the strongest personal opinions might be a good way to stimulate lively discussion.

The "Basic Principles" document is not so much a debate provoker as it is a serious statement about nongradedness, as defined by a jury of national experts. Even so, it is likely that many teachers will want to challenge, or at least better understand, some of the thirty-six statements. Unless and until there is both a good understanding of, and a reasonable commitment to, the basic principles, there remains the need for patient but vigorous discussion.

In the retreat setting, or during some other meeting in the early stages, the Awareness Task Force might also find it useful to introduce some outrageous statements as a stimulant to fruitful argument. The following list, to which other thought-provoking sentences or phrases could readily be added, has triggered lively (and often amusing) conversation in workshop groups.

A Few Outrageous Statements

(1) You can't know it all (by yourself).

(2) You can't teach it all (by yourself).

(3) The kids don't need to know it all (to survive).

(4) All contents overflow their boundaries.

(5) Things have to connect, to make sense.

(6) Kids come in all types and sizes (praise be).

(7) The curriculum is much too full of unimportant stuff.

(8) Working alone has severe limitations, both for kids and grownups.

(9) Fragmentation endangers the brain.

(10) Sequences rarely are defensible.

(11) Learning should please and excite.

(12) Old notes deserve respectful burial.

(13) Curriculum desegregation makes sense.

(14) A great concept is: teachers as co-learners.

(15) A greater concept is: kids as co-learners.

(16) The curriculum is too full of really bad stuff.

One way of arranging discussion would be to ask each person to identify several statements that he/she would be especially enthusiastic about defending, and also to identify those statements with which he/she is least comfortable. The sharing of these reactions would be a good way to discover where there are already shared views, and where some sensitive issues will have to be addressed.

It might also be useful to ask the group to reflect on the relationship of those statements, none of which apparently addresses nongradedness directly, to the basic principles. Enlarging the group's understanding of quality educational services broadly defined is one of the most important steps that can be taken toward abandoning graded structure.

Achieving Consensus: "We Agree"

One of the best features of the IGE training sequence was the generation of what were called "we agree" statements. As members of the school, or school district, or other groups making preparations for launching new IGE-oriented programs completed their explorations and discussions, they were urged to sit down together, or assign a task force to do so in their behalf, and hammer out some sentences representing the concepts/practices/procedures/ideas to which they all wholeheartedly subscribed. Some of these had to do with philosophy, some with administrative matters, some with curriculum and instruction, and some with "what is best for the child." Each list thus generated was then carefully reviewed, amended, and edited as necessary to make everyone feel comfortable with it. It was then promulgated as a *consensus platform* to guide all future actions.

Sometimes the final act in the "we agree" process was a ceremony, perhaps with lighted candles and a solemn atmosphere, during which the "platform" was read aloud and all members pledged their allegiance to it. The notion of total commitment was not taken lightly, and there is ample testimony from IGE participants that the "we agree" statement had profound meaning for them during their efforts to translate the platform into operational terms.

We believe that teachers, parents, administrators, and others are much more likely to put their hearts and their full energy into a nongraded effort if they have been helped through the awareness activities to a complete understanding of what nongradedness is all about and if, as when joining a lodge or a church group, they are required to express their beliefs and announce their loyalty to it.

GETTING READY

Although the awareness stage is in several respects the most important part of "getting ready," it is primarily aimed at preparing the heads and the hearts of the participants for the many "hands-on" activities that lie ahead. Now we turn to discussion of those activities, and again we propose that their successful accomplishment can best be assured through the assignment of working groups or task forces, each with a particular area of responsibility. We will propose that there be five such task forces, although local or district-wide conditions might suggest that either more or fewer working groups will be required.

The five groups we propose would be responsible for: (1) organizational planning; (2) operational resources; (3) the school-home partnership (parent involvement); (4) curriculum planning; and (5) revitalizing teaching and learning. It should be remembered that we envision a steering committee responsible for coordinating the entire action plan, and therefore each of the groups would receive guidance, and where appropriate direction, in the pursuit of its functions.

Whether the Awareness Task Force would continue as a separate group, or join with one of the above groups (especially the parent involvement group), or be discontinued with a vote of thanks for work accomplished, is a decision that may need to be made. Let us turn, then, to a possible agenda for each of the "new" working groups (although they may, in fact, have been working on their tasks in one way or another for several years).

Making the Transition: Organizational Planning

There are at least five topics/problems/activities with which this task force might be concerned. They are as follows.

Facilitating the Transition from a Self-Contained Classroom Pattern to Ventures in Teaching

Teachers with team teaching experience, either elsewhere or locally, can be called upon for emotional/intellectual support, procedural advice, and suggestions. Small steps can be taken to help the uninitiated to become comfortable about becoming working partners with other teachers. Consultation and other assistance can be provided as newly formed teams begin to function. Developing an effective modus operandi, team by team, will be the focus of many meetings and informal discussions.

Building a Strong Work Culture and Symbol System

Adults, no less than children and youth, enjoy making connections with each other and dealing successfully with challenges. "Team spirit" is a concept that applies no less to school work groups than it does to sports teams, military units, corporation divisions, or emergency squads. A school staff launching a brave new venture needs to have pride in itself, faith in its mission, confidence in its prospects for success, and a strong sense of shared responsibility. The success of any one of its members, or any one of its committees or task forces, or any one of its instructional subunits, is everyone else's success as well. Having a logo or logos, slogans, mottos, mascots, "pride songs," and other symbols of their mission and units will help the school personnel to feel good about what they're trying to do, how they're going about it, and why they think it's worth trying.

Defining the Roles to Be Played by Specialists

In the nongraded school, not only the classroom teachers but all professional specialists will be playing somewhat different roles, and the new role requirements need to be worked out with special care. The library/media staff, counselors, specialists in related disciplines (notably art, music, physical education), special education personnel, and others will relate to their "regular-classroom teacher" colleagues and their pupils in some new ways. Especially challenging may be working out patterns for instructing multi-age groups as the situation permits and requires. Likely is that there will be many more efforts to develop multidisciplinary (integrated) curriculum units. New approaches to block scheduling may provide both opportunities and complications in the view of specialists, and the negotiation of flexible but attractive timetables will require patience and skill.

Skillful and productive scheduling of space, people, and time is one of the most demanding and one of the trickiest tasks in the management/operation of a school even under familiar conditions. When a rather dramatic change is being contemplated, it is all the more necessary to think hard, long, and creatively to come up with an acceptable plan. A good ground rule is to regard every plan as an experiment (or at least a pilot), and to have it understood by all that frequent changes in scheduling will probably be needed, not only in the early stages but probably forever. The building of attitudes that support this notion will be a very important early (and continuing) step.

Creating Alternative Mechanisms for Pupil Grouping
and Pupil Movement

Even in the absence of teaming and multi-age arrangements, non-gradedness requires much more careful thinking about how children should be grouped together and how each child's day should/can be choreographed. Our view is that teachers should take care not to lock children into instructional groups, and instead should think about *all* pupil groupings as temporary arrangements subject to frequent adjustment. Helping to develop guidelines for grouping decisions and for regulating the flow of each day is a very important function for the organizational planning task force.

Dealing with Logistics

In addition to examining the logistical problems related to the items above, the task force seeks to insure that the spatial/physical resources within the school are used in the most efficient and appropriate manner possible. By contrast with the conventional graded and self-contained school, where special purpose domains are sometimes left empty, the team-organized nongraded school emphasizes the joint ownership of available square footage and features a great deal of space sharing and untypical space usage. Creating a flexible, tolerant attitude within the staff concerning access to space can help a great deal not only in providing more instructional options but also in promoting a genuine family spirit. The same holds for furniture, equipment, and various supplies, in the logistical distribution and management of which there could well arise some sensitive "ownership" problems.

Collecting and Developing Operational Resources

The emphasis in this category is not on physical resources such as will be examined by the organizational planning task force, but rather upon the tools, procedures, materials, and human resources needed to operate the instructional program. These will include the following.

Locating and/or Inventing Assessment Tools and Procedures

With the emphasis more on diagnosis than upon accounting for results, this task force will try to build a library or reference shelf of printed material and other devices that will help teachers better to understand the needs and the progress of individual children and also of class/team/school groups.

Designing Progress-Reporting Procedures and Practices

Here the concepts introduced in Chapter 8 need to be translated into operational terms. Again the desirability of building a library/reference shelf of ideas and materials, some borrowed from other schools offering nongraded programs, comes to mind. Forms to be used, guidelines for staff reviews of pupil progress, guidelines for teacher-pupil conferencing, guidelines for teacher-parent conferencing, and record-keeping systems will all be on the agenda for the task force.

Pupil Progress Portfolio Development

Assuming that the staff will adopt the portfolio approach, or a variant thereof, for progress reporting as well as archival purposes, the task force needs to make plans for this essential activity. Collecting portfolio examples from other school districts, deciding upon a format, providing training for teachers in assembling and utilizing portfolios, and considering necessary materials and equipment will be the major activities carried out.

Inventory of Instructional Resources

Under the roof of every school is a veritable treasure house of instructional materials and resources, ranging all the way from rocks, sticks, math manipulatives, and science kits through books and magazines to sophisticated computers, printers, and copy machines. Some of these, such as equipment in the office and books in the media center, are obviously common property. Others are stored in the cabinets or closets of individual teachers, for example microscopes or autoharps, and may seem more like private property. In the aggregate, they represent a considerable public investment, and broader teacher knowledge of the innumerable resources that could be drawn upon might benefit the instructional program.

An increasing problem in a things-oriented instructional program is the adequacy and accessibility of storage space. It would be well to aggregate items in particular spaces, for example a reading materials closet, a math materials closet, a science closet, and so on.

While it would be unproductive to inventory every paper clip (so to speak), it seems possible that an inventory day, during which lists are made of the full range of property on hand, would awaken the staff to options of which they were not aware, and help them to feel better equipped to meet the almost infinite learning needs of their children.

Perhaps even more important could be the taking of a personal resources inventory. The teachers on a given staff have enormous but often hidden or unrecognized *talents*, including knowledge bases and technical/strategic skills that can be put to greater schoolwide use not only in the instructional program but also in staff development activities. Furthermore, from their travel experiences and from having participated in all sorts of life experiences under many different conditions, the teachers as an aggregate represent a rich resource. Often colleagues do not realize that Mrs. Chapman grew up in Singapore; that Miss Elliott's father owns an art gallery; that the chief custodian's sister has published sixteen children's stories; and that Mrs. McCabe inherited an autograph and signature collection from an aunt in Rhode Island that includes every president between George Washington and Calvin Coolidge except for Zachary Taylor and the ill-fated William Henry Harrison and James Garfield.

Similarly, efforts to inventory the unusual talents and interests of parents and other community members can be very productive. A safe generalization is that perhaps because of busing, neither teachers nor children are much aware of the interesting people and places that surround them in the school neighborhood.

Therefore, a very useful activity (in which, by the way, the students might well be centrally involved) could be canvassing that neighborhood to discover its resources and to become more aware of possibilities for field trips and other off-campus learning experiences. This brings to mind the discovery by a principal in Newton, Massachusetts that there was a retirement home nearby, some of whose residents were delighted to come to the school and tell or read stories to the children, help them with their projects, and in a sense provide a "grandparent" type of experience. Visits by the children to the retirement home, where they in turn could tell or read stories, sing some of their favorite songs, and bring some cheer into the older persons' lives, were similarly rewarding.

Promoting the School-Home Partnership

The committee or task force responsible for parental involvement has an interesting and vital assignment. There are at least three dimensions of the task, and these relate not only to how parents can be helped to support growth and learning in the home, but also to how they can become active partners in the school enterprise.

Parental Orientation to Nongradedness

Because nearly all parents have had no other experience than gradedness, with its promotion-retention emphasis and its use of competitive marking systems, they need and deserve a thorough orientation to the proposed new way of doing things in the school. It is to be hoped that at least their representatives, and all others who are interested, will be invited to participate in the awareness activities and, as feasible, in task force work as well. Orientation sessions, study groups, morning teas, evening meetings – all such means should be used to help parents acquire the information they need and to build enthusiasm for the nongraded approach.

When parents are reminded of how their own children developed at different rates from birth to school entrance, they quickly grasp that this uneven development continues even into school and *requires* that the school adapt to their child's needs.

Since word of mouth is the most powerful form of news distribution (both good and bad), it is helpful when large numbers of parents become salespersons for nongradedness within their neighborhoods. In some communities, the PTA (or its equivalent) has adopted a "welcome wagon" approach to the orientation of new parents. With the help of real estate agents, or at least by noting the addresses of newly enrolled pupils, the parent representatives make an effort to call upon each new family to "spread the good word," offer assurance that the nongraded plan is better for the children and popular among parents, and answer questions.

Parental Involvement in School Activities

As was noted above, parents often have talents, hobbies, and backgrounds that can become valuable resources for the school program. Serving as aides and volunteers, in a variety of capacities, is often a welcome opportunity for them. Helping out with special projects, for example the inventory of community resources, can also provide them with a greater sense of partnership with teachers.

Perhaps the best way for parents to become educational partners is for them to fulfill their role, within the family, as educators. Parents sometimes do not realize how many things they can do to support academic progress, such as reading to their children and becoming involved in homework supervision. School staffs can facilitate such support activities through seminars or study sessions on "The Parent as Teacher," and by regularly sending information to parents about current curriculum goals and activities. A weekly photocopied newsletter from the teacher and or team, describing for example the new interdisciplinary unit on the children of Mexico, could be of much interest to parents and also suggestive of things (such as the National Geographic video) that could be seen and discussed at home.

Parental Participation in the Public Information Efforts

In addition to involvements such as the "welcome wagon" effort, some parents have both talent and interests with respect to public relations and could be enlisted in the writing of news stories, parent/school handbooks or brochures, and scripts for slide shows or videos for use with community groups. Especially during the first few years, it is likely that service clubs and other organizations will be pleased to feature presentations on the nongraded program. Articulate parents could well be included in such presentations. The local druggist or chiropractor is sure to have much curiosity about the new and unfamiliar arrangement, and positive information, especially when offered by taxpaying citizens rather than the professionals on the payroll, will likely have a persuasive impact on him or her.

Curriculum Updating

Even though the review and revision of curriculum is a perennial and essential task in every school district, it is probable that 99 percent of American school districts are significantly behind schedule insofar as updating is concerned. One supposes that the outdated curriculum could conceivably still be followed after switching to nongraded arrangements, under which there might be more success with it, but one also supposes that putting more thought into meeting the real needs of individual children will lead to awareness of necessary improvements.

Multi-aged grouping practices, in particular, will require teachers to reconsider many traditional sequences and to rearrange and integrate topics and materials in new ways. Working in teams, similarly, will create fresh opportunities for building integrated units of study, blending and combining previously separate contents, and allowing teachers to utilize their special talents and interests in more productive ways.

One specific and immediate activity, in schools where a nongraded program is being launched, could be the development of two (or more) interdisciplinary "units" that can be launched during the first few months. A possible theme for one of these could be "Exploring Our Own Back Yard." This might be taken literally in at least three ways: making descriptive reports on the school building and its contents (human as well as physical), collecting similar data about the school site (including area dimensions, varieties of plants and trees, unique topological features, birds, insects and animals sighted, etc.), and looking at the total geographic area, or a designated portion thereof, served by the school.

A variant of the latter could be for each child (perhaps with parental assistance) to take a "census" of the neighborhood area within which his/her own residence is located, and then for each class (or preferably team) to organize the resulting data. As some examples, it might be discovered that this multi-aged team of 106 children identified 631 family pets, including 37 dogs (broken down by breed, or color, or age, or whatever), 48 cats, 17 gerbils (and more on the way), 18 white mice, 11 snakes(!), 165 goldfish, etc. That same group may have located 431 trees, of which 183 were maples, 69 were oaks, etc. Ditto for flowers; for colors of houses; for skateboards, bicycles, backboards, musical instruments, jungle gyms, television sets, boats, or whatever else could be tallied and described. The sheer variety of interesting items within their collective environments is likely to surprise, and hopefully delight, the children.

It might be noted that the "census" activities could also include taking note of anomalies or problems in the neighborhood. For example, notes on the quantities and types of trash found on urban streets might be put to good use in social action efforts.

It is easy to see how such an exercise could involve learnings at many different developmental levels in mathematics, language, social studies, science, art, music, physical education, and other content areas.

Culminating activities could involve songs, plays, murals, TV documentaries, "census" reports, and all sorts of other products. The explorers, though of differing ages, would have come to know and respect each other in a working situation, and it is to be hoped that some of the most fascinating discoveries will have been made, and shared with enthusiasm, by the youngest children in the class or team.

An immediate activity when moving to multi-aged grouping will be to assign themes to certain years so children do not experience repeated themes. A two-year sequence is needed if the multi-aging spans two years; three-year sequence for three years, etc.

Revitalizing Teaching and Learning

It might be helpful for one task force to have as its responsibility the identification and development of ways to help teachers be more successful as the facilitators of learning (as contrasted with deliverers of content) and to help children become active and enthusiastic explorers (as contrasted with docile vessels for knowledge being poured into them). Among the topics the task force should focus upon might be:

(1) Promoting cooperative learning (pupil-pupil interaction)
(2) Promoting peer tutoring and mentoring among children
(3) Helping *groups* of pupils to thrive by teaching them ways and means of working productively together
(4) Helping the teacher to involve pupils in program planning and decision making
(5) Helping teachers to replace traditional reward/motivation practices with more appropriate practices; urging teachers to abandon the making of comparisons between children and their work

PREPARING TO LAUNCH

Well in advance of the date when the new nongraded program gets officially under way, it needs to be determined whether a separate task force should be created for this purpose, or whether the steering committee or other group should be responsible for seeing that the program gets off to a good start. Ideally, planning for the launch should begin a year or so in advance, since it is important that much of the work of the five task forces mentioned in the foregoing section should be completed or at least well under way. Even if the official launch needs to be postponed for a year or more, success is far likelier if good organizational planning has been done, adequate resources have been made available, parents and the community are well tuned in, good curriculum plans are at the ready, and teachers have a confident sense of how to work with multi-age groups in some new ways.

Out of preliminary planning should come:

(1) Operational definitions, in handbooks or other useful form

(2) An information program for parents and community

(3) An information program for pupils. As the transition from gradedness to nongradedness is made, children need to become familiar and comfortable with the new vocabulary that will be used, the new relationships that they will have with each other and with their teachers, the ways that they will utilize spaces and resources, and the new opportunities that are expected to unfold for them as the school enters a new phase.

(4) Some "milestone events" that will bring the staff together to review and to celebrate progress being made by the various task forces or working groups, to recognize and reward those individuals and groups who are being especially creative and productive during the planning years, and of course to ventilate and deal with problems or concerns that may be troubling some members

The Launch Itself

Eventually the dramatic moment will arrive. Likely this will be at the beginning of a new school year. In our view, the launch ought to have a festive, celebratory flavor, and it is appropriate to make it as memorable and inspirational as possible. Like a huge wedding or a Fourth of July ceremony, it should have its solemn dimension (we take this important step together; we pledge our loyalty; we know it won't always be easy; etc.) and it should also have a happy, even triumphal, dimension (we are doing a wonderful thing; we are proud of this opportunity).

This might be a good time to build schoolwide spirit through some total-school assembly programs or special events. On the opening day, for example, after brief roll-taking everyone might be taken into the auditorium or lunchroom or, weather permitting, the playground area for a ceremony. Welcome to a new era at McKinley Elementary School.

Farewell to Our Past

Originally offered almost in jest, the idea of including a burial ceremony for the Olde Graded School on the program at launch time is one that has been adopted in several places, with wonderful results. Imagine the expressions on the faces of children, parents, and others in attendance when a makeshift and amusingly decorated "coffin" (once a large fruit crate from the supermarket) is slowly carried onto the stage by "pallbearers" in appropriately funereal costumes (bedsheets representing ghosts, or Father Time with a sickle, or a Dracula cape). When turned around, this coffin has huge black letters reading "The Olde Graded School." Perhaps there can also be some somber or eerie music to accompany the procession. Then, in sequence, shrouded messengers place in the coffin cards about 10″ × 20″ with bold but blood-stained letters, reading "First Grade," "Second Grade," "Third Grade," etc. This is followed by also placing in the coffin, cards with "Promotion," "Failure," "ABCDF," and "Basal Readers." Perhaps a comically dressed "Terminator" then recites a poem or brief essay acknowledging that "what we now bury, never to rise again, may once have been useful practices, but now we hope they will forever rest in peace. May the lamp of knowledge now burn more brightly because the angry wind of gradedness will blow no more."

The lid is placed on the coffin, a few old flowers are cast upon it, and the pallbearers whisk the coffin away. Perhaps arms are raised and the word "Hallelujah" is vigorously exclaimed. An embellishment could be the placing of a tombstone, with a phrase such as "The Olde Graded School, buried with respect on September 3, 199X."

This sort of jollity might be offensive to some in the community, and teachers might feel safer conducting such a ceremony in a more private setting, such as a faculty retreat. On the other hand, if the community is involved in the ceremony, it would surely get the attention of everybody in the audience, and the fact that certain words and practices have been officially entombed would surely be remembered within the community for a long time.

After the Launch

It is impossible to predict how long it will be before an authentic, smoothly operating, and well-accepted nongraded program might be found in place. Experience suggests that even under the best possible circumstances, several years of development will be required. Inevitably there will arise some unanticipated problems. Some teachers will find themselves wishing that they could retreat to their old self-contained classrooms, at least for a while. Some parents will fail to understand the why or the how of the new program. Some of the operational mechanisms will have to be repaired or replaced.

Especially inevitable, it seems, is that while working closely together the teachers will come to realize how terribly outdated and inappropriate are/were some of the courses of study and instructional approaches to which they had until recently been quite loyal. In their zeal to update the program as thoroughly as possible, the teachers may start burning themselves out. The steering committee therefore may need to counsel a more patient approach to curriculum rebuilding, and perhaps to work out a five-year timetable or some other more manageable schedule for the development of new curricula.

Specifically, the authors recommend that no more than one major curriculum area should be revised per year. Year one should be to develop a themes schedule, and during the following four years it may be possible to tackle the four major content areas (reading, math, science, and social studies) in whatever order the staff selects. Refining of the themes sequence will probably continue through all five years.

The more successful are the efforts to develop full-fledged teacher teaming, the likelier it is that groups of teachers will be able to cope with program-management problems that arise. All the same, the principal in partnership with the steering committee should be constantly available for "troubleshooting." On the opposite side of the trouble coin is *SUCCESS* written in large letters, and the leadership team should exploit every opportunity for recognizing and celebrating the accomplishments of staff members both individually and collectively. Monthly awards ceremonies, framed certificates in the corridor, pins and buttons saluting the bearer, special desserts publicly presented in the lunchroom—these and hundreds of other types of recognition can be used to applaud work well done and shining examples of community-mindedness in action.

These celebrations, incidentally, will sometimes be private within the school, but sometimes should be shared with the community. Just as in the pre-launch days there was a concerted effort to inform and persuade the community, after the launch it is important to keep the community fully aware of the progress of the program not only in general terms but in as many specific ways as possible.

Extensions

Thus far in this chapter we have not implied that the new nongraded program was limited to the (former) K–3 level, although it seems probable that in most schools taking this significant step the primary grades will be the first to be changed. In schools where a more bold move was made, and where *all* gradedness was "buried," we trust that all of the suggestions in this chapter will have proved applicable to (former) grades four to six as well.

If an intermediate nongraded program remains for future development, there will be an important continuing role to be played by the steering committee and by the five or more task forces. Coexistence with a fledgling nongraded primary program will almost certainly provide both information and motivation. Especially toward the end of the first year, with a cohort of youngsters approximately nine years old preparing to enter the intermediate world, it will seem natural to let the nongraded concept flow upward. Nongradedness is no less viable or less important in (former) grades four to six than in the primary, and the philosophical/procedural groundwork already established should make the transition less difficult for intermediate teachers than it may have been for their primary-level colleagues.

One strategy that has been used successfully in the upward adoption of nongradedness has been to let some of the primary teachers move "up" with their children into the (former) fourth grade, with some or all of the (former) fourth grade teachers accepting membership in the primary team. A possible variant is to create, in that manner, either a four-year multi-age (i.e., "grades one to four") unit, or two two-year units (i.e., first to second and third to fourth) for the transition year. One year later, the original three-year primary team pattern could be reestablished and the formerly fourth grade group could be blended with the "fifth grade" group as a two-year unit. By the *next* year, the former sixth graders would have been moved up into middle school or junior high school, and the intermediate unit augmented by the approximately nine-year-old students who have completed the primary years would then be a three-year multi-age group.

If the middle school happens to include sixth grade, the transitional arrangements suggested above would take one year less, or it might even be that the transition could be accomplished in one year altogether.

CONCLUSION

Although we have never claimed that burying nongradedness is a simple matter, we have agreed that to do so is urgently important and that getting started is facilitated by breaking down the various tasks into manageable pieces. Crucial to the entire process is community-wide understanding of why gradedness needs to be scrapped, why nongradedness is a desirable and workable arrangement, how individual children as well as the society can be better served in a nongraded environment, and how the transition can and will be carried out. The creation of such understanding, as managed by an awareness task force or its equivalent, is a major first step.

Additional steps include organizational planning, with particular attention to changes in the ways teachers will work together; pulling together the operational resources, both human and material, that will be needed; promoting the partnership between the school and the home; updating the instructional program; and revitalizing teaching and learning.

Proceeding with almost theatrical intensity, we have proposed that launching the nongraded program ought to include some very special, public events that help everyone involved to feel that a new age is dawning. A part of this could be a ritual farewell to the Old Age. As the New Age becomes a reality, careful attention must be paid to resolving problems, noting and celebrating accomplishments, and otherwise keeping everyone's morale and involvement at a high level.

Finally, this chapter dealt briefly with extending the nongraded program throughout the elementary school years. Probably a sequel to this volume could be *Nongrading the Middle School*, since gradedness is no less anachronistic in the lives of pre-adolescents than it is for those in primary and intermediate levels.

Nongradedness was defined, at the outset of this volume, as an idea whose time has come. It represents only a small part of the effort that must be made if American schools are to serve their country and its children in the best possible way. But it is an important part; and once nongradedness is in place, many other and more important good things can occur. The launching of nongraded programs, in thousands upon thousands of elementary schools, is therefore an event of potentially great significance. We hope that this volume will have helped such events to happen.

APPENDIX A: RESPONSE SHEET – INVENTORY OF EDUCATIONAL BELIEFS AND IDEAS

(Answers are shown in boldface type.)

Response Code:　　A = Agree;　? = Uncertain;　D = Disagree

CATEGORY	RESPONSES											
Nongrading and Continuous Progress	1.	A	?	**D**	26.	A	?	**D**	51.	**A**	?	D
	2.	**A**	?	D	27.	A	?	**D**	52.	A	?	**D**
	3.	**A**	?	D	28.	A	?	**D**	53.	A	?	**D**
	4.	**A**	?	D	29.	A	?	**D**	54.	**A**	?	D
	5.	A	?	**D**	30.	A	?	**D**	55.	A	?	**D**
Individual Difference	6.	A	?	**D**	31.	A	?	**D**	56.	A	?	**D**
	7.	**A**	?	D	32.	A	?	**D**	57.	A	?	**D**
	8.	A	**?**	D	33.	A	?	**D**	58.	A	?	**D**
	9.	A	?	**D**	34.	**A**	?	D	59.	**A**	?	D
	10.	A	?	**D**	35.	A	**?**	D	60.	**A**	?	D
Pupil	11.	A	?	**D**	36.	A	?	**D**	61.	A	?	**D**
	12.	**A**	?	D	37.	A	?	**D**	62.	A	?	**D**
	13.	**A**	?	D	38.	A	?	**D**	63.	A	?	**D**
Curriculum Methods and Materials	14.	A	**?**	D	39.	A	?	**D**	64.	**A**	?	D
	15.	A	?	**D**	40.	A	**?**	D	65.	A	?	**D**
	16.	**A**	?	D	41.	**A**	?	D	66.	**A**	?	D
	17.	A	?	**D**	42.	**A**	?	D	67.	A	?	**D**
Team Teaching	18.	A	?	**D**	43.	**A**	?	D	68.	A	?	**D**
	19.	A	?	**D**	44.	A	?	**D**	69.	A	?	**D**
	20.	A	?	**D**	45.	**A**	?	D	70.	A	?	**D**
	21.	A	?	**D**	46.	**A**	?	D	71.	A	**?**	D
	22.	**A**	?	D	47.	A	?	**D**	72.	A	?	**D**
Site-Based Management	23.	A	**?**	D	48.	A	**?**	D	73.	**A**	?	D
	24.	**A**	?	D	49.	**A**	?	D	74.	A	?	**D**
	25.	A	?	**D**	50.	**A**	?	D	75.	A	?	**D**

APPENDIX B: RESEARCH STUDIES COMPARING NONGRADED AND GRADED SCHOOLS PUBLISHED AFTER 1968

Research Study	Sample Size	Duration in Years	Location	Academic Achievement		Mental Health	
				Results	Test	Results	Test
1. Perrin (1969)	288	3	Arkansas	(+) (+) +	Metropolitan Iowa Lower SES Students		
2. Sie (1969)	124	1	Iowa	0	Stanford		
3. Otto (1969, 1971) and Chandler (1969)	400	3	Texas	0 0	Iowa (intermediate) Metropolitan (primary)	(−)	Children's School Questionnaire (anxiety)
4. Ward (1970)	797	2	Texas	+	Metropolitan (primary)	+	Draw-a-Man (anxiety)
5. McLoughlin (1969, 1970)	3,898	3	New York	0 +	Metropolitan More complete primary in normal 3 years	0 +	Pupil Portraits Fewer Retentions
6. Brody (1970)	603	2	Pennsylvania	+ +	Stanford—High Achievers Stanford—Low Achievers		
7. Brown (1968, 1970)	210	1	Pennsylvania	+	Iowa		

Research Study	Sample Size	Duration in Years	Location	Academic Achievement		Mental Health	
				Results	Test	Results	Test
8. Eells (1970)	1,368	5	Massachusetts	+ +	Iowa More NG years, greater gains		
9. Purkey et al. (1970) TT, OS	939	1	Florida			+	Coopersmith Self-Esteem Inventory
10. Jeffreys (1970) TT, OS	88	1	Maryland	0	Iowa		
11. Saunders (1970)	333	1	Connecticut			+	Ohio Social Acceptance Scale (emotionally disturbed less rejected)
12. Morris (1971)	117	5	Pennsylvania	+ + +	Iowa Stanford Boys		
13. Bowman (1971) TT	457	2	North Carolina	+	Metropolitan	0	Piers-Harris Children's Self-Concept Scale

(continued)

+ = Results clearly favor nongraded organization.
(+) = Results generally favor nongraded organization.
0 = No trend in results.
(−) = Results generally favor graded organization.
− = Results clearly favor graded organization.

TT = Team Teaching.
OS = Open-Space Schools.
NG = Nongraded.
SES = Social Economic Status.
IGE = Individually Guided Education.

APPENDIX B: RESEARCH STUDIES COMPARING NONGRADED AND GRADED SCHOOLS PUBLISHED AFTER 1968 (continued)

Research Study	Sample Size	Duration in Years	Location	Academic Achievement		Mental Health	
				Results	Test	Results	Test
14. Case (1971) TT	269	1	Maryland	+	Stanford	0	Ohio Social Acceptance Scale
				+	Blacks	0	Gordon's How I See Myself Blacks
						+	
15. Deeb (1971)	744	1	Michigan			0	Brookover Self-Concept of Ability Scale
16. Engel and Cooper (1971)	40	1	Nova Scotia	+	California		
17. Gumpper (1971)	2 Schools	1	Pennsylvania	(−)	Stanford	+	Piers-Harris Children's Self-Concept Scale
				0	Durrell	−	Anxiety Scale C
						0	Illinois Index of Self-Derogation

Research Study	Sample Size	Duration in Years	Location	Academic Achievement		Mental Health	
				Results	Test	Results	Test
18. Junell (1971)	150	7	Washington			+	Bill's Index of Adjustment and Value
						+	Borg's School Inventory
						0	California Test of Personality
						+	Boys
						+	Below-Average Ability
19. Marcus (1971) TT	60	3	Tennessee	+	California		
				+	Disadvantaged		
20. Remacle (1971)	128	1	South Dakota	+	Iowa	+	School Morale Scale – Grade 5
						(−)	School Morale Scale – Grade 6
							Bill's Index of Adjustment and Value
						(+)	Grade 5
						0	Grade 6

(continued)

+ = Results clearly favor nongraded organization.
(+) = Results generally favor nongraded organization.
0 = No trend in results.
(−) = Results generally favor graded organization.
− = Results clearly favor graded organization.

TT = Team Teaching.
OS = Open-Space Schools.
NG = Nongraded.
SES = Social Economic Status.
IGE = Individually Guided Education.

APPENDIX B: RESEARCH STUDIES COMPARING NONGRADED AND GRADED SCHOOLS PUBLISHED AFTER 1968 (continued)

Research Study	Sample Size	Duration in Years	Location	Academic Achievement		Mental Health	
				Results	Test	Results	Test
21. Wilt (1971)	2 Schools	1	Missouri	0 –	Iowa Boys	0	Michigan Student Questionnaire
22. Killough (1971) OS	300	3	Texas	+	SRA		
23. Vogel and Bowers (1972)	473	1	Illinois	– +	Stanford Draw-a-Person (conceptual maturity)	– + –	Describe Your School Russell Sage School Relations Planning Operations
24. McCoy (1972)	177	1	Oklahoma	+ +	Metropolitan Spache Scales	0	California Test of Personality

				Academic Achievement		Mental Health	
Research Study	Sample Size	Duration in Years	Location	Results	Test	Results	Test
25. Ramayya (1972)	160	6	Nova Scotia	+	Canadian TBS	+	Malorif Self-Esteem Inventory
				+	Boys (except math)	0	Sarason Test Anxiety Scale
						0	General Anxiety Scale
						0	Loevinger Ego-Development
						−	My Classroom Inventory (boys)
26. Snake River (1972) TT	200	1	Idaho	0	SRA	(+)	Moreland Rating Scale
						0	Anderson Self-Concept Scale

(continued)

+ = Results clearly favor nongraded organization.
(+) = Results generally favor nongraded organization.
0 = No trend in results.
(−) = Results generally favor graded organization.
− = Results clearly favor graded organization.

TT = Team Teaching.
OS = Open-Space Schools.
NG = Nongraded.
SES = Social Economic Status.
IGE = Individually Guided Education.

APPENDIX B: RESEARCH STUDIES COMPARING NONGRADED AND GRADED SCHOOLS PUBLISHED AFTER 1968 (continued)

Research Study	Sample Size	Duration in Years	Location	Academic Achievement Results	Academic Achievement Test	Mental Health Results	Mental Health Test
27. Givens (1972)	100	1	Missouri	0	Iowa	+	Instructional Objectives Exchange Teachers, Learning School
				0	Blacks	0	Peers, Social Climate, School Structure
28. Bradford (1972) IGE	394	1	Michigan	+	Metropolitan	+	Piers-Harris Children's Self-Concept Scale
29. Burchyett (1973) TT	535	1	Michigan	0	Standard Achievement Test	+	Motivation
				+	Creative Thinking		
30. Herrington (1973)	951	1	Florida	+	Stanford	0	Self-Concept
				+	Low SES Schools		
31. Reid (1973)	100	4	Alabama	0	Stanford	+	School Morale Scale

| | | | | Academic Achievement | | Mental Health | |
Research Study	Sample Size	Duration in Years	Location	Results	Test	Results	Test
32. Walker (1973)	337	12	Kentucky Tennessee	(+)	California	(+) (+) (+)	Coopersmith Self-Esteem Inventory School Morale Scale Slow Progress Students
33. Carter (1973)	800	6	Michigan			+ +	Coopersmith Self-Esteem Inventory Morse Pupil Attitude Questionnaire
34. Lorton (1973) IGE, TT	486	3	Ohio	0	Metropolitan	+	School Morale Scale
35. Bradford (1973) IGE	2 Schools	1	Michigan	(+) +	Metropolitan (reading) Metropolitan (math)	+	Piers-Harris Children's Self-Concept Scale

(continued)

APPENDIX B: RESEARCH STUDIES COMPARING NONGRADED AND GRADED SCHOOLS PUBLISHED AFTER 1968 (continued)

Research Study	Sample Size	Duration in Years	Location	Academic Achievement		Mental Health	
				Results	Test	Results	Test
36. Schneiderhan (1973) IGE, OS, TT	484	1	Minnesota	0	Iowa	0 0	IOX School Sentiment Index IOX Self-Appraisal Inventory
37. Burtley (1974) IGE, TT	292	2	Illinois	+ +	Metropolitan Blacks		
38. Henn (1974) IGE	14,030	2	Ohio	0	Ohio Survey Test		
39. Dalton (1974)	2 Schools	1	South Dakota	0	Creative Thinking	0	Self-Concept
40. Lawson (1974)	338	1	Indiana	+	California	0 (+)	Strickland-Norwich Personal Reaction Grades 1 and 3 Grade 5
41. Turman and Blatt (1974)	650	3	California	(+)	Standard Achievement Test		

Research Study	Sample Size	Duration in Years	Location	Academic Achievement		Mental Health	
				Results	Test	Results	Test
42. Lair (1975)	12 Schools	1	Texas	0	California	0	Self-Concept and Motivation Inventory
						0	School Attitude Test
43. Schnee and Park (1975) OS, TT	1,200	1	Oklahoma	+	Metropolitan (reading)		
				+	Iowa (reading)		
				0	Metropolitan (math)		
				0	Iowa (math)		
44. Wisecarver (1975)	48	1	Tennessee				Gordon's How I See Myself
						−	School Attitude
						0	Academic Adequacy
						0	Interpersonal Adequacy

(continued)

+ = Results clearly favor nongraded organization.
(+) = Results generally favor nongraded organization.
0 = No trend in results.
(−) = Results generally favor graded organization.
− = Results clearly favor graded organization.

TT = Team Teaching.
OS = Open-Space Schools.
NG = Nongraded.
SES = Social Economic Status.
IGE = Individually Guided Education.

APPENDIX B: RESEARCH STUDIES COMPARING NONGRADED AND GRADED SCHOOLS PUBLISHED AFTER 1968 (continued)

Research Study	Sample Size	Duration in Years	Location	Academic Achievement Results	Academic Achievement Test	Mental Health Results	Mental Health Test
45. Patterson (1975) IGE	1,214	3	TN, SD, CO, IA, MI, IL, MN			+ −	Children's Personality Questionnaire Self-Concept Anxiety
46. Brooks and Hounshell (1975)	303	3	N. Carolina	(−)	Stanford (science)	+	Children's Locus of Control Scale
47. Mobley (1976)	120	3	Georgia	+ −	Coop (reading) Coop (math)	+	I Feel . . . Me Feel (self-concept)
48. Bell, et al. (1976)	134	3	Canada	− −	Canadian TBS Gates-MacGinitie	0 + +	Children's Personality Questionnaire Leadership Less Anxiety
49. Yarborough et al. (1976) and Yarborough and Johnson (1978)	563	6	Virginia	(+) (+) −	SRA Cognitive Abilities Test High Ability	0 0 0 +	California Test of Personality Nowicki-Strickland Scale Self-Social Symbols Tasks Low-Average Ability

| | Sample Size | Duration in Years | Location | Academic Achievement | | Mental Health | |
Research Study				Results	Test	Results	Test
50. Soumokil (1977) IGE, OS	102	2	Missouri	+ +	Iowa Disadvantaged	+ 0	Quality of School Life Intellectual Achievement Responsibility (locus of control)
51. Flowers (1977) IGE, OS	238	3	Colorado	0	Stanford	− −	Self-Esteem Inventory School Sentiment Index
52. Szymczuk (1977) IGE	1,586	5	Iowa	0 0 +	Stanford Gates MacGinite Boys		
53. Price (1977) IGE	3,566	5	Iowa	+ (+) +	Iowa (reading) Iowa (math) Low-aptitude students	(+) +	Quality of School Life Low-aptitude students

(continued)

+ = Results clearly favor nongraded organization.
(+) = Results generally favor nongraded organization.
0 = No trend in results.
(−) = Results generally favor graded organization.
− = Results clearly favor graded organization.

TT = Team Teaching.
OS = Open-Space Schools.
NG = Nongraded.
SES = Social Economic Status.
IGE = Individually Guided Education.

229

APPENDIX B: RESEARCH STUDIES COMPARING NONGRADED AND GRADED SCHOOLS PUBLISHED AFTER 1968 (continued)

Research Study	Sample Size	Duration in Years	Location	Academic Achievement		Mental Health	
				Results	Test	Results	Test
54. Chanick (1979) IGE	775	1	Colorado	(−)	California	+	Student Behavior
55. Klaus (1981) IGE	433	8	Missouri	+ 0	Iowa, grades 4–5 Iowa, grades 6, 11		
56. Milburn (1981)	700	5	British Columbia	(+) 0 +	Gates-MacGinite (reading) California (math) Slow Learners	+ +	Piers-Harris Children's Self-Concept Scale National Foundation for Educational Research Attitude Scale
57. Anderson (1981)	2 Schools	4	Louisiana	0	SRA	0 0	Coopersmith Self-Esteem Inventory Discipline Referrals
58. Higgins (1981)	253	1	Louisiana	+ +	Metropolitan—High Achievers Metropolitan—Low Achievers		

230

Research Study	Sample Size	Duration in Years	Location	Academic Achievement		Mental Health	
				Results	Test	Results	Test
59. Guarino (1982)	162	4	New Jersey	(+)	California	(+) (+)	Piers-Harris Children's Self-Concept Scale Less Anxiety
60. Ricciotti (1982) OS	114	6	Connecticut	(+) +	Gates-MacGinite More NG years, greater gains		
61. Schmitt (1983) OS	264	6	Pennsylvania	+ (+)	Gates MacGinte Stanford (math)	+	Fewer Discipline Referrals
62. Kuhlman (1985) IGE, OS	200	2	Kansas	0	Minimum Competency Test		
63. Gajadharsingh (1987)	4,407	1	Canada	+	Canadian TBS		
64. Brown and Martin (1989)	418	1	Canada	+	Canadian TBS		

+ = Results clearly favor nongraded organization.
(+) = Results generally favor nongraded organization.
0 = No trend in results.
(−) = Results generally favor graded organization.
− = Results clearly favor graded organization.

TT = Team Teaching.
OS = Open-Space Schools.
NG = Nongraded.
SES = Social Economic Status.
IGE = Individually Guided Education.

Standard instruments used to measure academic achievement (abbreviated in the Appendix) included the California Achievement Test, Canadian Tests of Basic Skills, Iowa Tests of Basic Skills, Metropolitan Achievement Test, Science Research Associates (SRA) Achievement Series, Spache Diagnostic Reading Scales, Gates-MacGinite Reading Test, Durrell Listening-Reading Tests, Stanford Achievement Test, and Cooperative Primary Test.

Biographies

BARBARA NELSON PAVAN is professor of Educational Administration at Temple University (Philadelphia) where she teaches courses on supervision, the principalship, and supervises their field placements in addition to her work with doctoral students. After completing her doctoral dissertation on nongradedness at Harvard University, she served as the second principal of the world-famous Franklin School in Lexington, Massachusetts, which was the first nongraded/team teaching school in the United States. Lately, she has been assisting school districts including some in Connecticut, Kentucky, Maryland, Pennsylvania and Tennessee to implement nongradedness.

She has been a classroom teacher, preservice instructor at Queens College (NY), teaching fellow at Harvard, and past president of the Council of Professors of Instructional Supervision. She earned her B.A. in Psychology from Adelphi University and her M.S. from SUNY at New Paltz.

Her publications on nongradedness are found in *Educational Leadership, Elementary School Journal, ERIC, Phi Delta Kappan, Principal, Texas Tech Journal of Education,* and *Wingspan.* Her most recent article describing research on nongraded schools was published by *Educational Leadership* in October 1992.

ROBERT H. ANDERSON was born and raised in Milwaukee, Wisconsin, where the school system has long been heavily influenced by educational thought in Germany and where, in the early 1940s, ungraded primary programs were introduced. After serving as a teacher and a coach (grades 4–8), as a naval officer in WWII, and as principal of an elementary-junior high school in Illinois, he became the first superintendent of School District 163 in Park Forest, Illinois 1949–1954. He was selected for the post because the Board of Education wanted to start a nongraded primary program, an idea about which Anderson had both knowledge and enthusiasm. It was probably the first officially-designated nongraded program in the United States.

Anderson then spent nineteen years on the faculty of the Harvard Graduate School of Education, where he participated in the development of team teaching, followed by ten years as Dean, College of Education, Texas Tech University. Upon his "retirement" he became full-time president of Pedamorphosis, Inc., a funded nonprofit corporation promoting educational change. He also has a part-time professorial appointment in the University of South Florida, Tampa.

He holds two degrees from the University of Wisconsin and the Ph.D. from the University of Chicago, where he was a fellow student with John I. Goodlad. Including this volume and two others simultaneously in press, Anderson has authored or co-authored fourteen books, plus some 200 other publications. He has worked professionally in all fifty states and thirty-one foreign countries. His recognitions include election to the Laureate Chapter of Kappa Delta Pi and an honorary degree from Harvard.

Index

SUPPLEMENT ONE

INVENTORY OF EDUCATIONAL BELIEFS AND IDEAS

Edited and Compiled by Robert H. Anderson, Barbara N. Pavan and Arthur J. Schwartz (5th Edition) 1991

Directions – To check your views on what is known or believed about teaching practices, schools and how they should be organized, and how children grow and develop, respond on the attached answer sheet according to this code:

A = Agree, the statement tends to be true, and I tend to agree with it.

B = Disagree, the statement seems *not* to be true, and I do not agree with it.

? = Uncertain, I doubt that we know whether or not this statement is true.

---

1. Students who move in and out of nongraded programs may be placed at a disadvantage when they move to a middle or junior high school.

2. A school in which grade labels and related organizational practices are used, can in fact be superior to a school that has officially abandoned the grade structure.

3. A nongraded program is essential for students even beyond the primary level.

4. Student evaluation records that consist of frequent anecdotal notations and dated samples of a child's work may be a more effective "reporting system" than the traditional letter grades.

5. A nongraded or continuous progress program can be built on a system of "defined levels."

6. It could be harmful to children if their school work during the first three or four years is nearly always successful.

7. Discipline problems tend to increase when teachers assume most of the responsibility for directing the learning process.

8. Children can learn without liking their teachers.

9. A competitive learning environment increases motivation, achievement, and self-improvement.

10. Understanding the culture and ethnicity of students matters little in creating instructional strategies.

11. Strong research evidence supports the recommendation that elementary school classes should not exceed (approximately) twenty-five pupils.

12. Multi-age classes allow students to develop both leadership and followership skills.

13. Studies have provided evidence that "age segregation" in classrooms increases competition and aggression of students.

14. The use of computer-assisted instruction may increase the isolation and alienation of students, even in the nongraded school.

15. In an open classroom, the materials provided have a prescribed usage determined by the curriculum.

16. While the student takes an active part in an activity-centered or open classroom, the teacher is equally active in stimulating children's interest.

17. Sequenced curriculum materials are very helpful and should be followed by all students, especially in the skill areas of mathematics and reading.

18. A visit to an "open space" school building will show evidence of nongrading, team teaching, and flexibility in action.

19. Typically, teachers are trained and prepared to make the most effective use of non-professional assistants in the schools.

20. One of the purposes of team teaching is to make possible the easy scheduling of a greater number of "homogeneous" groups of children than is possible in self-contained class programs.

21. Team teaching is difficult when the team members have a variety of opinions and ideas to contribute to lesson planning.

22. Teachers often feel lonely and unappreciated.

23. The recent wave of site-based management schools will have little effect on incorporating new and innovative instructional strategies.

24. When innovations are being considered, classroom teachers should be involved in preliminary planning and in all phases of implementation.

25. Most parents tend to understand the philosophy and goals behind a nongraded or team-teaching school.

26. A "nongraded first grade" and "nongraded reading" are acceptable forms of nongradedness.

27. Research studies in nongradedness have increased steadily from the early 1960s right up to the present.

28. There are concepts and skills that must be mastered at each grade level if the pupil is to progress in school.

29. Used with care and discretion, ABCDF report cards can be a useful mechanism in the school's educational and public relations program.

30. The main reason to have a strong evaluation and assessment program is so that the school can fully inform the parents of the child's progress and status.

31. Elementary-aged students should not be involved in making up rules of behavior and discipline under which they will operate—this process should occur mainly at the high school level.

32. Children in the primary unit (formerly grades 1-2-3) rarely need to have continued exposure to kindergarten type experiences.

33. Learning goals are obscured when a variety of activities are being carried on simultaneously during a given class period.

34. Usually, children are not given sufficient responsibility for establishing and pursuing their learning goals.

35. The teacher-student relationship, more than any other single factor, determines how much learning will actually take place.

36. Group cohesiveness is lost when children in a classroom are not of approximately the same age.

37. In the typical school, setting up classroom groups by ability is necessary and desirable.

38. There is a direct relation between promotion/retention practices and student performance.

39. Textbooks are used the same way in nongraded and graded schools.

40. A "cooperative learning" environment will increase the academic achievement of every student in the classroom.

41. The availability of materials for students is crucial to the success of individualized programs.

42. It is highly desirable for all children to formulate their own individual learning goals with guidance from their teachers.

43. Some teachers keep their classroom doors tightly shut to avoid criticism and evaluation of their teaching.

44. School buildings with self-contained classrooms cannot house team teaching and nongradedness.

45. Team teaching programs cannot function effectively unless the role of the principal changes to that of group facilitator.

46. About 90 percent of the professional knowledge a career teacher can possess will have to be acquired after entering the profession as a newly certified teacher.

47. Flexible scheduling means having periodic changes in a "set" schedule.

48. In moving into a nongraded structure, it is best to nongrade the primary division first.

49. The majority of elementary school buildings are either obsolete or greatly inhibit team teaching concepts, collaborative learning, and other new instructional strategies.

50. Staff development, training, and coaching are crucial if a nongraded, team-taught program is to succeed.

51. A portfolio of a student's work can be an effective assessment tool.

52. A student evaluation should concentrate on the weaknesses of the student—and offer strategies to improve the problem areas.

53. Uniform achievement standards must be maintained if a school is to be considered a good school.

54. The greatest single difficulty in accomplishing the goals of the "nongraded school" involves solving the curriculum problems that this organizational scheme raises.

55. A nongraded program enables a school to "cover" the standardized curriculum faster and better.

56. The most appropriate type of competition in the school is where children compete with themselves.

57. The teacher should try to keep a close watch over all children to make sure they are doing what they are supposed to do.

58. Teachers should never say to a student, "I don't know."

59. Modern concepts of curriculum and instruction see teachers as resource persons rather than transmitters of knowledge.

60. Student failure is often due to teacher attitude and low expectations.

61. Research studies have shown a positive causal relationship between the self-contained classroom and the personal-social-emotional well-being of younger children.

62. In general, gifted children or slow-learning children are best served in special, separate classes.

63. Academic achievement should be the chief criterion for pupil placement in a nongraded program.

64. The curriculum should be organized to develop the understanding of concepts and methods of inquiry rather than to emphasize specific content learning.

65. As a general rule, a "messy" classroom reinforces children's bad habits.

66. A cooperative learning procedure promotes more positive cross-sex and cross-ethnic relationships than does individualistic or competitive learning.

67. Since manipulative materials are so important in open and nongraded classrooms, there must be enough of each item for each child.

68. Having more than one teacher will probably confuse a good many children.

69. Teacher empowerment has more to do with issues of money and recognition than with curriculum or instruction.

70. Fear of failure is a greater "motivator" than "guaranteed success."

71. Hierarchical structure is a necessary ingredient of full-fledged team teaching.

72. Team teaching is a form of departmentalization.

73. Strategically, before officially launching a nongraded program in a

school, it is very helpful to first implement a cooperative, team teaching model.

74. Parents are usually reluctant to accept children's greater freedom of choice and movement in a school that adopts the "open classroom" or nongraded approach.

75. Unless one is nearly certain of the results, a new school program should not be tried out.

INVENTORY OF EDUCATIONAL BELIEFS AND IDEAS
RESPONSE SHEET
(Circle One)

A = Agree   ? = Uncertain   D = Disagree

RESPONSES

---

1. A ? D	26. A ? D	51. A ? D
2. A ? D	27. A ? D	52. A ? D
3. A ? D	28. A ? D	53. A ? D
4. A ? D	29. A ? D	54. A ? D
5. A ? D	30. A ? D	55. A ? D
6. A ? D	31. A ? D	56. A ? D
7. A ? D	32. A ? D	57. A ? D
8. A ? D	33. A ? D	58. A ? D
9. A ? D	34. A ? D	59. A ? D
10. A ? D	35. A ? D	60. A ? D
11. A ? D	36. A ? D	61. A ? D
12. A ? D	37. A ? D	62. A ? D
13. A ? D	38. A ? D	63. A ? D
14. A ? D	39. A ? D	64. A ? D
15. A ? D	40. A ? D	65. A ? D
16. A ? D	41. A ? D	66. A ? D
17. A ? D	42. A ? D	67. A ? D
18. A ? D	43. A ? D	68. A ? D
19. A ? D	44. A ? D	69. A ? D
20. A ? D	45. A ? D	70. A ? D
21. A ? D	46. A ? D	71. A ? D
22. A ? D	47. A ? D	72. A ? D
23. A ? D	48. A ? D	73. A ? D
24. A ? D	49. A ? D	74. A ? D
25. A ? D	50. A ? D	75. A ? D

SUPPLEMENT TWO

PRINCIPLES OF NONGRADEDNESS
(Revised from Pavan, 1972, pp. 39–43.)

A. *Goals of Schooling*

1. The ultimate school goal is to develop self-directing, autonomous individuals.
2. The school seeks to develop individual potentialities to the maximum possible.
3. Each individual is unique and is accorded dignity and respect. Differences in people are valued. Therefore the school strives to increase the variability of individual differences rather than to stress conformity.
4. Development of the child is considered in many areas, including aesthetic, physical, emotional, and social as well as cognitive.
5. Each child needs to develop the skills for productive and responsible membership and leadership in civic, social, and work groups.
6. The school environment is designed so that children enjoy learning, experience work effort as rewarding, and develop positive self-concepts.

B. *Organization*

7. Individuals work in varied situations where there will be opportunities for maximum progress. Advancement, retention, and pro-

motion procedures are flexible. Classes or teams of children are identified with labels free of grade-level implications.

8. A child's placement may be changed at *any time* if it is felt to be in the best interest of the child considering all five phases of development: aesthetic, physical, cognitive, emotional, and social.

9. Grouping and subgrouping patterns are extremely flexible. Learners are grouped and regrouped on the basis of one specific task or interest and the groups are disbanded when that object is reached.

10. Each child has opportunities to work with groups of many sizes, including one-person groups, formed for different purposes.

11. The specific task, materials required, and student needs determine the number of students that may be profitably engaged in any given educational experience.

12. Children and adults of varying personalities, backgrounds, abilities, interests, and ages work together in teams as co-learners in the collaborative school enterprise.

C. Curriculum

13. Children formulate their own learning goals with guidance from their teachers.

14. The unique needs, interests, abilities, learning rates, styles and patterns determine the child's individual curriculum. Conformity and rigidity are not demanded.

15. Broad thematic units integrating several subject matter disciplines are utilized, rather than the presentation of isolated bits of information.

16. Sequences of learning are determined for individual students since:
    • No predetermined sequence is appropriate to all learners.
    • Individual differences in level of competence and in interest are constantly in flux.
    • There are no logical or inherently necessary sequences in the various curriculum areas.

17. The curriculum is organized to develop understanding of concepts and methods of inquiry, more than retention of specific content learning.

18. Learning experiences based on the child's expressed interest will motivate the child to continue and complete a task successfully much more frequently than will teacher-contrived techniques.

D. Instruction

19. All phases of human growth — aesthetic, physical, cognitive, emotional, and social — are considered when planning learning experiences for a child.

20. Teachers are the facilitators of learning. They aid in children's development by helping them formulate goals and diagnose problem areas. They suggest alternative plans of action, provide resource materials, and give encouragement or support or prodding as needed.

21. Different people learn in different ways, so multiple learning alternatives should be available.

22. Successful completion of challenging experiences promotes greater confidence and motivation to learn than does fear of failure.

23. The process is more important than the product. The skills of learning to learn, especially inquiry, evaluation, interpretation, synthesis, and application are stressed.

24. Children strive to improve their performance and develop their potential rather than to compete with others.

E. Materials

25. A wide variety of textbooks, trade books, supplemental materials, workbooks, and teaching aids are available and readily accessible in sufficient quantities.

26. Varied materials are available to cover a wide range of reading abilities.

27. Alternate methods and materials are available at any time so that the children may use the learning styles and materials most suitable to their present needs and the task at hand (including skill building, self-teaching, self-testing, and sequenced materials).

28. Children are not really free to learn something they have not been exposed to. Teachers are responsible for providing a broad range of experiences and materials that will stimulate many interests in the educational environment.

29. Learning is the result of the student's interaction with the environment; therefore the child must be allowed to explore, to experiment, to mess around, to play, and have the freedom to err.

30. Children work with materials on the level appropriate to their present attainment and move as their abilities and desires allow them.

F. Assessment

31. Assessing and reporting must consider all five areas of the child's development: aesthetic, physical, cognitive, emotional, and social.

32. Assessment is continuous, cooperative, and comprehensive to fulfill its diagnostic purpose.

33. The child is directly involved in assessing and interpreting academic (and other) progress, and in shaping plans for future activity and growth.

34. Children's work is assessed in terms of their past achievements and their own potential, not only by comparison to group norms. Expectations differ for different children.

35. Teachers accept and respond to the fact that growth patterns are irregular and occur in different areas at different times.

36. Instead of letter or numerical grades to summarize student progress, multiple sources of documentation are utilized for reporting purposes.

PRINCIPLES OF NONGRADEDNESS
RESPONSE SHEET

Crucial = 3   Important = 2   Minor Importance = 1   Not Important = 0

A.   GOALS OF SCHOOLING
   1. Self-directing individuals   3   2   1   0
   2. Maximize individual potential   3   2   1   0
   3. Variability vs. conformity   3   2   1   0
   4. Development—c, a, p, e, s   3   2   1   0
   5. Group skills   3   2   1   0
   6. School atmosphere   3   2   1   0_____

B.   ORGANIZATION
   7. Individual placement   3   2   1   0
   8. Change as needed   3   2   1   0
   9. Flexible groups   3   2   1   0
   10. Many sizes   3   2   1   0
   11. Task, materials, needs   3   2   1   0
   12. Co-learner teams   3   2   1   0_____

C.   CURRICULUM
   13. Goals by student with teacher   3   2   1   0
   14. Individual curriculum   3   2   1   0
   15. Integrated themes   3   2   1   0
   16. Individual sequence   3   2   1   0
   17. Concepts/content   3   2   1   0
   18. Individual interests   3   2   1   0_____

D.   INSTRUCTION
   19. Plan—c, a, p, e, s   3   2   1   0
   20. Teacher role   3   2   1   0
   21. Different styles   3   2   1   0
   22. Success/failure   3   2   1   0
   23. Process/product   3   2   1   0
   24. Improve/compete   3   2   1   0_____

E.   MATERIALS
   25. Variety   3   2   1   0
   26. Reading range   3   2   1   0
   27. Alternative methods   3   2   1   0
   28. Stimulating environment   3   2   1   0
   29. Manipulation, error   3   2   1   0
   30. Appropriate level   3   2   1   0_____

F.   ASSESSMENT
   31. All areas—c, a, p, e, s   3   2   1   0
   32. Continuous, diagnostic   3   2   1   0
   33. Student involvement   3   2   1   0
   34. Potential, achievement   3   2   1   0
   35. Irregular growth   3   2   1   0
   36. Multiple data sources   3   2   1   0_____

Grand Total_____